THEORY

OF

MEANING

CENTRAL ISSUES IN PHILOSOPHY SERIES

BARUCH A. BRODY
series editor

~~~~~~

Baruch A. Brody
MORAL RULES AND PARTICULAR CIRCUMSTANCES

Hugo A. Bedau
JUSTICE AND EQUALITY

Mark Levensky
HUMAN FACTUAL KNOWLEDGE

George I. Mavrodes
THE RATIONALITY OF BELIEF IN GOD

Robert Sleigh
NECESSARY TRUTH

David M. Rosenthal
THE MENTAL AND THE PHYSICAL

Richard Grandy
THEORIES AND OBSERVATIONS IN SCIENCE

Gerald Dworkin
*DETERMINISM, FREE WILL, AND MORAL
RESPONSIBILITY*

David P. Gauthier
MORALITY AND RATIONAL SELF-INTEREST

Charles Landesman
THE FOUNDATIONS OF KNOWLEDGE

Adrienne and Keith Lehrer
THE THEORY OF MEANING

edited by

ADRIENNE AND KEITH LEHRER
University of Rochester

THEORY
OF
MEANING

Prentice-Hall, Inc., Englewood Cliffs, New Jersey

To our parents
Evelyn and Julius Kroman
and
Stelle and Al Lehrer.

© 1970 by Prentice-Hall, Inc., Englewood Cliffs, N.J.

Library of Congress Catalog Card Number: 72–117011

Printed in the United States of America

C 13–914598–2
P 13–914580–X

Current Printing (last digit):

10 9 8 7 6 5 4 3 2 1

PRENTICE-HALL INTERNATIONAL, INC., London
PRENTICE-HALL OF AUSTRALIA, PTY. LTD., Sydney
PRENTICE-HALL OF CANADA, LTD., Toronto
PRENTICE-HALL OF INDIA PRIVATE LIMITED, New Delhi
PRENTICE-HALL OF JAPAN, INC., Tokyo

Foreword

The Central Issues in Philosophy series is based upon the conviction that the best way to teach philosophy to introductory students is to experience or to *do* philosophy with them. The basic unit of philosophical investigation is the particular problem, and not the area or the historical figure. Therefore, this series consists of sets of readings organised around well-defined, manageable problems. All other things being equal, problems that are of interest and relevance to the student have been chosen.

Each volume contains an introduction that clearly defines the problem and sets out the alternative positions that have been taken. The selections are chosen and arranged in such a way as to take the student through the dialectic of the problem; each reading, besides presenting a particular point of view, criticizes the points of view set out earlier.

Although no attempt has been made to introduce the student in a systematic way to the history of philosophy, classical selections relevant to the development of the problem have been included. As a side benefit, the student will therefore come to see the continuity, as well as the breaks, between classical and contemporary thought. But in no case has a selection been included merely for its historical significance; clarity of expression and systematic significance are the main criteria for selection.

BARUCH A. BRODY

Contents

KEITH LEHRER

Meaning in Philosophy

Philosophers in the past have offered theories of meaning to support other kinds of theories. Only recently have they come to recognize the importance of a theory of meaning for understanding the various uses of language. One primary function of former theories of meaning was to bolster a theory of knowledge called *empiricism*. According to empiricism, sentences which contain assertions about matters of fact can only be known to be true or false empirically, and to know something empirically is to know it by observing the world. We shall first consider those theories of meaning that were employed in support of empiricism, noting the shortcomings of such theories, and subsequently consider the way in which theories of meaning have taken on a broader role in understanding language.

Imagine a philosopher confronted with diverse theories about everything in the universe, carefully supported with intricate and ingenious arguments but wholly in conflict with one another and lacking any empirical proof. One philosopher, for example, may assert that reality is composed entirely of minds; another that reality is neither mind nor matter; and other philosophers may defend still other theses about reality. Might not one conclude that there is more ingenuity than sense in all this?

One who decides that these conflicting theories may really be meaningless and that all meaningful theories must be subject to the test of observation is within the school of empiricist philosophy. John Locke, for example, maintains that knowledge concerning matters of fact must be obtained from experience. If our knowledge of such matters of fact is obtained from experience, then the meaning of the words and sentences which we use to formulate this knowledge must, according to Locke, be derived from the same source. Indeed, experience must be the source of all our ideas, whether they are formulated in words or left unexpressed. Once it is conceded that all our ideas are derived from experience, then it seems apparent that any knowledge which involves such ideas can only be achieved by turning once again to the source of those ideas, experience. Hence all theories about factual matters must undergo the test of observation or be rejected without a hearing. There is one way to factual knowledge, the empirical way.

This theory of knowledge gains much plausibility from the doctrine that the meaning of what we say consists of ideas which are derived from experience. We shall explore here not the viability of this theory of knowledge but rather the merits of the theory of meaning used to support it. The theory that the meaning of what we say consists of an idea has the merit of enabling us to explain how people understand the meaning of the words they utter. For, if the meaning consists of an idea in the speaker's mind, then it is easy enough to see how he could understand such a meaning.

As George Berkeley illustrates, however, Locke has some difficulty with the meaning of general terms, such as the term "man" in the sentence "John is a man." Locke maintains that, though we may experience or observe many men, we do not observe that general characteristic which they all share, the characteristic of being a man. We observe only particular things: this man, that star, this pretty girl, that speck of dust. Though we may observe that things have general characteristics, those general characteristics are not themselves observable. When I observe that Jane is a girl, I observe Jane, but I do not observe the general girliness which is a characteristic of all other girls as well.

This theory, which limits observation to particulars, is not beyond dispute, but it is important to notice the resultant conclusion that the meaning of "man" and other general terms must be some particular. This conclusion leads in turn to Locke's doctrine of abstract ideas, which is attacked by Berkeley and William Alston. In his attack on this doctrine, Berkeley insists that the meaning of a general term includes both a particular and the understanding that the term applies to other particulars of the same kind. Berkeley adheres to the thesis that the meaning of a term is an idea because he maintains that everything is an idea except for the minds that have them. The suggestion that meaning is an idea as well as the thesis that it is a particular is unwarranted, however. These theses are unjustified even if one adopts the basic tenets of empiricism. First, we can observe facts as well as objects. I can observe Jane and the fact that Jane is a girl. Thus the meaning of the term "girl" might be construed by an empiricist as that general characteristic which I observe in Jane. There is no need to account for the meaning of the term by interposing some idea of mine between the term and the characteristic. Of course, I have an idea of the characteristic, but that idea is not the characteristic, any more than my idea of John is John. When I say "Jane is a girl," I am ascribing a characteristic to her; it would therefore be consistent with empiricism to interpret the meaning of the term "girl" as being the characteristic ascribed to Jane.

The preceding argument shows that empiricism need not subscribe to the doctrine that meanings are ideas. The problem remains, however, of formulating a theory of meaning to support empiricism. Such a theory was formulated by a group of philosophers known as logical positivists or logical empiricists. The positivists used as a starting point Berkeley's second criticism of Locke. Berkeley had pointed out that Locke's theory of meaning was suited to only one use of language, that of making factual assertions. But language has other uses: asking questions, giving commands, expressing attitudes, and so forth. Recognizing these other uses, the logical positivists sought to defend empiricism by constructing a theory of cognitive meaning—a theory of meaning concerning those statements which are claims to knowledge.

The positivists, as Moritz Schlick illustrates, maintain that a sentence is cognitively meaningful if and only if it is logically possible to verify the statement in experience. Any statement which, as a simple matter of logic, cannot be verified in experience lacks cognitive meaning. This contention, though plausible, proves to be ineffective as a pillar of empiricism. For there are many statements lacking in empirical content which nevertheless satisfy the preceding condition of cognitive meaning. Consider the statement, "All things are made up of minds." Or consider the statement, "Time is unreal; there is no such thing as past, present, or future." Both these statements have had their proponents, and neither is known to be true by experience or observation. How are we to show that it is logically impossible to verify such statements through experience? Where is the contradiction in the assertion that such a statement is found to be true in experience? It may be difficult to imagine what experiences could verify such strange statements as these, but such difficulty fails to prove that such verification is logically impossible. Instead of the simple criterion of meaningfulness, we need some theory of cognitive meaning which would enable us to separate the cognitively meaningful from the nonmeaningful.

Such a theory is found in writings of other positivists, most notably Rudolph Carnap. Carnap proposes that the cognitive meaning of a statement is the set of truth conditions of the statement. He gives the following example. Suppose that Pierre says, "*Mon crayon est noir.*" If we know French we understand the meaning of the sentence. Our understanding consists of our knowledge of truth conditions; we know that the sentence is true if and only if a certain object, Pierre's pencil, has a certain color, black. From our knowledge of the meaning or truth conditions of the sentence we can tell what we must do to find out whether the sentence is true or false; we must observe the color of Pierre's pencil.

As this example illustrates, the truth conditions are conditions that hold if and only if an object we can observe has (or lacks) some property we can observe it to have (or lack). In this description of cognitive meaning, a sentence has cognitive meaning if and only if the meaning of the sentence can be formulated in terms of truth conditions, conditions we can observe to hold or fail to hold.

This attempt to construe meaning as truth conditions fails for two reasons. First, some things are highly theoretical in character. As a result, the sentences expressing knowledge of such things must be considered cognitively meaningful even though such sentences lack truth conditions of the requisite type. For example, consider the statement "The neutrino has less mass than the electron." This statement is known to be true. But neither the neutrino nor the electron can be observed. Hence there are no conditions that hold if and only if we observe the neutrino to have less mass than the electron. The neutrino and the electron are theoretical entities and, though the theories are confirmed by observation, the meaning of such theoretical statements cannot be a set of truth conditions that hold if and only if certain observable objects have (or lack) some property we can observe them to have (or lack). Thus, the positivist theory of meaning is inadequate as a theory of cognitive meaning, because it would rule out as meaningless all statements of theoretical knowledge.

Second, the positivist theory of meaning lacks a necessary kind of generality. Compare the assertion, "My crayon is black," with the question, "Is my crayon black?" According to Carnap, our knowledge of truth conditions constitutes our understanding of the meaning of the former statement. But, if that is so, then how are we to explain the obvious relation of meaning between the assertion and the question? The question has no truth conditions, and consequently its meaning is not a set of truth conditions. Yet the meaning of the two sentences is clearly related. Indeed, anyone who understands the meaning of one will, if he understands the grammar of English, also understand the meaning of the other. This example illustrates an important shortcoming in the theory of cognitive meaning defended by the positivists—namely, that the acceptance of such a theory would render us incapable of explaining or understanding the relations of meaning that pertain among sentences fulfilling diverse linguistic functions. As Berkeley points out, we use sentences to question, to command, and so forth. A theory that isolates one of these functions of language and makes the meaning of sentences depend on only that one function deprives us of a general understanding of the various ways in which the meaning of words enables us to use language. We must seek instead a theory that will enable us to achieve broader objectives.

The preceding remarks are an indication of the kinds of objectives appropriate to a theory of meaning. Like any theory, a theory of meaning is accepted on the basis of its explanatory utility. The question is: what is a theory of meaning supposed to explain? According to empiricists and positivists, it was to explain which sentences we could know to be true from observation and which we could not. A broader objective is more sensible. Any use of a sentence, whether to assert, question, command, or express, depends on the meaning of the words uttered. Moreover, to consider the matter from the standpoint of the listener rather than the speaker, it is because the listener understands the meaning of words uttered that he understands what is asserted, asked, commanded, or expressed. Thus, a theory of meaning should be part of a theory of language explaining how language can fulfill its various linguistic functions.

Consideration of these more general aims has led some philosophers to explore the possibility that the meaning of words can be equated with the use to which these words are put. As John R. Searle argues, this solution is wrong. If I yell "Coffee is ready!" to wake someone, then the use of the words is to wake a person. But it is not part of the meaning of the words that they are so used. There are many uses of words that are obviously not part of their meaning. Even more conventional uses of words saying, for example, "The car is red," to tell someone the color of the car—do not constitute the meaning of those words. Because the words have the meaning they do I can use them to tell someone the color of a car. Their meaning is essential to my use of them. But, to say that my use of these words is part of their meaning is an error, like saying that the ax which I use to chop trees is nothing more than the uses to which the ax is put. This assertion is, of course, absurd, since we can see that though the ax is essential to the cutting, the ax is one thing and the use of it another. Similarly, the meaning of words is essential to some uses of the words, but the meaning of the words is one thing and their use another.

We have argued that a theory of meaning should be part of a theory of language explaining how words fulfill various linguistic functions—asserting, questioning, and so forth—and how a listener understands such acts of speech. A theory of meaning will not suffice by itself to explain such matters, however. Factors other than the meaning of words are necessary for the words to accomplish their purpose, for example, the grammar of the language and the context of the utterance. If I utter a string of words, my success or failure in asserting something will depend on the order in which I say the words. If I say "Did sleep Joe," I will probably accomplish nothing, whereas if I say "Did Joe sleep?" I will have asked a question, and if I say "Joe did sleep," I will have asserted something. The grammar of our language limits the conventional ways we can use words. Put less negatively, grammar or syntax specifies certain word-orders as acceptable for a given linguistic function.

The ordering of words need not be perfectly grammatical for the words to accomplish their purpose if the context of utterance provides enough information for understanding the ungrammatical utterance. A person saying "I vase like" may be understood by people who know the speaker is new to the language and who see his pleasure in handling a vase. Contextual information can compensate for many linguistic anomalies. A theory of language may be justified in ignoring such contextual factors, however, important as they are, because the grammar and meaning of words are the most constant and stable factors influencing the use and understanding of language.

We have isolated two factors important to a theory of language, meaning and grammar. Recent work in theory of language by philosophers and linguists has been concentrated on both theories of grammar and theories of meaning. This work is represented in the articles by Charles C. Fries, Jerrold J. Katz, and John Lyons, reprinted below. In these theories of meaning, the meaning of a word is regarded as a highly theoretical entity, something more like an electron: an entity whose existence explains what we observe by virtue of a theory which describes it. These theories of meaning present certain problems. Many speakers know little or nothing about electrons, although they all know the meaning of the words they utter. If the meaning of a word is an abstract theoretical entity like an electron, then how can a speaker who is uninitiated into modern theories of meaning know the meaning of the words he speaks? This question motivates those empiricist theories of meaning which assert that the meaning of the words is an idea in the mind of the speaker. If every speaker knows the meaning of the words he speaks (at least most of the time!), then, concludes the empiricist, the meaning must be something in his mind, an idea.

The empiricist line of thought, described above, is fallacious. To recognize its inadequacy, it is necessary to distinguish between knowing the meaning of a word and knowing that such and such is the meaning of the word. For example, a man might know the meaning of "brother" and not know that "male sibling" is the meaning of the word. Knowing the meaning of a word is not knowing that such and such is the meaning of the word; it is instead knowing how to do something. An analogy may be helpful. Suppose a man knows the shortest route from Rochester to Sodus Bay because he drives it frequently, and suppose that the route is N.Y. 31. The man who knows the shortest route may well not know *that* route N.Y. 31 is the shortest route. Similarly, a man may know the meaning of the word "brother" without knowing *that* an analysis given in a theory is the meaning of the word.

We have now cleared the way for a theory of meaning that construes the meaning of a word as a theoretical entity. Such a theory should *not* be concocted to fit some preconceived theory of knowledge, however. On the contrary, the only relevant test of such a theory is how well it serves to explain our use of language. It should help to explain how words fulfill the functions of language in the variety of speech acts language is used to perform and to explain how the listener understands the utterances he constantly confronts. A theory of meaning together with a theory of grammar which would enable us to explain, for example, how you understand what is written in this book and how the authors use language to achieve this purpose, would be a remarkable contribution to human knowledge. These are the goals of recent theories of meaning characterized in the next chapter.

ADRIENNE LEHRER

Meaning in Linguistics

The goal of the linguist is to study and describe languages as systems by which people communicate with one another. A theory of meaning is a necessary part of linguistic theory because the messages that are communicated are meaningful. Since the linguist looks primarily at systems of communication, he is interested not so much in the content of what people say as in the code, that is the language, they use to transmit their messages. Factually false statements like "Mount Everest is in Europe" and silly ones like "The cat is on the mat but the frog is on the log" must be accounted for just as much as those expressing great scientific truths and profound moral insights.

An important distinction among sentences is that between meaningful and meaningless ones. An adequate linguistic description should be able to show explicitly what is wrong with sentences like "I saw a splendid odor," "Cats can dogs," and "All spinsters are married to handsome men." Perhaps no definite line can be drawn between false and meaningless sentences. The sentence "Rocks think profound thoughts" can be analyzed either as factually false or as linguistically absurd.

We may expect a linguistic theory to take account of sentences which are odd in many contexts but meaningful in special situations, for example, poetry ("Thou wast the deep glen/Thou wast the mountain top"); children's stories ("Papa Bear said to Goldilocks . . ."); science fiction ("Then Super President turned into a

9

solid steel brick"); and conventional kinds of "deviance" such as metaphor, puns, and paradoxes. If a sentence is judged to be meaningful, either in normal or in special contexts, we can then proceed to describe the meaning of the sentence.

In addition to the words themselves, the settings of utterances, the identity of the speakers, the places where they come from, and other kinds of nonlinguistic information contribute to the meaning of sentences. For example, "I'm going up the river," when spoken by someone sitting in a canoe, will be interpreted differently from the same sentence spoken by someone handcuffed and being pushed into a paddy wagon. "A cupful of flour," when spoken in Great Britain, refers to ten ounces, whereas in the United States the phrase refers to only eight ounces.

Without denying the relevance of factors like settings, beliefs, cultural norms, shared knowledge, and so forth, linguists have found it methodologically useful to put aside extralinguist considerations in analyzing meaning. These other factors can be brought in when needed as the linguistic analysis proceeds, and eventually extralinguistic information can be systematically related to the results of linguistic analysis.

One present concern of linguists investigating semantic structures involves putting together the lexical and grammatical aspects of a language. The meaning of a sentence depends not only on the words in it, but also on their arrangement. "John hit Bill" means something different from "Bill hit John." Yet it is not possible to assign meaning accurately to abstract grammatical patterns. In "John hit Bill" the subject is the initiator of the action, that is, the agent; in "John received a letter" the grammatical subject is not the agent. The article by Fries in this volume discusses the role of words and grammatical constructions in the meaning of sentences.

The complex relationship between the vocabulary and grammar of a language constitutes one of the most interesting current research areas of linguistics. For example, causality can be expressed in English by a variety of patterns. "John made Mary sad" can alternatively be expressed as "John saddened Mary." "John made Mary happy" has no similar formulation. That is, we cannot say "John happiened Mary," "John made Mary die" is rather odd; the normal expression would be "John killed Mary." A semantic description should show the diverse ways of expressing approximately the same thing. The problem involves more than synonymy. Words which are synonyms are words of the same part of speech (*e.g.*, nouns, verbs) which can be interchanged without altering the meaning or grammatical structure of a sentence. In the sentences above and in paraphrases generally, there are grammatical changes as well as lexical ones.

The meaning of words is varied and complex, and different kinds of concepts are required to characterize adequately the whole vocabulary. Anyone who looks through a dictionary will notice many kinds of information contained in the definitions. Sometimes factual information and/or pictures are provided about the referents of words as in the case of certain plants and animals. Sometimes a list of synonyms and/or antonyms is given. For some words, like "to," "for," or "but," there are no definitions, but there are phrases or sentences in which the words are used.

In the study of the vocabulary structure in a language (that is, the relationship of words to one another and to the grammar), several theoretical problems are worth mentioning. The first problem is: What is the best size unit or segment of language to use for semantic analysis? It is better to concentrate on as small a segment as possible, since there will be fewer units to deal with than if longer segments are selected. The number of words in a language is smaller than the number of phrases, clauses, and sentences. From the meaning of minimal semantic units (which are finite in number) and the grammatical structures (which are described by a finite set of rules), we can derive the meaning of an infinite number of sentences. We need additional rules to show how the meaning of sentences can be so derived. These rules, which have been called *projection rules*, are discussed by Katz in his article in this volume.

Words are traditionally considered the best unit of semantic analysis. But sometimes smaller units can be used, for instance the "re-" in "resell," "remake," and "remarry." The *morpheme* is the smallest meaningful segment of a language; there is a great overlap between morphemes and words in English. "Dog" is one word and one morpheme. "Resell" is one word but two morphemes.

Morphemes and words are basically units of grammatical analysis. Though they frequently serve as units of semantic analysis as well, they do not always do so. In some cases morphemes may be too small a segment for semantic analysis. Roots and affixes like "-ceive," "-fect," "in-," and "de-" are morphemes, yet it is extremely difficult to abstract meaning from them that can be accurately predicted when they are combined to form new words, such as "refect" or "inceive."

Even words may sometimes be too small a segment. Phrases like "get up" ("awake") or "kick the bucket" ("die") are cases in which units larger than words are necessary. It is not always easy to decide when a phrase is to be taken as a minimal semantic unit, but considerations of simplicity and generality are relevant. For example, in the expression "red herring" it would be possible to define "red" so that it includes a sense (in addition to its commoner senses) that is possible only in juxtaposition with "herring," and "herring" can be similarly defined. To do so would be uneconomical, however. Thus "red herring" can be considered a minimal semantic unit.

A second problem of semantic analysis is whether we can reasonably establish distinct senses of words. Dictionaries divide the word *fish* into several senses, including (1) any legless water animal with a particular shape (which may be described or illustrated), and (2) a more limited class of legless water animals which have gills, lay eggs, and so forth. In the second sense whales are excluded. Shall we say that we are dealing with two different meanings or shall we say that "fish" covers a wide range of meaning? If we decide to establish discrete senses, why not set up a number of senses for the verb "eat": one referring to foods like spaghetti, another to things like ice cream cones, another to soup, and so forth, since the act of eating can be performed in several different ways. Linguists and lexicographers have assumed that discrete senses can be established in some satisfactory manner, although the criteria for doing so are not clear.

The third problem involves distinguishing between different senses of the same word and different words which happen to have the same sound. For example, the word "horn" can refer to both a musical instrument and a part of an animal, but sometimes what is being noted by this word is an animal's horn used to produce sound. Are there two different words or is there one word with two or three distinct senses? Is "hammer" in "I have a hammer" the same as in "He wants to hammer this nail?" In resolving the problem grammatical considerations as well as semantic ones are sometimes brought in, but linguists are still seeking adequate criteria for making decisions.

Three general approaches to semantic analysis have been proposed: collocational studies, field theories, and componential analysis. These approaches are not particularly in conflict; rather they emphasize different aspects of meaning and direct the linguist to look at different facts. Many semanticists have based their theories on two or on all three approaches.

Collocational analysis involves a study of the co-occurrence of individual lexical items with other individual lexical items. For example, in sampling a large corpus, say one hundred books on various subjects, one would discover that the word "night" collocates with, that is, occurs in the same clause with, "dark," "black," "time," "mid," "clear," and "fall." Some of these words in turn collocate with "day," "morning," and so forth, in addition to "night." In this way, one can construct collocational classes. "Dark," "black," "time," "mid," "clear," and so forth form a collocational class because they all collocate with "night." "Day, night, morning," and so forth form another collocational class because they occur with "mid-." Collocational analysis differs from grammar in that grammar deals with classes of items, not individual words. The grammatical classes *noun, verb, adjective,* and so forth, contain thousands of words which have no important semantic interrelationships. However, these grammatical classes can be subclassified, for example, into animate and inanimate nouns, and collocational classes may overlap with grammatical subclasses. But often collocations cut across grammatical classes. For example, "argue" and "strong" collocate in different grammatical capacities, as "He argued strongly" (verb-adverb), "The strength of his argument was considerable" (noun-noun), and "His argument was strengthened by the facts he cited" (noun-verb).

Collocational analysis has been proposed as an end in itself. Firth, for instance, has claimed that a list of collocations for each word is a part of its meaning. (J. R. Firth, "A Synopsis of Linguistic Theory, 1930–1955," in *Studies in Linguistic Analysis,* Special Volume of the Philological Society, Oxford: Blackwell, 1957). It seems more reasonable to assume, however, that this approach will provide hypotheses about the meaning of words, since a list of collocation does not explain why some lexical items frequently co-occur or conversely why some never occur. Collocations occur or fail to occur for a variety of reasons: "spic" almost always occurs with "span" because the form "spic-and-span" constitutes an idiomatic phrase which should not be segmented for semantic analysis. "Red," "green," "yellow," and "golden" collocate with "apple," but "purple," "silver," and "gray" do not because of certain facts about apples. One finds in a corpus "travel on foot" but not "walk on foot" (*i.e.*, one's own foot) because the latter is redundant whereas the former is not. "Walk," by virtue of its meaning, implies "on foot."

The second approach, the *field theory,* sets forth the view that in order to understand the meaning of a word, one must also understand a set of semantically related words. This set constitutes a lexical or semantic field. A field is something like a general subject area, and the linguist must look at the relationships among words within each field. Examples of lexical fields that have been investigated are kinship, colors, plants, diseases, and cooking. The first step in this kind of analysis is to determine what words are in a field. For instance, kinship terms in English include: "mother," "father," "child," "parent," "brother," "sister," "aunt," "uncle," "cousin," "nephew," "niece," "grandmother," and so forth. In fact the size of the class can be increased indefinitely since one can prefix "great-" to "grandmother," "grandfather," "grandchild," and so forth, any number of times ("great grandmother," "great great grandmother," and so forth).

A recent and complete account of field theories can be found in Lyons, *Structural Semantics* and in *Introduction to Theoretical Linguistics,* Chapter 9 and 10. Lyons defines the meaning of terms as "certain relations that hold between the items in a particular lexical subsystem." (*Structural Semantics,* 57.) That is, all the words in a lexical field are related, but not necessarily in the same way. According to Lyons, a semantic field must contain a specification of what "certain relations" are. They include synonymy, antonymy, class inclusion, and several others.

Incompatibility is an important semantic relation. Terms are incompatible if the assertion of one implies a denial of the others in the set. Most of the kinship terms above are incompatible. To say "John is my brother" implies that "John is not my sister, mother, aunt," and so forth. "Mother" and "parent" or "father" and "parent" are not incompatible, however.

Associated with incompatibility is *antonymy*, a relation applicable to pairs. Antonyms can be subclassified as gradable or nongradable. Nongradable antonyms are absolute and do not contain degrees; examples are "single-married" and "dead-alive." Gradable antonyms, on the other hand, do contain degrees of comparison. For example, with the pair "small-large," the sentence "Cats are larger than mice" implies "Mice are smaller than cats."

Class inclusion is a relation of one-way implication. It can be illustrated by terms like "father" and "parent" or "apple" and "fruit." "Father" implies "parent" but not *vice versa*.

Synonymy is a relation of bilateral implication applicable to terms which can be substituted for each other in most sentence contexts. "Mother" and "mama" are synonyms. Stylistic differences between terms do not invalidate the concept of synonymy.

Other kinds of semantic relations are needed to account for sets of terms like "second," "minute," "hour," and for pairs like "give-take," "buy-sell." Some lexical fields will include many of these relations, whereas others will not. Some relations may not even be necessary for analyzing certain languages. The linguist must establish whatever semantic relations are necessary to analyze the vocabulary of a particular language.

A third approach to semantic analysis is *componential analysis*. Usually linguists and anthropologists who have used this method have also implicitly accepted the field theory by beginning their analyses with a set of related lexical items. Rather than stating the relationship between the lexemes, however, they isolate certain usually-recurring *components*. Consider the following table of English words:

sheep	ram	ewe	lamb
horse	stallion	mare	colt
chicken	rooster	hen	chick

It is possible to establish certain components common to several of the above words. For example, (Sheep), (Horse), and (Chicken) can be isolated as species components, differentiating the rows, and (Generic), (Male), (Female), and (Young) can be isolated as the components differentiating the columns. "Ram" can then be analyzed as having the components (Sheep) and (Male). "Hen" can be analyzed as having the components (Chicken) and (Female). Other components must be added, however: (Animal) to both "ram" and "hen"; (Mammal) to "ram," (Bird) to "hen." The semantic theory of Katz, reprinted in this volume, uses a version of componential analysis for the dictionary part of semantic analysis. Lyon's article criticizes certain aspects of componential analysis.

There is disagreement about just what these isolated components are. Some linguists have suggested that the components are the most basic words in the vocabulary of a language, whereas others, Katz among them, treat the components as primitive abstract units or meanings and possible units of human conceptualization. *Semantic marker* and *sememe* are other terms that have been applied to semantic components. Proponents of componential analysis have argued that this approach will simplify the task of relating language to nonlinguistic phenomena (things, events, situations, *etc.*)

In an analysis of the meaning of sentences, components can be assigned to each word in the sentence, but some components must be added on the basis of the grammatical construction as well. For example, in "The man hit the ball," the component (Agent) would be assigned to "man" in addition to its inherent components. In "I see the man," (Object) would be assigned to "man" and (Agent) would be assigned to "I."

Each of these three approaches directs our attention to a different aspect of meaning. The approaches are complementary and all contribute to the description of the semantics of a language. Whatever form semantic theory finally takes, it seems likely that the results of collocational, field, and componential analyses will be utilized.

WILLIAM ALSTON

Theories of Meaning

THE PROBLEM OF MEANING

The present chapter is concerned with the nature of linguistic meaning. This is a problem of philosophical analysis, which is best formulated as follows: "What are we saying about a linguistic expression when we specify its meaning?" [1] That is, we are trying to give an adequate characterization of one of the uses of "mean" and its cognates.

There are many other uses of "mean," some of which might be confused with our sense.

(1) That is no mean accomplishment. (insignificant)
(2) He was so mean to me. (cruel)
(3) I mean to help him if I can. (intend)
(4) The passage of this bill will mean the end of second class citizenship for vast areas of our population. (result in)
(5) Once again life has meaning for me. (significance)
(6) What is the meaning of this? (explanation)
(7) He just lost his job. That means that he will have to start writing letters of application all over again. (implies)

* Reprinted from *Philosophy of Language* (Englewood Cliffs: Prentice-Hall, Inc., 1964) by permission of the author and publisher.

[1] Although this is the canonical form, I shall not hesitate to employ the other forms, "What is linguistic meaning?" and "How is the concept of linguistic meaning to be analyzed?" as stylistic variants.

In these cases we are talking about people, actions, events, or situations rather than about words, phrases, or sentences. The cases in which we apply, or seem to apply, "means" to a linguistic expression, but where "mean" does not have the sense we are examining are rare; but it is here that confusion is most likely to occur.

(8) Keep off the grass. This means you.

Here it seems plausible to regard "this" as referring to the sentence, "Keep off the grass." But it is clear that we are *not* saying what the sentence means. An English-French phrase book would not contain the entry: Keep off the grass—*vous*. This is the use in which "mean" means very much the same as "refer." It is more commonly used of people, as in "Who do you mean?"—"I mean Susie." But, as in (8), it can be used of linguistic expressions. Again consider:

(9) Lucky Strike means fine tobacco.

Here we are not talking about a linguistic expression, although it may seem at first sight as if we are. We are not giving the meaning of the phrase, "Lucky Strike." No dictionary could possibly contain such an entry. (If *Webster's* did contain this entry, the American Tobacco Company would undoubtedly be delighted.) This is an example of the same use we have in:

That look on his face means trouble.
When he begins complaining, that means he is getting better.

In all these cases, we are saying that one thing or event is a reliable indication of the existence of another.

There is one sense in which we all know perfectly well what we are saying when we say what a word means. We succeed in communicating with each other by saying things like " 'Procrastinate' means *put things off*," [2] "He doesn't know what 'suspicious' means," and so on. In general, we know how to support, attack, and test such statements, we know when such statements are warranted and when they are not, we know what practical implications accepting such a statement would have, and so on. What we lack, in advance

---

[2] A word about the notation. We shall regularly italicize what follows "means" in "E means. . . ." (or what follows "is" in "The meaning of E is. . . .") This is intended to reflect the fact that when expressions are put into this slot, they have a unique kind of occurrence, for which we shall use the term "exhibit."

of a philosophical investigation, is an explicit and coherent account of these abilities.

TYPES OF THEORIES OF MEANING

The literature on this subject contains a bewildering diversity of approaches, conceptions, and theories, most of which can be grouped into three types, which I shall call "referential," "ideational," and "behavioral." The referential theory identifies the meaning of an expression with that to which it refers or with the referential connection, the ideational theory with the ideas with which it is associated, and the behavioral theory with the stimuli that evoke its utterance and/or the responses that it in turn evokes. Each of these kinds of theory exists in more forms than I shall have time to consider. But I shall try to choose forms of each that will clearly exemplify its basic features.

THE REFERENTIAL THEORY

The referential theory has been attractive to a great many theorists because it seems to provide a simple answer that is readily assimilable to natural ways of thinking about the problem of meaning. It has seemed to many that proper names have an ideally transparent semantic structure. Here is the word "Fido"; there is the dog the word names. Everything is out in the open; there is nothing hidden or mysterious. Its having the meaning it has is simply constituted by the fact that it is the name of that dog.[3] It is both tempting and natural to suppose that a similar account can be given for all meaningful expressions. It is thought that every meaningful expression names something or other, or at least stands

[3] A more penetrating account of proper names would show that this is a singularly unfortunate model for an account of meaning. It is questionable whether proper names can be correctly said to have meaning. They are not assigned meanings in dictionaries. One who does not know what "Fido" is the name of is not thereby deficient in his grasp of English in the way he would be if he did not know what "dog" means. And the fact that "Fido" is used in different circles as the name of a great many different dogs does not show that it has a great many different meanings or that it is a highly ambiguous word.

to something or other in a relation something like naming (designating, labelling, referring to, *etc.*). The something or other referred to does not have to be a particular concrete, observable thing like Fido. It could be a kind of thing (as with "common names" like "dog"), a quality ("perseverance"), a state of affairs ("anarchy"), a relationship ("owns"), and so on. But the supposition is that for any meaningful expression, we can understand what it is for it to have a certain meaning by noting that there is something or other to which it refers. "Words all have meaning, in the simple sense that they are symbols that stand for something other than themselves." [4]

The referential theory exists in a more and a less naïve version. Both versions subscribe to the statement that for an expression to have a meaning is for it to refer to something other than itself, but they locate meaning in different areas of the situation of reference. The more naïve view is that the meaning of an expression is that to which the expression refers;[5] the more sophisticated view is that the meaning of the expression is to be identified with the relation between the expression and its referent, that the referential connection constitutes the meaning.

MEANING AND REFERENCE

The first form of the theory can easily be shown to be inadequate by virtue of the fact that two expressions can have different meanings but the same referent. Russell's classic example of this point concerns "Sir Walter Scott" and "the author of *Waverley.*" These two expressions refer to the same individual, since Scott is the author of *Waverley*, but they do not have the same meaning. If they did, the statement that Scott is the author of *Waverley* would be known to be true just by knowing the meaning of the constituent terms. It is a fundamental principle that whenever two referring expressions have the same meaning, for example, "my only uncle"

---

[4] Bertrand Russell, *Principles of Mathematics* (London: Cambridge University Press, 1903), p. 47.

[5] It is difficult to find a full-blown presentation of this version in the works of reputable philosophers. But since it exercises an enormous influence on popular thinking about language, it is worthwhile to exhibit its defects.

and "the only brother either of my parents has," then the identity statement with these terms as components, "My only uncle is the only brother either of my parents has," is necessarily true just by virtue of the meanings of these expressions. But this is not the case with "Scott is the author of *Waverley*." This statement is a particularly good example because the identity of the author of these novels was at first kept secret, so that many people could understand the sentence "Scott is the author of *Waverley*" (Scott was already a famous poet) without knowing whether it was true. In general, anything to which we can refer can be referred to by many expressions that do not have the same meaning at all, for example, John F. Kennedy can be referred to as "the President of the U.S.A. in 1962," "the U.S. President assassinated in Dallas." Such examples show that it cannot simply be the fact that an expression refers to a certain object that gives it the particular meaning it has.

The converse phenomenon—same meaning but different referents —can be demonstrated, not for different expressions, but for different utterances of the same expression. There is a class of terms, sometimes called "indexical terms," for example, "I," "you," "here," "this," which systematically change their reference with changes in the conditions of their utterance. When Jones utters the word "I," it refers to Jones; when Smith utters it, it refers to Smith. But this fact doesn't mean that "I" has different meanings corresponding to these differences. If a word like "I" had a distinguishable meaning for every person to whom it has ever been used to refer, it would be the most ambiguous word in English. Think of how many different meanings we would have to learn before we could be said to have mastered the use of the word; in fact, every time a new speaker of English learned to use the word, it would acquire a new meaning. But this is fantastic. The word has a single meaning—*the speaker*. And it is because it always has this meaning that its referent systematically varies with variations in the conditions of utterance.

DO ALL MEANINGFUL EXPRESSIONS REFER TO SOMETHING?

Because of these readily appreciable difficulties, the more careful versions of the referential theory take the second alternative. Even though Russell, for example, often talks as if the meaning of an expression *is* what it stands for, we also find him saying things like: "When we ask what constitutes meaning, . . . we are asking, not who is the individual meant, but what is the relation of the word to the individual which makes the one mean the other." [6] This version cannot be disposed of by pointing out that reference and meaning do not always vary together. For it may be that although "Scott" and "the author of *Waverley*" refer to the same person, they are not related to that referent in the same way, though it is difficult to say whether they are until we have some account of the sort of relation in question. But at this point a more fundamental difficulty comes into view. No sort of referential theory will be adequate as a general account of meaning unless it is true that all meaningful linguistic expressions do refer to something. And if we take a careful look at the matter, it will be seen that this is not the case.

First of all, there are conjunctions and other components of language, which serve an essentially connective function. Do words like "and," "if," "is," and "whereas" refer to anything? It seems not. Referential theorists usually reply to this objection by denying that "syncategorematic" [7] terms like these have meaning "in isolation," or that they have meaning in the primary sense in which nouns, adjectives, and verbs have meaning. It is possible, of course, that in the end we may be driven to the position that there is no one sense in which all linguistic units to which we ordinarily assign meaning, have meaning. But to admit this before we have made an earnest effort to find a single sense would be a counsel of despair. It certainly seems that in saying " 'Procrastinate' means *put things off*" and " 'If' means *provided that*" we are saying things which, in some important respect, are the same sort of thing; we are, so to say, speaking in the same logical tone of voice. And we should not

---

[6] *Analysis of Mind* (London: George Allen & Unwin, Ltd., 1921), p. 191.

[7] This term was introduced by medieval logicians to apply to words like conjunctions, which were regarded as not standing for anything and so as not having meaning "in isolation." These were the linguistic units that were left over after one had gone through everything that could be assigned to Aristotle's ten "Categories," a classification of terms made by Aristotle. Thus, the remnants were terms that were used only *with* (syn—categorematic) the categories.

lightly give up the attempt to spell out explicitly what is common. Moreover, the idea that every meaningful linguistic expression refers to something encounters rough going even in those stretches of language where the referential theorist feels most secure. Proponents of this theory generally take it as obvious that nouns like "pencil," adjectives like "courageous," and verbs like "run" refer to something or other. It is not always recognized that it is sometimes difficult to find a plausible candidate for the referent. To what does "pencil" refer? Not to any particular pencil, for the word "pencil" can be used in talking about any pencil whatsoever. If saying what the word refers to is to bring out what gives it its semantic status, what enables it to function as it does, then we cannot limit its reference to any particular pencil or to any particular group of pencils. The most plausible suggestion would be that it refers to the class of pencils, that is, to the sum total of all those objects correctly called "pencils." Likewise, "courageous" might be said to refer to a certain quality of character, the quality of courage. And "run" could be said to refer to the class of all acts of running. It is to be noted that in order to find anything that might conceivably be a referent for words of these sorts (which make up the great bulk of our vocabulary), we have had to bring in entities of a rather abstract sort—classes and qualities. This should not disturb us, unless we are attached to the groundless idea that words cannot be meaningful unless they refer to concrete observable physical objects.

There is no doubt that "pencil" is related in some important way to the class of pencils, but does it *refer* to that class? One reason for denying that it does is this. If we want to pick out the class of pencils as what we are talking about, preparatory to going on to say something about it, the word "pencil" will not serve our purpose. If, for example, we want to say that the class of pencils is very large, we will not succeed in doing so by uttering the sentence "Pencil is very large." The word "pencil" simply will not do the job of referring to the class of pencils. The same point can be made for adjectives and verbs. If we wanted to pick out the quality of courage in order to say something about it, for example, that it is all too rare in these times, we could not use the adjective "courageous" to do so. We would not say "Courageous is all too rare in these times." Again, I would not say that what I just did belongs to the class of acts of running by uttering the sentence "What I just did belongs to run."

This point reflects the fact that referring is only one of the functions that linguistic expressions perform, a function assigned to some sorts of expressions and not to others. What distinguishes referring from other functions is the fact that it serves to make explicit what a given bit of discourse is about. Thus:

W refers to $x =_{df} W$ can be used in a sentence, S, to make it explicit that S is about x.

There are other contexts in which expressions are used to refer to something, for example, in lists, or in labels. But we may take the function of making explicit what a sentence is about as the defining characteristic of referring. Types of expressions that normally have this function include proper names like "Winston Churchill"; abstract nouns like 'courage"; phrases combining a concrete noun or noun phrase with an article or demonstrative, like "the pencil," "this pencil," "the pencil in my pocket"; and concrete nouns in the plural, like "pencils," and "dogs." If referring is one linguistic job among others and is assigned only to some types of expressions, no account of meaning that presupposes that all meaningful units refer to something can be correct. More specifically, it cannot be the case that to say a word has a certain meaning is to say it refers to something.

But perhaps it is just that "refer" is an unfortunate term for what the referential theorist really has in mind. In the preceding discussion, we used the term "stand for" at one place; and there are other terms that occur in expositions of this kind of theory, such as "designate," "signify," "denote." Perhaps there is some more generic notion, such as "standing for," which is such that every meaningful linguistic unit stands for something. Referring would then be only one species of this genus, along with denoting, connoting, and any others there may be.

DENOTATION AND CONNOTATION

Is it the case that there is some one semantically important relation that each meaningful linguistic unit has to something or other? Now there is no doubt that expressions like "pencil" and "courageous," which do not, in the strict sense, *refer* to anything, stand in relations that are crucial for their meaning. Thus, "pencil," though it does not *refer* to the class of pencils, does *denote* that class; which is simply to say that the class of pencils is the class of all those things to which the word "pencil" can be correctly applied. And, clearly, it is crucial for its having the meaning it has that it denote this class rather than some other. If it denoted another class, for example, the class of chairs, it would not have the same meaning, and vice versa. Again, although the adjective "courageous" does not *refer* to the disposition to remain steadfast in the face of danger, it does *connote* that disposition, in the logician's sense of "connote"; which is to say that the possession of that disposition by someone is the necessary and sufficient condition of the term "courageous" being correctly applied to that person. Thus, it would seem that many expressions that do not refer to anything, nevertheless, do denote and/or connote something. Let us pause for a moment to give explicit definitions of these terms as they are being used here.

W denotes the class, $C =_{df}$. C is the class of all those things of which W can truly be asserted.

W connotes the property, $P =_{df}$. The possession of P by something is a necessary and sufficient condition of W being correctly asserted of it (that is, of its belonging to the denotation of W).[8]

However, it is not at all clear that every nonreferring expression has a denotation and a connotation. Consider prepositions like "into," "at," and "by." There is no doubt that each has a meaning, in most cases a number of meanings. For example, one of the meanings of "at" is *in the direction of;* however, "at" can hardly be said to refer, denote, or connote. We can see that referring is out, by the same argument as that given previously; we cannot use "at" to pick out what we are going to talk about in a given sentence. To see that denotation and connotation are out as well, recall that "de-

---

[8] Note that this use of "denotation" and "connotation" (some logicians use "extension" and "intension" instead) is very different from the literary use, in which denotation is something like the standard meaning of a word, whereas connotation comprises the associations, which may well vary somewhat from person to person, to which this meaning gives rise.

note" and "connote" are defined in terms of an expression being applied to or asserted of something; hence, we can speak of an expression denoting or connoting only where it makes sense to speak of it being applied to or asserted of something. If you try to assert "at" of something, you draw a blank. Having said that it is at, you have said nothing. To make sense you must supplement this at least to the extent of saying, for example, that it was thrown *at the wall*. But then, what you have asserted of the thing in question is not "at," but rather "thrown at the wall." This *phrase* could be said to denote or connote, but not the preposition itself.

It may be that at this point we are once more being victimized by the poverty of the existing semantic terminology. It does seem plausible to suppose that there is some distinguishable aspect of the situation we are talking about when we utter sentences containing "at," to which the word "at" is related in some way not wholly unlike the way nouns or adjectives are related to what they connote or denote. We might try to formulate this aspect as *direction toward something*. We might then try to introduce a term that would designate the relation a preposition would have to such aspects of talked-about situations. But even if this is possible for prepositions, it still seems that such parts of speech as conjunctions and modal auxiliaries like "should," "would," and "might" will resist such treatment. It seems impossible to identify independently any aspect of talked-about situations to which "and," "if," or "should" is related in a way that is anything at all like reference, denotation, or connotation. There are those who have been so hypnotized by the referential theory as to insist, contrary to appearances, that such expressions do stand for something. It has been said that "and" stands for a conjunctive function, "or" stands for a disjunctive function, and so forth. But this view runs into the difficulty that there is no way of explaining what a "conjunctive function" is, except by saying, for example, that it is what we are asserting to hold between the fact that it is raining and the fact that the sun is shining when we say "It is raining and the sun is shining." And this means that we cannot identify a "conjunctive function" except by reference to the way we use "and" and equivalent expressions. Thus, we have not really gotten at an independently specifiable referent for "and" in the way we can for "Winston

Churchill." There we can specify what it is this name stands for, namely, the prime minister of Great Britain during the latter part of World War II, without having to bring into the specification talk about the way the name is used. In other words, to say that "and" stands for a "conjunctive function" is just to talk in a misleading way about the kind of function "and" has in sentences. No real extralinguistic reference has been demonstrated. Thus, there seems to be no escape from the conclusion that such expressions as conjunctions stand in no semantically interesting relations to extralinguistic entities.

Over and above the point that not all meaningful expressions stand for something in any sense of that term, there is a question as to whether the various types of "standing for" we have been considering have anything important in common. Is there anything semantically interesting that is common to referring, denoting, and connoting? If there is not, then there is no one sense of "stand for" in which all the expressions that have these various relations to the extralinguistic stand for something. And it seems that there is not. Of course we can say that what they all have in common is that they are all relationships that (1) hold between expressions and what the expressions are used to talk about, and (2) are crucial for the meaning of the expressions. (The second requirement is necessary because otherwise the fact that the word "pencil" is very unlike the class of pencils would be a relation of the sort in question.) But by bringing in requirement (2) we are making the account viciously circular; since the generic notion of "standing for" is brought in to give an account of the notion of meaning, we can hardly bring the notion of meaning into an explanation of it. And unless we do, it seems impossible to find anything significant that is in common to referring, denoting, and connoting. This leaves us with the conclusion that (even if we forget about such items as conjunctions) the principle, "To say that a word has a certain meaning is to say that it stands for something other than itself," is either straightforwardly false, or does not employ "stands for" in any one sense. And this means that we have failed to make explicit any single sense of the term "meaning" in which all words have meaning.

The upshot of this discussion is that we cannot give a generally adequate idea of what it is for a linguistic expression to have a certain meaning by explaining this in terms of referring, or in terms of any relation or set of relations like referring. The referential theory is based on an important insight—that language is used to talk about things outside (as well as inside) language, and that the suitability of an expression for such talk is somehow crucial for its having the meaning it has. But in the referential theory, this insight is ruined through oversimplification. The essential connection of language with "the world," with what is talked about, is represented as a piecemeal correlation of meaningful linguistic units with distinguishable components of the world. What the preceding discussion has shown is that the connection is not so simple as that. Speech does not consist of producing a sequence of labels, each of which is attached to something in "the world." Some of the meaningful components of the sentences we use to talk about the world can be connected in semantically important ways to distinguishable components of the world, but others cannot. Hence, we must look elsewhere for an account of what it is for an expression to have meaning, remembering that the account must be framed in such a way as to give due weight to the fact that language is somehow connected with the world.

MEANING AS A KIND OF ENTITY

If the referential theory of meaning is based on the fundamental insight that language is used to talk about things, the ideational and behavioral theories are based on an equally fundamental insight—that words have the meaning they do only because of what human beings do when they use language. These theories focus on aspects of what goes on in communication, in an effort to get at those features of the use of language that give linguistic units the meanings they have. These theories may or may not saddle themselves with the assumption we found to be fatally involved in the referential theory—that every meaningful linguistic unit stands for something, in some one sense of "stands for." When they do make this assumption, as is often the case, they bring in associations of ideas or stimulus-response connections as ways of explicating this relation of standing for. Thus, one may suppose a word stands for *x* by virtue of being associated with an idea of *x* (ideational theory), or by virtue of having the potentiality of giving rise to responses similar to those to which *x* gives rise (behavioral theory). These theories, however, are not necessarily cast in this form; and since the assumption just mentioned has already been amply criticized in connection with the referential theory, I shall, in considering the ideational and behavioral theories, concentrate on problems that would be there even if this assumption were not made.

Before examining these theories it would be well to note a certain deficiency in the way the problem of meaning and theories of meaning are often stated. More often than not, when people set out to clarify the concept of meaning they do so by asking, "What sort of entity is a meaning and how does an entity of this sort have to be related to a linguistic expression in order to be the meaning of that expression?" Theories of meaning are quite often expressed as answers to this kind of question. Thus, the referential theory generally takes the form of an identification of the meaning of *E* with that to which *E* refers, or alternatively with the relation between *E* and its referent; the ideational theory identifies the meaning of *E* with the idea(s) that give rise to it and to which it gives rise; and behavioral theories typically identify the meaning of an expression with the situation in which it is uttered, with responses made to its utterance, or both. There is something fundamentally wrong with this way of conceiving the problem. This can be seen by noting that we run into absurdities as soon as we take seriously the idea of identifying a meaning with anything otherwise specified (that is, specified in terms that do not include "meaning" or any of its synonyms or near synonyms). No matter what sort of entity we try to identify meanings with, we find many things that we would be prepared to say about an entity of that sort but would not be prepared to say about a meaning, and vice versa. Since many things are true of one but not true of the other, they cannot be identical. Suppose that, following out the behavioral theory, we attempt to identify the meaning of "Look out!" with such activities as ducking, falling prone, and fending. That the meaning is not identical with such activities can be shown by the fact that although it is true that I sometimes engage in such activities, it can hardly be true that I sometimes engage in the meaning of "Look out!" It makes no sense to talk of engaging in a meaning. Again it may be true that I have forgotten the meaning of "Look out!" without its being true that I have forgotten the activities of ducking, falling prone, and fending. Such examples show that meanings and activities belong to radically different categories; something can be true of one without there even being any sense in the supposition that it is true of the other. This same point will hold of anything else with which we try to identify meanings. The cruder form of the referential theory (in which the meaning is said to be the referent) is most obviously in trouble in this respect, for anything whatsoever can be a referent; at least, we cannot mention anything that is not a referent, for we have referred to it in the act of mentioning it. This means that the identification of the meaning of an expression with its referent could be maintained only if anything could be true of a meaning that was true of anything whatever; a random sample of referents will suffice to show that this is not the case. For example, the phrase "the father of pragmatism" refers to C. S. Peirce. If the meaning of that phrase were identical with its referent, we would have to be able to say, both intelligibly and truly, that the meaning of "the father of pragmatism" was married twice and that the meaning often wrote reviews for the *Nation*. Meanings, however, do not get married and they do not write reviews. And so it goes.

The moral of all this is that it is a basic mistake to suppose that "meanings" are entities of a sort that are otherwise specifiable. If we are to speak of meanings as a class of entities at all, we shall have to recognize that they are so unique as not to admit of being characterized in any other terms. The almost universal tendency to raise the problem of meaning in this form may come from the supposition that in specifying the meaning of a word, what we are doing is identifying the entity that is so related to that word as to be its meaning. That is, it is very natural to regard:

(1) The meaning of "procrastinate" is *put things off*.

as having the same logical form as:

(2) The capital of France is Paris.

and, consequently, to think that just as in (2) we are specifying the entity so related to France as to be its capital, so in (1) we are specifying the entity so related to "procrastinate" as to be its meaning. The simplest way of seeing that this is not what we are doing is to note that, in general, what follows "is" in statements like (1) is not a specification of any entity whatsoever. This is true of (1); "put things off" is not a phrase that has the function of specifying a certain entity of which we might then go on to ask and answer certain questions. The generalization is much more obviously true of:

(3) The meaning of "if" is *provided that.*

Here it is perfectly clear that there is no such entity as "provided that." This is so, not because no such thing happens to exist, but because it makes no sense to suppose that it does, for the phrase "provided that" simply does not have the function of designating some entity that may or may not exist.

Then what are we doing when we say what a word means? What we are doing is *exhibiting* another expression that we are claiming has at least approximately the same use as the one whose meaning we are specifying.[9] The primary reason for saying things like (1) and (3) is to help someone learn how to use the expression whose meaning we are specifying; when we provide a specification of meaning, we seek to accomplish this end by telling the person that this expression is used in the same way as another one that, we suppose, the person already knows how to use. Thus, (1) is roughly equivalent to "Use 'procrastinate' in the way you are accustomed to use 'put things off,' and you will be all right." We will be misled by superficial grammatical similarities if we suppose that what we are really doing is picking out a particular example of a special kind of entity called "meanings."[10]

If this account of meaning-statements is accurate, the problem of meaning should be formulated as follows: "How must one expression be related to another in order that the one can be exhibited in a specification of the meaning of the other?" If we can agree to use

<hr />

[9] For some qualifications to this conclusion see M. Scriven, "Definitions, Explanations, and Theories," *Minnesota Studies in the Philosophy of Science,* Vol. II (Minneapolis: University of Minnesota Press, 1958).

[10] For a more extended presentation of this point, see W. P. Alston, "The Quest for Meanings," *Mind,* Vol. LXXII (Jan. 1963).

the term "have the same use" as a label for that relationship, whatever it may turn out to be in detail, then the crucial question can be stated: "What is it for two expressions to have the same use?" And since whenever E_1 can be exhibited in a specification of the meaning of E_2, E_1 and E_2 would be said to have at least approximately the same meaning, to be at least approximately synonymous, we can formulate what is essentially the same question by asking, "What is it for two expressions to be synonymous?"

This point concerning the right way to raise the problem of meaning has absolutely no implications as to what *kind* of theory is or is not adequate; any of the standard types of theory can be formulated as an answer to this question. Thus, the referential theory can be stated by saying that two expressions have the same use if and only if they refer to the same object (or perhaps refer to the same object in the same way). The ideational theory would be that two expressions have the same use if and only if they are associated with the same idea(s); and the behavioral theory would hold that two expressions have the same use if and only if they are involved in the same stimulus-response connections. Henceforth, I shall proceed as if the theories were in this form, even when they are not explicitly so put.

THE IDEATIONAL THEORY

The classic statement of the ideational theory was given by the seventeenth century British philosopher, John Locke, in his *Essay Concerning Human Understanding*, section 1, Chapter 2, Book III. "The use, then, of words is to be sensible marks of ideas; and the ideas they stand for are their proper and immediate signification." This kind of theory is in the background whenever people think of language as a "means or instrument for the communication of thought," or as a "physical and external representation of an internal state," or when people define a sentence as a "chain of words expressing a complete thought." The picture of communication involved is set forth with great clarity by Locke in the passage immediately preceding the sentence just quoted.

> Man, though he has great variety of thoughts, and such, from which others, as well as himself, might receive profit and delight; yet they

are all within his own breast, invisible and hidden from others, nor can of themselves be made to appear. The comfort and advantage of society not being to be had without communication of thoughts, it was necessary that man should find out some external sensible signs, whereof those invisible ideas, which his thoughts are made up for, might be made known to others. . . . Thus we may conceive how words which were by nature so well adapted to that purpose, come to be made use of by men, as the signs of their ideas; not by any natural connexion that there is between particular articulate sounds and certain ideas, for then there would be but one language amongst all men; but by a voluntary imposition, whereby such a word is made arbitrarily the mark of such an idea.

According to this theory, what gives a linguistic expression a certain meaning is the fact that it is regularly used in communication as the "mark" of a certain idea; the ideas with which we do our thinking have an existence and a function that is independent of language. If each of us were content to keep all his thoughts to himself, language could have been dispensed with; it is only because we feel a need to convey our thoughts to each other that we have to make use of publicly observable indications of the purely private ideas that are coursing through our minds. A linguistic expression gets its meaning by being used as such an indication.

Let us see what would have to be the case for this theory to work. For each linguistic expression, or rather for each distinguishable sense of a linguistic expression, there would have to be an idea such that when any expression is used in that sense, it is used as an indication of the presence of that idea. This presumably means that whenever an expression is used in that sense, (1) the idea must be present in the mind of the speaker, and (2) the speaker must be producing the expression in order to get his audience to realize that the idea in question is in his mind at that time.[11] Finally, (3)

---

[11] On a less stringent version of the theory, there can be occasions on which the expression is used in that sense without the idea being consciously in the mind of the speaker, provided that the speaker could call up the idea if any question arose as to what he had meant. These occasions would be those on which we are using words "automatically," "unthinkingly," without having our minds on what we are saying. But even this form of the theory maintains that the above conditions are satisfied whenever we say anything with our minds on what we are saying; and, furthermore, it maintains that this is the primary kind of situation, from which the automatic use of words is derivative. That is,

insofar as communication is successful, the expression would have to call up the same idea in the mind of the hearer, with analogous qualifications as to an "unthinking" grasp of what was being said that might hold on some, though not on all, occasions.

These conditions are not in fact satisfied. Take a sentence at random, for example, "When in the course of human events, it becomes necessary for one people to . . . ," and utter it with your mind on what you are saying; then, ask yourself whether there was a distinguishable idea in your mind corresponding to each of the meaningful linguistic units of the sentence. Can you discern an idea of "when," "in," "course," "becomes," and so forth, swimming into your ken as each word is pronounced? In the unlikely event that you can, can you recognize the idea that accompanies "when" as the same idea that puts in an appearance whenever you utter "when" in that sense? Do you have a firm enough grip on the idea to call it up, or at least know what it would be like to call it up, without the word being present? In other words, is it something that is identifiable and producible apart from the word? Do you ever catch the idea of "when" appearing when you utter other words—"until," "rheostat," or "epigraphy"?

What is disturbing about these questions is not that they have one answer rather than another, but that we do not know how to go about answering them. What are we supposed to look for by way of an idea of "when"? How can we tell whether we have it in mind or not? Just what am I supposed to try for when I try to call it up out of context? The real difficulty is that we are unable to spot "ideas" as we would have to in order to test the ideational theory.

There is, to be sure, a sense of "idea" in which it is not completely implausible to say that ideas are involved in any intelligible bit of speech. This is the sense "idea" has in such expressions as "I get the idea," "I have no idea what you are saying," and "He isn't getting his ideas across." In that sense of the term, I don't

---

a given person could not meaningfully use a given word without having the corresponding idea in his mind, unless he fairly often produced it with the conscious intention of making it known that a certain idea was consciously in his mind.

understand what someone is saying unless I get the idea. But that is because the phrase "get the idea" would have to be explained as equivalent to "see what the speaker meant by his utterance" or "know what the speaker is saying." "Idea" in this sense is derivative from such notions as "meaning" and "understanding," and so can provide no basis for an explication of meaning. If we are to have an explication of meaning in terms of ideas, we must be using "idea" so that the presence or absence of an idea is decidable independent of determining in what senses words are being used. Ideas would have to be introspectively discriminable items in consciousness. Locke was trying to satisfy this requirement when he took "idea" to mean something like "sensation or mental image." But the more we push "idea" in the direction of such identifiability, the clearer it becomes that words are not related to ideas in the way required by the theory.

The ideational theory will not work even for words that have an obvious connection with mental images, for example, "dog," "stove," and "book." A little introspection should be sufficient to convince the reader that insofar as his use of the word "dog" is accompanied by mental imagery, it is by no means the case that the mental image is the same on each occasion the word is used in the same sense. At one time it may be the image of a collie, on another the image of a beagle, on one occasion the image of a dog sitting, on another the image of a dog standing, and so on. Of course a determined defender of the theory could claim that this fact is sufficient to show that the word is not being used in quite the same sense on these different occasions; however, if one takes this way out, he has simply lost contact with the concept of meaning he set out to explicate. For it is perfectly clear that such differences in mental imagery need not, and undoubtedly will not, be reflected in any difference in what one is saying. Conversely, one can have indistinguishable mental images accompanying different words with quite different meanings. Thus, the image of a sleeping beagle might accompany the utterance of the words "beagle," "hound," "dog," "mammal," "animal," "organism," "sports," "hunting," and so on. Clearly, this example does nothing to show that all these words were being used in the same sense.

MEANING AS A FUNCTION OF
SITUATION AND RESPONSE

The behavioral theory of meaning also concentrates on what is involved in using language in communication, but it differs from the ideational theory in focusing on publicly observable aspects of the communication situation. There are several reasons for the attractiveness of such a project. One deficiency of the ideational theory that was not explicitly mentioned above stems from the fact that we do not look for ideas in the minds of speakers and listeners in order to settle questions about what a word means in the language or about the sense in which a speaker used a term on a given occasion. If I am not sure as to the exact sense in which you used the word "normal" in something you just said, it would be absurd for me to try to find out by asking you to carefully introspect and tell me what imagery accompanied your utterance of the word. It is not at all clear just what we do look for in settling such questions; however, the fact that there is a broad consensus concerning what various words mean strongly suggests that meaning is a function of aspects of the communication situation that are open to public inspection. Moreover, the success of psychology in explaining some aspects of human behavior in terms of regular connections between observable stimuli and responses naturally gives rise to a hope of being able to give the same kind of treatment of verbal behavior.

The simplest forms of the behavioral theory are to be found in the writings of linguists who, not surprisingly, take over ideas from behaviorally minded psychologists with little awareness of the complexities involved. Thus, Leonard Bloomfield says that the ". . . meaning of a linguistic form . . ." is ". . . the situation in which the speaker utters it and the response which it calls forth in the hearer." [12] The crudity of this definition is mitigated by the qualifying statement: "We must discriminate between the nondistinctive features of the situation . . . and the distinctive, or linguistic meaning (the semantic features) which are common to all the situations that call forth the utterance of the linguistic form." [13]

[12] *Language* (London: George Allen & Unwin, Ltd., 1935), p. 139.
[13] *Ibid.*, p. 141.

The requirements for the adequacy of this kind of theory are similar to those for the ideational theory. If it is to work, there must be features that are common and peculiar to all the situations in which a given expression is uttered in a given sense, and there must be features common and peculiar to all the responses that are made to the utterance of a given expression in a given sense. (Furthermore, these common elements must be actually employed as criteria for assigning the sense in question to that expression. But if the preceding requirements are not satisfied, we do not have to worry about this one.) Again, this seems not to be the case. Certainly, for a single word like "shirt," there is nothing of interest that is common and peculiar to the situations in which the following utterances are made or to the responses they call forth.

> Bring me my shirt.
> This shirt is frayed.
> I need a new shirt.
> Shirts were rarely worn before the fourteenth century.
> What a lovely shirt!
> Do you wear a size 15 shirt?

Perhaps we would do better to start with sentences, leaving subsentential units for later treatment. But even here the prospects are discouraging.

(1) Bring me another cup of coffee, please.
(2) My shirt is torn.
(3) What a superb steak!

If we abandon counsels of perfection and overlook a few exceptions, we can find situational features that are common to *most* of the occasions on which each of the preceding sentences are uttered. For example (using S as an abbreviation for "the speaker" and H as an abbreviation for "the hearer"):

(1) S has recently had a cup of coffee.
   H is in a position to bring S a cup of coffee.
(2) S possesses a shirt.
   S is doing something to call H's attention to one of his shirts.
(3) S is doing something to call H's attention to some particular steak.
   S is enthusiastic about the steak.

Items like these, however, will not do the job, for several reasons.

First, these uniformities hold equally for quite different sentences with quite different meanings. Thus, the situational features listed for sentence (1) hold just as often for the sentence "No more coffee, please," and the situational features for sentence (2) are equally correlated with the sentence "Bring me my torn shirt."

Second, we have been considering the favorable cases. With declarative sentences that have to do with states of affairs remote from the situation of utterance, we are hard pressed to find any common situational features, at least any that seem likely to have an important bearing on the meaning of the sentence. Consider the sentences:

(4) The disarmament conference is about to collapse.
(5) Mozart wrote *Idomeneo* at the age of 25.
(6) Affirming the consequent produces a fallacious argument.

Each of these sentences can be uttered in a wide variety of situations, and there is little or nothing of relevance that they have in common. There are certain temporal limitations for (4) and (5). Thus, (4) is usually uttered while a disarmament conference is going on, and (5) is uttered only after 1781. But it is obvious that these uniformities are radically insufficient to distinguish these sentences from many others with quite different meanings.

Third, in all these cases we are going to have great difficulty in finding any interesting features common to the overt responses made to the utterance of the sentences. Imperatives look most promising in this respect, for they clearly call for a specific response from the hearer. But in what proportion of the cases in which an imperative is heard and understood is the standard compliance forthcoming? Think of the variety of responses that a parent's "Come in now" will elicit.

> No response. Whatever activity was in progress proceeds as if the utterance had not been made.
> Explicit refusal to comply.
> Demand for justification.
> Criticism of the parent for issuing the command.
> Justification of noncompliance.
> Plea for mercy.
> Change of subject.

Running in the opposite direction.
Compliance.

If the response last mentioned were made in a substantial proportion of cases, the life of a parent would be much easier. And imperatives constitute the favorable case. With assertions, it is much more difficult to suggest even a plausible candidate for a common response.

MEANING AS A FUNCTION OF
BEHAVIORAL DISPOSITIONS

Psychologists and psychologically oriented philosophers who have taken this kind of approach to meaning have tried to develop more sophisticated accounts. Interestingly enough, they have pretty much confined themselves to responses to linguistic utterances and have said little about the situation of utterance as a determinant of meaning. Presumably this is so because they have generally started with natural signs, where there is no intentional production of the sign. In concentrating on responses, men like the philosopher, Charles Morris, and the psychologist, Charles Osgood,[14] recognize that having a certain meaning cannot be simply identified with regularly evoking a certain overt response, for, as noted previously, (a) we can have meaningful utterances that evoke no response at all, and (b) where there are overt responses, they can vary widely among themselves without any variation in meaning. Something more elaborate is called for. This, Morris tries to provide in the concept of a disposition to respond.[15] To say that someone has a disposition to make a certain response, *R*, is simply to say that there are conditions, *C*, under which he will do *R*. It is to assert a certain hypothetical proposition of him—"if *C*, then *R*." Now, even though there is no one response that is universally, or even generally, elicited by the utterance of "Come in now," it may be that this utterance regularly produces a *disposition* to come in if

[14] See his *Method and Theory in Experimental Psychology* (New York: Oxford University Press, 1953), Chap. 16.
[15] See his *Signs, Language, and Behavior* (Englewood Cliffs, N.J.: Prentice-Hall, Inc., 1946), especially Chap. 1.

the hearer has a strong inclination to obey the speaker. In other words, it may be that this utterance brings it about that a certain hypothetical proposition comes to be true, namely, that if the hearer is generally inclined to obey the speaker, he will come into the house. This is what Morris is banking on. If this is generally the case, then we can specify something of a behavioral character that is common to all utterances of a given sentence even though there be nothing overt that is common.

Unfortunately, this version of the behavioral theory fares almost as badly as the simpler one. There are several reasons why it breaks down.

(1) If we try to specify the particular disposition(s), the regular production of which would give a particular sentence the meaning it has, we can think of some plausible candidates for certain kinds of sentences, for example, imperatives like "Come in now," and declarative sentences that have to do with matters of fact that have a direct bearing on the hearer's future conduct. As an example of the latter, consider "Your son is ill." We might think of this sentence as regularly producing a disposition to go where the hearer believes his son to be if he has a great deal of concern for him. But when we consider utterances having to do with matters more remote from practical concerns of the moment, things do not go so well. What semantically important dispositions are produced by historical utterances like "Mozart wrote *Idomeneo* at the age of 25"? It may be said that this produces a disposition to say "25" if one is asked "At what age did Mozart write *Idomeneo?*" But if this is the only kind of disposition we can specify, we are in trouble. For presumably the meaning of a sentence has something to do with its connection with the sorts of things it is used to talk about; consequently, the meaning of a sentence that is not about language can hardly be a function of purely linguistic dispositions.

(2) In fact, it is only in one sort of case that an utterance like "Your son is ill" will produce a disposition to go to where one believes one's son to be if one has a great deal of concern for one's son. This kind of case is one in which the hearer believes that the speaker is providing correct information and the hearer has not previously acquired that information. If I do not believe you when

you say "Your son is ill," your utterance will certainly not produce any such disposition. And if I were already aware of the fact, no such disposition will be produced by your utterance. I will already have been so disposed if I am going to be.

(3) Even in the ideal case there are problems. For one thing, we may have to make a given disposition extremely, perhaps indefinitely, complicated before there is any plausibility in supposing that it is regularly produced by the utterance of a certain sentence. Thus, even if I understand and believe someone when he tells me that my son is ill, and even if I were not previously aware of this, this utterance will not lead me to go to him, even given concern on my part, if I am in jail and cannot escape, or if I am at the crucial stage of some enormous business transaction that will affect my financial situation for years (and I have not been told that he is *seriously* ill), or if I have very strong religious scruples against travelling on a certain day, and so on. With a little ingenuity, we could keep going indefinitely in listing factors that, if present, would prevent the antecedent from giving rise to the consequent. Of course, for each of these possible interferences we could save the claim that the utterance generally produces the disposition in question by stipulating the absence of this interfering factor in the antecedent. Thus, the utterance of "Your son is ill" will produce in a hearer a disposition to go to his son if he has a great deal of concern for him, if he is not physically prevented from doing so, if he has no religious scruples against doing what is necessary for accomplishing this. . . . However, it is not at all clear that we can ever complete this list.

Thus far in my discussion of Morris, I have ignored the fact that he has saddled himself with the assumption that every meaningful expression is a "sign" of something. Despite the indefensibility of this assumption, we can see why a behavioral response theory needs it. For if we were to allow *any* disposition produced to have a bearing on the meaning of the sentence, we would be dragging in things that have nothing to do with meaning. Suppose that uttering "The sun is 97,000,000 miles from the earth" produces a disposition to open one's mouth in amazement if one were previously unaware of this. It is obvious that this disposition-production has nothing to do with the meaning of the sentence. We can imagine a lot of other sentences with widely different meanings having the same effect, for example, "The pyramids are several thousand years old." With the assumption that every expression is a "sign" of something, we can limit the relevant dispositions to those that are dispositions to the kinds of responses that are involved in some important way with the object. No doubt it is extremely difficult to see just what such responses would be in the case of "objects" like the distance of the sun from the earth and the age of the pyramids. In fact, the difficulty of deciding which "responses" are to be called relevant to a given "object" constitutes one of the main weaknesses in Morris' theory.

SUMMARY OF DISCUSSION
OF BEHAVIORAL THEORY

Whether we consider relatively crude versions that regard meaning as a function of common features of situations in which expressions are uttered and responses made to those utterances, or relatively sophisticated versions in terms of dispositions to response produced by utterances, we will be unable to find situation and response features that are distributed in the way the theory requires. Meaning simply does not vary directly with the kinds of factors highlighted in these theories.

Like the others, the behavioral theory is based on an insight that it perverts through oversimplification. Just as the meaningful use of language has something to do with reference to the "world," and just as in some way we do express and communicate our thoughts in using language, so it is also a significant fact that units of language get their meaning through being *used* by people, through the fact that they are involved in various sorts of behavior. Behavioral theories err in conceiving this behavioral involvement in oversimplified terms. They suppose that a word or sentence has a certain meaning by virtue of being involved, as response and/or stimulus, in stimulus-response connections that are basically similar, except for complexity, to a simple reflex like the knee jerk. Unfortunately, no such connections have ever been found, except for those that are obviously not determinative of meaning, like the fact that a sudden loud utterance of "Look out!" typically elicits a start. Some more adequate characterization of linguistic behavior is called for, one that will get at the units of behavior that are crucial for the meaning. . . .

JOHN STUART MILL

Of Names

§ 1. "A name," says Hobbes,[1] "is a word taken at pleasure to serve for a mark which may raise in our mind a thought like to some thought we had before, and which being pronounced to others, may be to them a sign of what thought the speaker had before in his mind." This simple definition of a name, as a word (or set of words) serving the double purpose of a mark to recall to ourselves the likeness of a former thought, and a sign to make it known to others, appears unexceptionable. Names, indeed, do much more than this; but whatever else they do, grows out of, and is the result of this: as will appear in its proper place.

Are names more properly said to be the names of things, or of our ideas of things? The first is the expression in common use; the last is that of some metaphysicians, who conceived that in adopting it they were introducing a highly important distinction. The eminent thinker, just quoted, seems to countenance the latter opinion. "But seeing," he continues, "names ordered in speech (as is defined) are signs of our conceptions, it is manifest they are not signs of the things themselves; for that the sound of this word *stone* should be the sign of a stone, cannot be understood in any sense but this, that he that hears it collects that he that pronounces it thinks of a stone."

---

* From *A System of Logic* (London, Longmans, 1843), Chapter 2.
[1] *Computation or Logic,* Chap. ii.

If it be merely meant that the conception alone, and not the thing itself, is recalled by the name, or imparted to the hearer, this of course cannot be denied. Nevertheless, there seems good reason for adhering to the common usage, and calling the word *sun* the name of the sun, and not the name of our idea of the sun. For names are not intended only to make the hearer conceive what we conceive, but also to inform him what we believe. Now, when I use a name for the purpose of expressing a belief, it is a belief concerning the thing itself, not concerning my idea of it. When I say, "the sun is the cause of day," I do not mean that my idea of the sun causes or excites in me the idea of day; or in other words, that thinking of the sun makes me think of day. I mean, that a certain physical fact, which is called the sun's presence (and which, in the ultimate analysis, resolves itself into sensations, not ideas) causes another physical fact, which is called day. It seems proper to consider a word as the *name* of that which we intend to be understood by it when we use it; of that which any fact that we assert of it is to be understood of; that, in short, concerning which, when we employ the word, we intend to give information. Names, therefore, shall always be spoken of in this work as the names of things themselves, and not merely of our ideas of things.

But the question now arises, of what things? And to answer this it is necessary to take into consideration the different kinds of names.

§ 2. It is usual, before examining the various classes into which names are commonly divided, to begin by distinguishing from names of every description, those words which are not names, but only parts of names. Among such are reckoned particles, as *of, to, truly, often;* the inflected cases of nouns substantive, as *me, him, John's;* and even adjectives, as *large, heavy.* These words do not express things of which anything can be affirmed or denied. We cannot say, Heavy fell, or A heavy fell; Truly, or A truly, was asserted; Of, or An of, was in the room. Unless, indeed, we are speaking of the mere words themselves, as when we say, Truly is an English word, or, Heavy is an adjective. In that case they are complete names, namely, names of those particular sounds, or of those particular collections of written characters. This employment of a word to denote the mere letters and syllables of which it is composed, was termed by the schoolmen the *suppositio materialis* of the word. In any other sense we cannot introduce one of these words into the subject of a proposition, unless in combination with other words; as, A heavy *body* fell, A truly *important fact* was asserted, A *member* of *parliament* was in the room.

An adjective, however, is capable of standing by itself as the predicate of a proposition; as when we say, Snow is white; and occasionally even as the subject, for we may say, White is an agreeable colour. The adjective is often said to be so used by a grammatical ellipsis: Snow is white, instead of Snow is a white object; White is an agreeable colour, instead of, A white colour, or, The colour white, is agreeable. The Greeks and Romans were allowed, by the rules of their language, to employ this ellipsis universally in the subject as well as in the predicate of a proposition. In English this cannot, generally speaking, be done. We may say, The earth is round; but we cannot say, Round is easily moved; we must say, A round object. This distinction, however, is rather grammatical than logical. Since there is no difference of meaning between *round,* and *a round object,* it is only custom which prescribes that on any given occasion one shall be used, and not the other. We shall, therefore, without scruple, speak of adjectives as names, whether in their own right, or as representative of the more circuitous forms of expression above exemplified. The other classes of subsidiary words have no title whatever to be considered as names. An adverb, or an accusative case, cannot under any circumstances (except when their mere letters and syllables are spoken of) figure as one of the terms of a proposition.

. . . .

For, as one word is frequently not a name, but only part of a name, so a number of words often compose one single name, and no more. These words, "the place which the wisdom or policy of antiquity had destined for the residence of the Abyssinian princes," form in the estimation of the logician only one name; one Categorematic term. A mode of determining whether any set of words makes only one name, or more than one, is by predicating something of it, and observing whether, by this predication, we make only one assertion or several. Thus, when we say, John Nokes, who was the mayor of the town, died yesterday—by this predication we make but one assertion; whence it appears that "John Nokes, who was the mayor of the town," is no more than one name. It is true that in this proposition, besides the assertion that John Nokes died yesterday, there is included another assertion, namely, that John Nokes was mayor of the town. But this last assertion was already made: we did not make it by adding the predicate, "died yesterday." Suppose, however, that the words had been, John Nokes *and* the mayor of the town, they would have formed two names instead of one. For when we say, John Nokes and the mayor of the town died yesterday, we make two assertions; one, that John Nokes died yesterday; the other, that the mayor of the town died yesterday.

It being needless to illustrate at any greater length the subject of many-worded names, we proceed to the distinctions which have been established among names, not according to the words they are composed of, but according to their signification.

§ 3. All names are names of something, real or imaginary; but all things have not names appropriated to them individually. For some individual objects we require, and consequently have, separate distinguishing names; there is a name for every person, and for every remarkable place. Other objects, of which we have not occasion to speak so frequently, we do not designate by a name of their own; but when the necessity arises for naming them, we do so by putting together several words, each of which, by itself, might be and is used for an indefinite number of other objects; as when I say, *this stone:* "this" and "stone" being, each of them, names that may be used of many other objects besides the particular one meant, though the only object of which they can both be used at the given moment, consistently with their signification, may be the one of which I wish to speak.

Were this the sole purpose for which names, that are common to more things than one, could be employed; if they only served, by mutually limiting each other, to afford a designation for such individual objects as have no names of their own; they could only be ranked among contrivances for economizing the use of language. But it is evident that this is not their sole function. It is by their means that we are enabled to assert *general* propositions; to affirm or deny any predicate of an indefinite number of things at once. The distinction, therefore, between *general* names, and *individual* or *singular* names, is fundamental; and may be considered as the first grand division of names.

A general name is familiarly defined, a name which is capable of being truly affirmed, in the same sense, of each of an indefinite number of things. An individual or singular name is a name which is only capable of being truly affirmed, in the same sense, of one thing.

Thus, *man* is capable of being truly affirmed of John, George, Mary, and other persons without assignable limit; and it is affirmed of all of them in the same sense; for the word man expresses certain qualities, and when we predicate it of those persons, we assert that they all possess those qualities. But *John* is only capable of being truly affirmed of one single person, at least in the same sense. For though there are many persons who bear that name, it is not conferred upon them to indicate any qualities, or anything which belongs to them in common; and cannot be said to be affirmed of them in any *sense* at all, consequently not in the same sense. "The king who succeeded William the Conqueror," is also an individual name. For, that there cannot be more than one person of whom it can be truly affirmed, is implied in the meaning of the words. Even *"the* king," when the occasion or the context defines the individual of whom it is to be understood, may justly be regarded as an individual name.

It is not unusual, by way of explaining what is meant by a general name, to say that it is the name of a *class*. But this, though a convenient mode of expression for some purposes, is objectionable as a definition, since it explains the clearer of two things by the more obscure. It would be more logical to reverse the proposition, and turn it into a definition of the word *class:* "A class is the indefinite multitude of individuals denoted by a general name."

It is necessary to distinguish *general* from *collective* names. A general name is one which can be predicated of *each* individual of a multitude; a collective name cannot be predicated of each separately, but only of all taken together. "The 76th regiment of foot in the British army," which is a collective name, is not a general but an individual name; for though it can be predicated of a multitude of individual soldiers taken jointly, it cannot be predicated of them severally. We may say, Jones is a soldier, and Thompson is a soldier, and Smith is a soldier, but we cannot say, Jones is the 76th regiment, and Thompson is the 76th regiment, and Smith is the 76th regiment. We can only say, Jones, and Thompson, and Smith, and Brown, and so forth (enumerating all the soldiers), are the 76th regiment.

"The 76th regiment" is a collective name, but not a general one: "a regiment" is both a collective and a general name. General with respect to all individual regiments, of each of which separately it can be affirmed; collective with respect to the individual soldiers of whom any regiment is composed.

§ 4. The second general division of names is into *concrete* and *abstract*. A concrete name is a name which stands for a thing; an abstract name is a name which stands for an attribute of a thing. Thus *John, the sea, this table,* are names of things. *White,* also, is a name of a thing, or rather of things. Whiteness, again, is the name of a quality or attribute of those things. Man is a name of many things; humanity is a name of an attribute of those things. *Old* is a name of things; *old age* is a name of one of their attributes.

I have used the words concrete and abstract in the sense annexed to them by the schoolmen, who, notwithstanding the imperfections of their philosophy, were unrivalled in the construction of technical language, and whose definitions, in logic at least, though they never went more than a little way into the subject, have seldom, I think, been altered but to be spoiled. A practice, however, has grown up in more modern times, which, if not introduced by Locke, has gained currency chiefly from his example, of applying the expression "abstract name" to all names which are the result of abstraction or generalization, and consequently to all general names, instead of confining it to the names of attributes. . . . A more wanton alteration in the meaning of a word is rarely to be met with; for the expression *general name,* the exact equivalent of which exists in all languages I am acquainted with, was already available for the purpose to which *abstract* has been misappropriated, while the misappropriation leaves that important class of words, the names of attributes, without any compact distinctive appellation. The old acceptation, however, has not gone so completely out of use, as to deprive those who still adhere to it of all chance of being understood. By *abstract*, then, I shall always, in Logic, mean the opposite of *concrete*: by an abstract name, the name of an attribute; by a concrete name, the name of an object.

Do abstract names belong to the class of general, or to that of singular names? Some of them are certainly general. I mean those which are names not of one single and definite attribute, but of a class of attributes. Such is the word *colour,* which is a name common to whiteness, redness, and so forth. Such is even the word whiteness, in respect of the different shades of whiteness to which it is applied in common; the word magnitude, in respect of the various degrees of magnitude and the various dimensions of space; the word weight, in respect of the various degrees of weight. Such also is the word *attribute* itself, the common name of all particular attributes. But when only one attribute, neither variable in degree nor in kind, is designated by the name; as visibleness; tangibleness; equality; squareness; milkwhiteness; then the name can hardly be considered general; for though it denotes an attribute of many different objects, the attribute itself is always conceived as one, not many. To avoid needless logomachies, the best course would probably be to consider these names as neither general nor individual, and to place them in a class apart.

It may be objected to our definition of an abstract name, that not only the names which we have called abstract, but adjectives, which we have placed in the concrete class, are names of attributes; that *white,* for example, is as much the name of the colour as *whiteness* is. But (as before remarked) a word ought to be considered as the name of that which we intend to be understood by it when we put it to its principal use, that is, when we employ it in predication. When we say snow is white, milk is white, linen is white, we do not mean it to be understood that snow, or linen, or milk, is a colour. We mean that they are things having the colour. The reverse is the case with the word whiteness; what we affirm to *be* whiteness is not snow, but the colour of snow. Whiteness, therefore, is the name of the colour exclusively: white is a name of all things whatever having the colour; a name, not of the quality whiteness, but of every white object. It is true, this name was given to all those various objects on account of the quality; and we may therefore say, without impropriety, that the quality forms part of its signification; but a name can only be said to stand for, or to be a name of, the things of which it can be predicated. We shall presently see that all names which can be said to have any signification, all names by applying which to an individual we give any information respecting that individual, may be said to *imply* an attribute of some sort; but they are not names of the attribute; it has its own proper abstract name.

§ 5. This leads to the consideration of a third great division of names, into *connotative* and *nonconnotative,* the latter sometimes, but improperly, called *absolute.* This is one of the most important distinctions which we shall have occasion to point out, and one of those which go deepest into the nature of language.

A nonconnotative term is one which signifies a subject only, or an attribute only. A connotative term is one which denotes a subject, and implies an attribute. By a subject is here meant anything which possesses attributes. Thus John, or London, or England, are names which signify a subject only. Whiteness, length, virtue, signify an attribute only. None of these names, therefore, are connotative. But *white, long, virtuous,* are connotative. The word white, denotes all white things, as snow, paper, the foam of the sea, and so forth, and implies, or as it was termed by the schoolmen, *connotes,*[2] the attribute *whiteness.* The word white is not predicated of the attribute, but of the subjects, snow, and so forth; but when we predicate it of them, we imply, or connote, that the attribute whiteness belongs to them. The same may be said of the other words above cited. Virtuous, for example, is the name of a class, which includes Socrates, Howard, the Man of Ross, and an indefinable number of other individuals, past, present, and to come. These individuals, collectively and severally, can alone be said with propriety to be denoted by the word: of them alone can it properly be said to be a name. But it is a name applied to all of them in consequence of an attribute which they are supposed to possess

---

[2] *Notare,* to mark; *connotare,* to mark *along with;* to mark one thing *with* or *in addition to* another.

in common, the attribute which has received the name of virtue. It is applied to all beings that are considered to possess this attribute; and to none which are not so considered.

All concrete general names are connotative. The word *man,* for example, denotes Peter, Jane, John, and an indefinite number of other individuals, of whom, taken as a class, it is the name. But it is applied to them, because they possess, and to signify that they possess, certain attributes. These seem to be, corporeity, animal life, rationality, and a certain external form, which for distinction we call the human. Every existing thing, which possessed all these attributes, would be called a man; and anything which possessed none of them, or only one, or two, or even three of them without the fourth, would not be so called. For example, if in the interior of Africa there were to be discovered a race of animals possessing reason equal to that of human beings, but with the form of an elephant, they would not be called men. Swift's Houyhnhnms would not be so called. Or if such newly-discovered beings possessed the form of man without any vestige of reason, it is probable that some other name than that of man would be found for them. How it happens that there can be any doubt about the matter, will appear hereafter. The word *man,* therefore, signifies all these attributes, and all subjects which possess these attributes. But it can be predicated only of the subjects. What we call men, are the subjects, the individual Stiles and Nokes; not the qualities by which their humanity is constituted. The name, therefore, is said to signify the subjects *directly,* the attributes *indirectly;* it *denotes* the subjects, and implies, or involves, or indicates, or as we shall say henceforth *connotes,* the attributes. It is a connotative name.

Connotative names have hence been also called *denominative,* because the subject which they denote is denominated by, or receives a name from, the attribute which they connote. Snow, and other objects, receive the name white, because they possess the attribute which is called whiteness; Peter, James, and others receive the name man, because they possess the attributes which are considered to constitute humanity. The attribute, or attributes, may therefore be said to denominate those objects, or to give them a common name.

It has been seen that all concrete general names are connotative.

Even abstract names, though the names only of attributes, may in some instances be justly considered as connotative; for attributes themselves may have attributes ascribed to them; and a word which denotes attributes may connote an attribute of those attributes. Of this description, for example, is such a word as *fault;* equivalent to *bad* or *hurtful quality.* This word is a name common to many attributes, and connotes hurtfulness, an attribute of those various attributes. When, for example, we say that slowness, in a horse, is a fault, we do not mean that the slow movement, the actual change of place of the slow horse, is a bad thing, but that the property or peculiarity of the horse, from which it derives that name, the quality of being a slow mover, is an undesirable peculiarity.

In regard to those concrete names which are not general but individual, a distinction must be made.

Proper names are not connotative: they denote the individuals who are called by them; but they do not indicate or imply any attributes as belonging to those individuals. When we name a child by the name Paul, or a dog by the name Cæsar, these names are simply marks used to enable those individuals to be made subjects of discourse. It may be said, indeed, that we must have had some reason for giving them those names rather than any others; and this is true; but the name, once given, is independent of the reason. A man may have been named John, because that was the name of his father; a town may have been named Dartmouth, because it is situated at the mouth of the Dart. But it is no part of the signification of the word John, that the father of the person so called bore the same name; nor even of the word Dartmouth, to be situated at the mouth of the Dart. If sand should choke up the mouth of the river, or an earthquake change its course, and remove it to a distance from the town, the name of the town would not necessarily be changed. That fact, therefore, can form no part of the signification of the word; for otherwise, when the fact confessedly ceased to be true, no one would any longer think of applying the name. Proper names are attached to the objects themselves, and are not dependent on the continuance of any attribute of the object.

But there is another kind of names, which, although they are individual names, that is, predicable only of one object, are really connotative. For, though we may give to an individual a name utterly unmeaning, which we call a proper name—a word which answers the purpose of showing what thing it is we are talking about, but not of telling anything about it; yet a name peculiar to an individual is not necessarily of this description. It may be significant of some attribute, or some union of attributes, which, being possessed by no object but one, determines the name exclusively to that individual. "The sun" is a name of this description; "God," when used by a monotheist, is another. These, however, are scarcely examples of what we are now attempting to illustrate, being, in strictness of language, general, not individual names: for, however they may be *in fact* predicable only of one object, there is nothing in the meaning of the words themselves which implies this: and, accordingly, when we are imagining and not affirming, we may speak of many suns; and the majority of mankind have believed, and still believe, that there are many gods. But it is easy to produce words which are real instances of connotative individual names. It may be part of the meaning of the connotative name itself, that there can exist but one individual possessing the attribute which it connotes: as, for instance, "the *only* son of John Stiles"; "the *first* emperor of Rome." Or the attribute connoted may be a connexion with some determinate event, and the connexion may be of such a kind as only one individual could have; or may at least be such as only one individual actually had; and this may be implied in the form of the expression. "The father of Socrates" is an example of the one kind (since Socrates could not have had two fathers); "the author of the Iliad," "the murderer of Henri Quatre," of the second. For, though it is conceivable that more persons than one might have participated in the authorship of the Iliad, or in the murder of Henri Quatre, the employment of the article *the* implies that, in fact, this was not the case. What is here done by the word *the,* is done in other cases by the context: thus, "Cæsar's army" is an individual name, if it appears from the context that the army meant is that which Cæsar commanded in a particular battle. The still more general expressions, "the Roman army," or "the Christian army," may be individualized in a similar manner. Another case of frequent occurrence has already been noticed; it is the following. The name, being a many-worded one, may consist, in the first place, of a *general* name, capable therefore in itself of being affirmed of more things than one, but which is, in the second place, so limited by other words joined with it, that the entire expression can only be predicated of one object, consistently with the meaning of the general term. This is exemplified in such an instance as the following: "the present prime minister of England." Prime Minister of England is a general name; the attributes which it connotes may be possessed by an indefinite number of persons: in succession however, not simultaneously; since the meaning of the name itself imports (among other things) that there can be only one such person at a time. This being the case, and the application of the name being afterwards limited by the article and the word *present,* to such individuals as possess the attributes at one indivisible point of time, it becomes applicable only to one individual. And as this appears from the meaning of the name, without any extrinsic proof, it is strictly an individual name.

From the preceding observations it will easily be collected, that whenever the names given to objects convey any information, that is, whenever they have properly any meaning, the meaning resides not in what they *denote,* but in what they *connote.* The only names of objects which connote nothing are *proper* names; and these have, strictly speaking, no signification.

If, like the robber in the Arabian Nights, we make a mark with chalk on a house to enable us to know it again, the mark has a purpose, but it has not properly any meaning. The chalk does not declare anything about the house; it does not mean, this is such a person's house, or This is a house which contains booty. The object of making the mark is merely distinction. I say to myself, All these houses are so nearly alike that if I lose sight of them I shall not again be able to distinguish that which I am now looking at, from any of the others; I must therefore contrive to make the appearance of this one house unlike that of the others, that I may hereafter know, when I see the mark—not indeed any attribute of the house —but simply that it is the same house which I am now looking at. Morgiana chalked all the other houses in a similar manner, and defeated the scheme. How? Simply by obliterating the difference of appearance between that house and the others. The chalk was still there, but it no longer served the purpose of a distinctive mark.

When we impose a proper name, we perform an operation in

some degree analogous to what the robber intended in chalking the house. We put a mark, not indeed upon the object itself, but, so to speak, upon the idea of the object. A proper name is but an unmeaning mark which we connect in our minds with the idea of the object, in order that whenever the mark meets our eyes or occurs to our thoughts, we may think of that individual object. Not being attached to the thing itself, it does not, like the chalk, enable us to distinguish the object when we see it; but it enables us to distinguish it when it is spoken of, either in the records of our own experience, or in the discourse of others; to know that what we find asserted in any proposition of which it is the subject, is asserted of the individual thing with which we were previously acquainted.

When we predicate of anything its proper name; when we say, pointing to a man, this is Brown or Smith, or pointing to a city, that it is York, we do not, merely by so doing, convey to the hearer any information about them, except that those are their names. By enabling him to identify the individuals, we may connect them with information previously possessed by him; by saying, This is York, we may tell him that it contains the Minster. But this is in virtue of what he has previously heard concerning York; not by anything implied in the name. It is otherwise when objects are spoken of by connotative names. When we say, The town is built of marble, we give the hearer what may be entirely new information, and this merely by the signification of the many-worded connotative name, "built of marble." Such names are not signs of the mere objects, invented because we have occasion to think and speak of those objects individually; but signs which accompany an attribute: a kind of livery in which the attribute clothes all objects which are recognised as possessing it. They are not mere marks, but more, that is to say, significant marks; and the connotation is what constitutes their significance.

As a proper name is said to be the name of the one individual which it is predicated of, so (as well from the importance of adhering to analogy, as for the other reasons formerly assigned) a connotative name ought to be considered a name of all the various individuals which it is predicable of, or in other words *denotes*, and not of what it connotes. But by learning what things it is a name of, we do not learn the meaning of the name: for to the same thing we may, with equal propriety, apply many names, not equivalent in meaning. Thus, I call a certain man by the name Sophroniscus: I call him by another name, The father of Socrates. Both these are names of the same individual, but their meaning is altogether different; they are applied to that individual for two different purposes; the one, merely to distinguish him from other persons who are spoken of; the other to indicate a fact relating to him, the fact that Socrates was his son. I further apply to him these other expressions: a man, a Greek, an Athenian, a sculptor, an old man, an honest man, a brave man. All these are, or may be, names of Sophroniscus, not indeed of him alone, but of him and each of an indefinite number of other human beings. Each of these names is applied to Sophroniscus for a different reason, and by each whoever understands its meaning is apprised of a distinct fact or number of facts concerning him; but those who knew nothing about the names except that they were applicable to Sophroniscus, would be altogether ignorant of their meaning. It is even possible that I might know every single individual of whom a given name could be with truth affirmed, and yet could not be said to know the meaning of the name. A child knows who are its brothers and sisters, long before it has any definite conception of the nature of the facts which are involved in the signification of those words.

In some cases it is not easy to decide precisely how much a particular word does or does not connote; that is, we do not exactly know (the case not having arisen) what degree of difference in the object would occasion a difference in the name. Thus, it is clear that the word man, besides animal life and rationality, connotes also a certain external form; but it would be impossible to say precisely what form; that is, to decide how great a deviation from the form ordinarily found in the beings whom we are accustomed to call men, would suffice in a newly-discovered race to make us refuse them the name of man. Rationality, also, being a quality which admits of degrees, it has never been settled what is the lowest degree of that quality which would entitle any creature to be considered a human being. In all such cases, the meaning of the general name is so far unsettled and vague; mankind have not come to any positive agreement about the matter. When we come to treat of Classification, we shall have occasion to show under what conditions this vagueness may exist without practical inconvenience; and cases will appear in which the ends of language are better promoted by it than by complete precision; in order that, in natural history for instance, individuals or species of no very marked character may be ranged with those more strongly characterized individuals or species to which, in all their properties taken together, they bear the nearest resemblance.

But this partial uncertainty in the connotation of names can only be free from mischief when guarded by strict precautions. One of the chief sources, indeed, of lax habits of thought, is the custom of using connotative terms without a distinctly ascertained connotation, and with no more precise notion of their meaning than can be loosely collected from observing what objects they are used to denote. It is in this manner that we all acquire, and inevitably so, our first knowledge of our vernacular language. A child learns the meaning of the words *man,* or *white,* by hearing them applied to a variety of individual objects, and finding out, by a process of generalization and analysis which he could not himself describe, what those different objects have in common. In the case of these two words the process is so easy as to require no assistance from culture; the objects called human beings, and the objects called white, differing from all others by qualities of a peculiarly definite and obvious character. But in many other cases, objects bear a general resemblance to one another, which leads to their being familiarly classed together under a common name, while, without more analytic habits than the generality of mankind possess, it is not immediately apparent what are the particular attributes, upon the possession of which in common by them all, their general resemblance depends. When this is the case, people use the name without any recognised connotation, that is, without any precise meaning; they talk, and consequently think, vaguely, and remain contented to attach only the same degree of significance to their own words, which a child three years old attaches to the words brother and sister. The child at least is seldom puzzled by the starting up of new individuals, on whom he is ignorant whether or not to confer the title; because there is usually an authority close at hand competent to solve all doubts. But a similar resource does not exist in the generality of cases; and new objects are continually presenting themselves to men, women, and children, which they are called upon to class *proprio motu*. They, accordingly, do this on no other principle than that of superficial similarity, giving to each new object the name of that familiar object, the idea of which it most readily recalls, or which, on a cursory inspection, it seems to them most to resemble: as an unknown substance found in the ground will be called, according to its texture, earth, sand, or a stone. In this manner, names creep on from subject to subject, until all traces of a common meaning sometimes disappear, and the word comes to denote a number of things not only independently of any common attribute, but which have actually no attribute in common; or none but what is shared by other things to which the name is capriciously refused. Even scientific writers have aided in this perversion of general language from its purpose; sometimes because, like the vulgar, they knew no better; and sometimes in deference to that aversion to admit new words, which induces mankind, on all subjects not considered technical, to attempt to make the original stock of names serve with but little augmentation to express a constantly increasing number of objects and distinctions, and, consequently, to express them in a manner progressively more and more imperfect.

To what a degree this loose mode of classing and denominating objects has rendered the vocabulary of mental and moral philosophy unfit for the purposes of accurate thinking, is best known to whoever has most meditated on the present condition of those branches of knowledge. Since, however, the introduction of a new technical language as the vehicle of speculations on subjects belonging to the domain of daily discussion, is extremely difficult to effect, and would not be free from inconvenience even if effected, the problem for the philosopher, and one of the most difficult which he has to resolve, is, in retaining the existing phraseology, how best to alleviate its imperfections. This can only be accomplished by giving to every general concrete name which there is frequent occasion to predicate, a definite and fixed connotation; in order that it may be known what attributes, when we call an object by that name, we really mean to predicate of the object. And the question of most nicety is, how to give this fixed connotation to a name, with the least possible change in the objects which the name is habitually employed to denote; with the least possible disarrangement, either by adding or subtraction, of the group of objects which, in however imperfect a manner, it serves to circumscribe and hold together; and with the least vitiation of the truth of any propositions which are commonly received as true.

This desirable purpose, of giving a fixed connotation where it is wanting, is the end aimed at whenever any one attempts to give a definition of a general name already in use; every definition of a connotative name being an attempt either merely to declare, or to declare and analyse, the connotation of the name. And the fact, that no questions which have arisen in the moral sciences have been subjects of keener controversy than the definitions of almost all the leading expressions, is a proof how great an extent the evil to which we have adverted has attained.

Names with indeterminate connotation are not to be confounded with names which have more than one connotation, that is to say, ambiguous words. A word may have several meanings, but all of them fixed and recognised ones; as the word *post*, for example, or the word *box*, the various senses of which it would be endless to enumerate. And the paucity of existing names, in comparison with the demand for them, may often render it advisable and even necessary to retain a name in this multiplicity of acceptations, distinguishing these so clearly as to prevent their being confounded with one another. Such a word may be considered as two or more names, accidentally written and spoken alike.

§ 6. The fourth principal division of names, is into *positive* and *negative*. Positive, as *man, tree, good;* negative, as *not-man, not-tree, not-good*. To every positive concrete name, a corresponding negative one might be framed. After giving a name to any one thing, or to any plurality of things, we might create a second name which should be a name of all things whatever, except that particular thing or things. These negative names are employed whenever we have occasion to speak collectively of all things other than some thing or class of things. When the positive name is connotative, the corresponding negative name is connotative likewise; but in a peculiar way, connoting not the presence but the absence of an attribute. Thus, *not-white* denotes all things whatever except white things; and connotes the attribute of not possessing whiteness. For the nonpossession of any given attribute is also an attribute, and may receive a name as such; and thus negative concrete names may obtain negative abstract names to correspond to them.

Names which are positive in form are often negative in reality, and others are really positive though their form is negative. The word *inconvenient,* for example, does not express the mere absence of convenience; it expresses a positive attribute, that of being the cause of discomfort or annoyance. So the word *unpleasant,* notwithstanding its negative form, does not connote the mere absence of pleasantness, but a less degree of what is signified by the word *painful,* which, it is hardly necessary to say, is positive. *Idle,* on the other hand, is a word which, though positive in form, expresses nothing but what would be signified either by the phrase *not working,* or by the phrase *not disposed to work;* and *sober,* either by *not drunk* or by *not drunken.*

There is a class of names called *privative.* A privative name is equivalent in its signification to a positive and a negative name taken together; being the name of something which has once had a particular attribute, or for some other reason might have been expected to have it, but which has it not. Such is the word *blind,* which is not equivalent to *not seeing,* or to *not capable of seeing,* for it would not, except by a poetical or rhetorical figure, be applied to stocks and stones. A thing is not usually said to be blind, unless the class to which it is most familiarly referred, or to which it is referred on the particular occasion, be chiefly composed of things which can see, as in the case of a blind man, or a blind horse; or unless it is supposed for any reason that it ought to see; as in saying of a man, that he rushed blindly into an abyss, or of philosophers or the clergy that the greater part of them are blind guides. The names called privative, therefore, connote two things: the absence of certain attributes, and the presence of others, from which the presence also of the former might naturally have been expected.

§ 7. The fifth leading division of names is into *relative* and *absolute,* or let us rather say, *relative* and *nonrelative;* for the word absolute is put upon much too hard duty in metaphysics, not to be willingly spared when its services can be dispensed with. It resembles the word *civil* in the language of jurisprudence, which stands for the opposite of criminal, the opposite of ecclesiastical, the opposite of military, the opposite of political—in short, the opposite of any positive word which wants a negative.

Relative names are such as father, son; ruler, subject; like; equal; unlike; unequal; longer, shorter; cause, effect. Their characteristic property is, that they are always given in pairs. Every relative name which is predicated of an object, supposes another object (or objects), of which we may predicate either that same name or another relative name which is said to be the *correlative* of the former. Thus, when we call any person a son, we suppose other persons who must be called parents. When we call any event a cause, we suppose another event which is an effect. When we say of any distance that it is longer, we suppose another distance which is shorter. When we say of any object that it is like, we mean that it is like some other object, which is also said to be like the first. In this last case both objects receive the same name; the relative term is its own correlative.

It is evident that these words, when concrete, are, like other concrete general names, connotative; they denote a subject, and connote an attribute; and each of them has or might have a corresponding abstract name, to denote the attribute connoted by the concrete. Thus the concrete *like* has its abstract *likeness;* the concretes, father and son, have, or might have, the abstracts, paternity, and filiety, or sonship. The concrete name connotes an attribute, and the abstract name which answers to it denotes that attribute. But of what nature is the attribute? Wherein consists the peculiarity in the connotation of a relative name?

The attribute signified by a relative name, say some, is a relation; and this they give, if not as a sufficient explanation, at least as the only one attainable. If they are asked, "What then is a relation?" they do not profess to be able to tell. It is generally regarded as something peculiarly recondite and mysterious. I cannot, however, perceive in what respect it is more so than any other attribute; indeed, it appears to me to be so in a somewhat less degree. I conceive, rather, that it is by examining into the signification of relative names, or, in other words, into the nature of the attribute which they connote, that a clear insight may best be obtained into the nature of all attributes: of all that is meant by an attribute.

It is obvious, in fact, that if we take any two correlative names, *father* and *son* for instance, though the objects *de*noted by the names are different, they both, in a certain sense, connote the same thing. They cannot, indeed, be said to connote the same *attribute:* to be a father, is not the same thing as to be a son. But when we call one man a father, another a son, what we mean to affirm is a set of facts, which are exactly the same in both cases. To predicate of A that he is the father of B, and of B that he is the son of A, is to assert one and the same fact in different words. The two propositions are exactly equivalent: neither of them asserts more or asserts less than the other. The paternity of A and the filiety of B are not two facts, but two modes of expressing the same fact. That fact, when analysed, consists of a series of physical events or phenomena, in which both A and B are parties concerned, and from which they both derive names. What those names really connote, is this series of events: that is the meaning, and the whole meaning, which either of them is intended to convey. The series of events may be said to *constitute* the relation.

•   •   •   •   •   •   •   •   •   •   •   •

§ 8. Names have been further distinguished into *univocal* and *equivocal:* these, however, are not two kinds of names, but two different modes of employing names. A name is univocal, or applied univocally, with respect to all things of which it can be predicated *in the same sense:* it is equivocal, or applied equivocally, as respects those things of which it is predicated in different senses. It is scarcely necessary to give instances of a fact so familiar as the double meaning of a word. In reality, as has been already observed, an equivocal or ambiguous word is not one name, but two names, accidentally coinciding in sound. *File* meaning a steel instrument, and *file* meaning a line of soldiers, have no more title to be considered one word, because written alike, than *grease* and *Greece* have, because they are pronounced alike. They are one sound, appropriated to form two different words.

An intermediate case is that of a name used *analogically* or metaphorically; that is, a name which is predicated of two things, not univocally, or exactly in the same signification, but in significations somewhat similar, and which being derived one from the other, one of them may be considered the primary, and the other a secondary signification. As when we speak of a brilliant light and a brilliant achievement. The word is not applied in the same sense to the light and to the achievement; but having been applied to the light in its original sense, that of brightness to the eye, it is transferred to the achievement in a derivative signification, supposed to be somewhat like the primitive one. The word, however, is just as properly two names instead of one, in this case, as in that of the most perfect ambiguity. And one of the commonest forms of fallacious reasoning arising from ambiguity, is that of arguing from a metaphorical expression as if it were literal; that is, as if a word, when applied metaphorically, were the same name as when taken in its original sense: which will be seen more particularly in its place.

JOHN LOCKE

Of Words

~~~~~~

OF THE SIGNIFICATION OF WORDS

(1) WORDS ARE SENSIBLE SIGNS NECESSARY FOR COMMUNICA-
TION. Man, though he have great variety of thoughts, and such
from which others as well as himself might receive profit and de-
light, yet they are all within his own breast, invisible, and hidden
from others, nor can of themselves be made appear. The comfort
and advantage of society not being to be had without communication of thoughts, it was necessary that man should find out some
external sensible signs, whereby those invisible ideas which his
thoughts are made up of might be made known to others. For this
purpose nothing was so fit, either for plenty or quickness, as those
articulate sounds which, with so much ease and variety, he found
himself able to make. The use, then, of words is to be sensible marks
of ideas, and the ideas they stand for are their proper and immediate
signification.

(2) WORDS ARE THE SENSIBLE SIGNS OF HIS IDEAS WHO USES
THEM. The use men have of these marks being either to record
their own thoughts for the assistance of their own memory, or, as
it were, to bring out their ideas, and lay them before the view of
others: words in their primary or immediate signification stand for
nothing but the ideas in the mind of him that uses them, how im-

---

* From *Essay Concerning Human Understanding*, 1690, Book III, Chaps. 2–3.

perfectly soever or carelessly those ideas are collected from the things which they are supposed to represent. Words being voluntary signs, they cannot be voluntary signs imposed by a man on things he knows not. That would be to make them signs of nothing, sounds without signification. A man cannot make his words the signs either of qualities in things, or of conceptions in the mind of another, whereof he has none in his own.

(3) Words, in every man's mouth, stand for the ideas he has, and which he would express by them. A child having taken notice of nothing in the metal he hears called "gold," but the bright shining yellow colour, he applies the word "gold" only to his own idea of that colour, and nothing else; and therefore calls the same colour in a peacock's tail, "gold." Another, that hath better observed, adds to shining yellow great weight: and then the sound "gold," when he uses it, stands for a complex idea of a shining yellow and very weighty substance. Another adds to those qualities fusibility: and then the word "gold" to him signifies a body, bright, yellow, fusible, and very heavy. Another adds malleability. Each of these uses equally the word "gold," when they have occasion to express the idea which they have applied it to: but it is evident that each can apply it only to his own idea; nor can he make it stand as a sign of such a complex idea as he has not.

(4) WORDS OFTEN SECRETLY REFERRED. But though words, as they are used by men, can properly and immediately signify nothing but the ideas that are in the mind of the speaker, yet they in their thoughts give them a secret reference to two other things.

FIRST, TO THE IDEAS IN OTHER MEN'S MINDS. First, They suppose their words to be marks of the ideas in the minds also of other men, with whom they communicate: for else they should talk in vain, and could not be understood, if the sounds they applied to one idea were such as by the hearer were applied to another, which is to speak two languages.

(5) SECONDLY, TO THE REALITY OF THINGS. Secondly, Because men would not be thought to talk barely of their own imaginations,

but of things as really they are; therefore they often suppose their words to stand also for the reality of things.

(6) Words by Use Readily Excite Ideas   Concerning words also it is farther to be considered: First, That they being immediately the signs of men's ideas, and by that means, the instruments whereby men communicate their conceptions, and express to one another those thoughts and imaginations they have within their own breasts, there comes, by constant use, to be such a connection between certain sounds and the ideas they stand for, that the names heard almost as readily excite certain ideas, as if the objects themselves which are apt to produce them did actually affect the senses. Which is manifestly so in all obvious sensible qualities, and in all substances that frequently and familiarly occur to us.

(7) Words Often Used without Signification   Secondly, That though the proper and immediate signification of words are ideas in the mind of the speaker, yet because, by familiar use from our cradles, we come to learn certain articulate sounds very perfectly, and have them readily on our tongues, and always at hand in our memories, but yet are not always careful to examine or settle their significations perfectly; it often happens that men, even when they would apply themselves to an attentive consideration, do set their thoughts more on words than things.

(8) Their Signification Perfectly Arbitrary   Words, by long and familiar use, as has been said, come to excite in men certain ideas, so constantly and readily, that they are apt to suppose a natural connexion between them. But that they signify only men's peculiar ideas, and that by a perfectly arbitrary imposition, is evident in that they often fail to excite in others (even that use the same language) the same ideas we take them to be the signs of: and every man has so inviolable a liberty to make words stand for what ideas he pleases, that no one hath the power to make others have the same ideas in their minds that he has, when they use the same words that he does. Whatever be the consequence of any man's using of words differently, either from their general meaning, or the particular sense of the person to whom he addresses

them, this is certain, their signification, in his use of them, is limited to his ideas, and they can be signs of nothing else.

OF GENERAL TERMS

(1) THE GREATEST PART OF WORDS GENERAL   All things that exist being particulars, it may perhaps be thought reasonable that words, which ought to be conformed to things, should be so too, I mean in their signification: but yet we find the quite contrary. The far greatest part of words, that make all languages, are general terms: which has not been the effect of neglect or chance, but of reason and necessity.

(2) FOR EVERY PARTICULAR THING TO HAVE A NAME IS IMPOSSIBLE   First, It is impossible that every particular thing should have a distinct peculiar name. For the signification and use of words depending on that connexion which the mind makes between its ideas and the sounds it uses as signs of them, it is necessary, in the application of names to things, that the mind should have distinct ideas of the things, and retain also the particular name that belongs to every one, with its peculiar appropriation to that idea. But it is beyond the power of human capacity to frame and retain distinct ideas of all the particular things we meet with: every bird and beast men saw, every tree and plant that affected the senses, could not find a place in the most capacious understanding.

(3) AND USELESS   Secondly, If it were possible, it would yet be useless, because it would not serve to the chief end of language. Men would in vain heap up names of particular things, that would not serve them to communicate their thoughts. Men learn names, and use them in talk with others, only that they may be understood: which is then only done when, by use or consent, the sound I make by the organs of speech excites, in another man's mind who hears it, the idea I apply it to in mine when I speak it. This cannot be done by names applied to particular things, whereof I alone having the ideas in my mind, the names of them could not be significant or intelligible to another who was not acquainted with all those very particular things which had fallen under my notice.

(4) Thirdly, But yet granting this also feasible (which I think is not), yet a distinct name for every particular thing would not be of any great use for the improvement of knowledge: which, though founded in particular things, enlarges itself by general views; to which things reduced into sorts under general names, are properly subservient.

(6) HOW GENERAL WORDS ARE MADE The next thing to be considered is, how general words come to be made. For, since all things that exist are only particulars, how come we by general terms, or where find we those general natures they are supposed to stand for? Words become general by being made the signs of general ideas: and ideas become general by separating from them the circumstances of time, and place, and any other ideas that may determine them to this or that particular existence. By this way of abstraction they are made capable of representing more individuals than one; each of which, having in it a conformity to that abstract idea, is (as we call it) of that sort.

(7) But to deduce this a little more distinctly, it will not perhaps be amiss to trace our notions and names from their beginning, and observe by what degrees we proceed, and by what steps we enlarge our ideas from our first infancy. There is nothing more evident than that the ideas of the persons children converse with (to instance in them alone), are, like the persons themselves, only particular. The ideas of the nurse and the mother are well framed in their minds; and, like pictures of them there, represent only those individuals. The names they first gave to them are confined to these individuals; and the names of "nurse" and "mamma" the child uses, determine themselves to those persons. Afterwards, when time and a larger acquaintance has made them observe that there are a great many other things in the world, that, in some common agreements of shape and several other qualities, resemble their father and mother, and those persons they have been used to, they frame an idea which they find those many particulars do partake in; and to that they give, with others, the name "man," for example. And thus they come to have a general name, and a general idea. Wherein they make nothing new, but only leave out

of the complex idea they had of Peter and James, Mary and Jane, that which is peculiar to each, and retain only what is common to them all.

(9) GENERAL NATURES ARE NOTHING BUT ABSTRACT IDEAS He that thinks general natures or notions are anything else but abstract and partial ideas of more complex ones, taken at first from particular existences, will, I fear, be at a loss where to find them. For, let anyone reflect, and then tell me wherein does his idea of "man" differ from that of "Peter" and "Paul," or his idea of "horse" from that of "Bucephalus," but in the leaving out something that is peculiar to each individual, and retaining so much of those particular complex ideas of several particular existences as they are found to agree in? Of the complex ideas signified by the names "man" and "horse," leaving out but those particulars wherein they differ, and retaining only those wherein they agree, and of those making a new distinct complex idea, and giving the name "animal" to it, one has a more general term, that comprehends with man, several other creatures. Leave out of the idea of "animal" sense and spontaneous motion, and the remaining complex idea, made up of the remaining simple ones of "body, life, and nourishment," becomes a more general one under the more comprehensive term, *vivens.*

(11) GENERAL AND UNIVERSAL ARE CREATURES OF THE UNDERSTANDING It is plain, by what has been said, that general and universal belong not to the real existence of things; but are the inventions and creatures of the understanding, made by it for its own use, and concern only signs, whether words or ideas. Words are general, as has been said, when used for signs of general ideas, and so are applicable indifferently to many particular things; and ideas are general when they are set up as the representatives of many particular things: but universality belongs not to things themselves, which are all of them particular in their existence, even those words and ideas which in their signification are general. When therefore we quit particulars, the generals that rest are only creatures of our own making, their general nature being nothing but the capacity they are put into by the understanding of signifying

or representing many particulars. For the signification they have is nothing but a relation that by the mind of man is added to them.

(12) ABSTRACT IDEAS ARE THE ESSENCES OF THE *Genera* AND *Species* The next thing therefore to be considered, is, what kind of signification it is that general words have. For as it is evident that they do not signify barely one particular thing, for then they would not be general terms, but proper names; so on the other side it is as evident they do not signify a plurality; for "man" and "men" would then signify the same, and the distinction of "numbers" (as grammarians call them) would be superfluous and useless. That then which general words signify, is a sort of things; and each of them does that by being a sign of an abstract idea in the mind; to which idea as things existing are found to agree, so they come to be ranked under that name; or, which is all one, be of that sort. Whereby it is evident, that the essences of the sorts, or (if the Latin word pleases better) *species* of things, are nothing else but these abstract ideas. For the having the essence of any species, being that which makes any thing to be of that species, and the conformity to the idea to which the name is annexed being that which gives a right to that name, the having the essence, and the having that conformity, must needs be the same thing: since to be of any species, and to have a right to the name of that species, is all one. As, for example: to be a man or of the species man, and to have right to the name "man," is the same thing. Again: to be a man, or of the species man, and have the essence of a man, is the same thing. Now, since nothing can be a man, or have a right to the name "man," but what has a conformity to the abstract idea the name "man" stands for; nor any thing be a man, or have a right to the species man, but what has the essence of that species; it follows, that the abstract idea for which the name stands, and the essence of the species, is one and the same. From whence it is easy to observe, that the essences of the sorts of things, and consequently the sorting of this, is the workmanship of the understanding that abstracts and makes those general ideas.

• • • • • • • • • • • • •

Of Language

(1) Philosophy being nothing else but the study of wisdom and truth, it may with reason be expected that those who have spent most time and pains in it should enjoy a greater calm and serenity of mind, a greater clearness and evidence of knowledge, and be less disturbed with doubts and difficulties than other men. Yet so it is, we see the illiterate bulk of mankind that walk the high road of plain common sense, and are governed by the dictates of nature, for the most part easy and undisturbed. To them nothing that is familiar appears unaccountable or difficult to comprehend. They complain not of any want of evidence in their senses, and are out of all danger of becoming skeptics. But no sooner do we depart from sense and instinct to follow the light of a superior prin- ciple, to reason, meditate, and reflect on the nature of things, but a thousand scruples spring up in our minds concerning those things which before we seemed fully to comprehend. Prejudices and errors of sense do from all parts discover themselves to our view; and, en- deavoring to correct these by reason, we are insensibly drawn into uncouth paradoxes, difficulties, and inconsistencies, which multiply and grow upon us as we advance in speculation, till at length, hav- ing wandered through many intricate mazes, we find ourselves just where we were, or, which is worse, sit down in a forlorn skepticism.

* From "Introduction" to *A Treatise Concerning the Principles of Human Knowledge*, 1710, edited by Colin Murray Turbayne.

(2) The cause of this is thought to be the obscurity of things, or the natural weakness and imperfection of our understandings. It is said the faculties we have are few and those designed by nature for the support and comfort of life, and not to penetrate into the inward essence and constitution of things. Besides, the mind of man being finite, when it treats of things which partake of infinity it is not to be wondered at if it run into absurdities and contradictions, out of which it is impossible it should ever extricate itself, it being of the nature of infinite not to be comprehended by that which is finite.

(3) But, perhaps, we may be too partial to ourselves in placing the fault originally in our faculties and not rather in the wrong use we make of them. It is a hard thing to suppose that right deductions from true principles should ever end in consequences which cannot be maintained or made consistent. . . . Upon the whole, I am inclined to think that the far greater part, if not all, of those difficulties which have hitherto amused philosophers and blocked up the way to knowledge, are entirely owing to ourselves —that we have first raised a dust and then complain we cannot see.

(4) My purpose therefore is to try if I can discover what those principles are which have introduced all that doubtfulness and uncertainty, those absurdities and contradictions, into the several sects of philosophy—insomuch that the wisest men have thought our ignorance incurable, conceiving it to arise from the natural dullness and limitation of our faculties. And surely it is a work well deserving our pains to make a strict inquiry concerning the first principles of human knowledge, to sift and examine them on all sides, especially since there may be some grounds to suspect that those lets and difficulties which stay and embarrass the mind in its search after truth do not spring from any darkness and intricacy in the objects or natural defect in the understanding so much as from false principles which have been insisted on, and might have been avoided.

.   .   .   .

(6) In order to prepare the mind of the reader for the easier conceiving what follows, it is proper to premise somewhat, by way of introduction, concerning the nature and abuse of language. But

the unraveling this matter leads me in some measure to anticipate my design by taking notice of what seems to have had a chief part in rendering speculation intricate and perplexed and to have occasioned innumerable errors and difficulties in almost all parts of knowledge. And that is the opinion that the mind has a power of framing *abstract ideas* or notions of things. He who is not a perfect stranger to the writings and disputes of philosophers must needs acknowledge that no small part of them are spent about abstract ideas. These are in a more especial manner thought to be the object of those sciences which go by the name of logic and metaphysics, and of all that which passes under the notion of the most abstracted and sublime learning, in all which one shall scarce find any question handled in such a manner as does not suppose their existence in the mind, and that it is well acquainted with them.

(7) It is agreed on all hands that the qualities or modes of things do never really exist each of them apart by itself and separated from all others, but are mixed, as it were, and blended together, several in the same object. But we are told the mind, being able to consider each quality singly, or abstracted from those other qualities with which it is united, does by that means frame to itself abstract ideas. For example, there is perceived by sight an object extended, colored, and moved: this mixed or compound idea the mind, resolving into its simple, constituent parts and viewing each by itself, exclusive of the rest, does frame the abstract ideas of extension, color, and motion. Not that it is possible for color or motion to exist without extension, but only that the mind can frame to itself by *abstraction* the idea of color exclusive of extension, and of motion exclusive of both color and extension.

(8) Again, the mind having observed that in the particular extensions perceived by sense there is something common and alike in all, and some other things peculiar, as this or that figure or magnitude, which distinguish them one from another, it considers apart or singles out by itself that which is common, making thereof a most abstract idea of extension, which is neither line, surface, nor solid, nor has any figure or magnitude, but is an idea entirely prescinded from all these. So likewise the mind, by leaving out of the particular colors perceived by sense that which distinguishes them one from another, and retaining that only which is common

to all, makes an idea of color in abstract, which is neither red, nor blue, nor white, nor any other determinate color. And, in like manner, by considering motion abstractedly not only from the body moved, but likewise from the figure it describes, and all particular directions and velocities, the abstract idea of motion is framed, which equally corresponds to all particular motions whatsoever that may be perceived by sense.

(9) And as the mind frames to itself abstract ideas of qualities or modes, so does it, by the same precision or mental separation, attain abstract ideas of the more compounded beings which include several coexistent qualities. For example, the mind, having observed that Peter, James, and John resemble each other in certain common agreements of shape and other qualities, leaves out of the complex or compounded idea it has of Peter, James, and any other particular man that which is peculiar to each, retaining only what is common to all, and so makes an abstract idea wherein all the particulars equally partake—abstracting entirely from and cutting off all those circumstances and differences which might determine it to any particular existence. And after this manner it is said we come by the abstract idea of *man* or, if you please, humanity, or human nature; wherein it is true there is included color, because there is no man but has some color, but then it can be neither white, nor black, nor any particular color, because there is no one particular color wherein all men partake. So likewise there is included stature, but then it is neither tall stature, nor low stature, nor yet middle stature, but something abstracted from all these. And so of the rest. Moreover, there being a great variety of other creatures that partake in some parts, but not all, of the complex idea of man, the mind, leaving out those parts which are peculiar to men, and retaining those only which are common to all the living creatures, frames the idea of *animal*, which abstracts not only from all particular men, but also all birds, beasts, fishes, and insects. The constituent parts of the abstract idea of animal are body, life, sense, and spontaneous motion. By "body" is meant body without any particular shape or figure, there being no one shape or figure common to all animals, without covering, either of hair, or feathers, or scales, and so forth, nor yet naked: hair, feathers, scales, and nakedness being the distinguishing properties of par-

ticular animals, and for that reason left out of the *abstract idea.* Upon the same account the spontaneous motion must be neither walking, nor flying, nor creeping; it is nevertheless a motion, but what that motion is it is not easy to conceive.

(10) Whether others have this wonderful faculty of abstracting their ideas, they best can tell; for myself I find indeed I have a faculty of imagining, or representing to myself, the ideas of those particular things I have perceived, and of variously compounding and dividing them. I can imagine a man with two heads, or the upper parts of a man joined to the body of a horse. I can consider the hand, the eye, the nose, each by itself abstracted or separated from the rest of the body. But then whatever hand or eye I imagine, it must have some particular shape and color. Likewise the idea of man that I frame to myself must be either of a white, or a black, or a tawny, a straight, or a crooked, a tall, or a low, or a middle-sized man. I cannot by any effort of thought conceive the abstract idea above described. And it is equally impossible for me to form the abstract idea of motion distinct from the body moving, and which is neither swift nor slow, curvilinear nor rectilinear; and the like may be said of all other abstract general ideas whatsoever. To be plain, I own myself able to abstract in one sense, as when I consider some particular parts or qualities separated from others, with which, though they are united in some object, yet it is possible they may really exist without them. But I deny that I can abstract one from another, or conceive separately, those qualities which it is impossible should exist so separated; or that I can frame a general notion by abstracting from particulars in the manner aforesaid—which two last are the two proper acceptations of "abstraction." And there are grounds to think most men will acknowledge themselves to be in my case. The generality of men which are simple and illiterate never pretend to abstract notions. It is said they are difficult and not to be attained without pains and study; we may therefore reasonably conclude that, if such there be, they are confined only to the learned.

(11) I proceed to examine what can be alleged in defense of the doctrine of abstraction, and try if I can discover what it is that inclines the men of speculation to embrace an opinion so remote from common sense as that seems to be. There has been a late, de-

servedly esteemed philosopher[1] who, no doubt, has given it very much countenance by seeming to think the having abstract general ideas is what puts the widest difference in point of understanding betwixt man and beast.

> The having of general ideas [he says] is that which puts a perfect distinction betwixt man and brutes, and is an excellency which the faculties of brutes do by no means attain unto. For, it is evident we observe no footsteps in them of making use of general signs for universal ideas; from which we have reason to imagine that they have not the faculty of abstracting, or making general ideas, since they have no use of words or any other general signs.

And a little after:

> Therefore, I think, we may suppose that it is in this that the species of brutes are discriminated from men, and it is that proper difference wherein they are wholly separated, and which at last widens to so wide a distance. For, if they have any ideas at all, and are not bare machines (as some would have them), we cannot deny them to have some reason. It seems as evident to me that they do, some of them, in certain instances reason as that they have sense; but it is only in particular ideas, just as they receive them from their senses. They are the best of them tied up within those narrow bounds, and have not (as I think) the faculty to enlarge them by any kind of abstraction.—*Essay on Human Understanding,* Book II, Chap. 11, §§ 10f.

I readily agree with this learned author that the faculties of brutes can by no means attain to abstraction. But then if this be made the distinguishing property of that sort of animals, I fear a great many of those that pass for men must be reckoned into their number. The reason that is here assigned why we have no grounds to think brutes have abstract general ideas is that we observe in them no use of words or any other general signs; which is built on this supposition—that the making use of words implies the having general ideas. From which it follows that men who use language are able to abstract or generalize their ideas. That this is the sense and arguing of the author will further appear by his answering the question he in another place puts: "Since all things

---

[1] John Locke (1632–1704). He published his revolutionary *Essay Concerning Human Understanding* in 1690. . . .

that exist are only particulars, how come we by general terms?" His answer is: "Words become general by being made the signs of general ideas." (*Essay on Human Understanding*, Book III, Chap. 3, § 6.) But it seems that a word becomes general by being made the sign, not of an abstract general idea, but of several particular ideas, any one of which it indifferently suggests to the mind. For example, when it is said, "the change of motion is proportional to the impressed force," or that, "whatever has extension is divisible," these propositions are to be understood of motion and extension in general; and nevertheless it will not follow that they suggest to my thoughts an idea of motion without a body moved, or any determinate direction and velocity, or that I must conceive an abstract general idea of extension which is neither line, surface, nor solid, neither great nor small, black, white, nor red, nor of any other determinate color. It is only implied that whatever motion I consider, whether it be swift or slow, perpendicular, horizontal, or oblique, or in whatever object, the axiom concerning it holds equally true. As does the other of every particular extension, it matters not whether line, surface, or solid, whether of this or that magnitude or figure.

(12) By observing how ideas become general we may the better judge how words are made so. And here it is to be noted that I do not deny absolutely there are general ideas, but only that there are any *abstract* general ideas; for, in the passages above quoted, wherein there is mention of general ideas, it is always supposed that they are formed by abstraction, after the manner set forth in sections (8) and (9). Now, if we will annex a meaning to our words and speak only of what we can conceive, I believe we shall acknowledge that an idea which, considered in itself, is particular, becomes general by being made to represent or stand for all other particular ideas of the same sort. To make this plain by an example, suppose a geometrician is demonstrating the method of cutting a line in two equal parts. He draws, for instance, a black line of an inch in length: this, which in itself is a particular line, is nevertheless with regard to its signification general, since, as it is there used, it represents all particular lines whatsoever; for that which is demonstrated of it is demonstrated of all lines or, in other words, of a line in general. And, as that *particular* line becomes general by

being made a sign, so the *name* "line," which taken absolutely is particular, by being a sign is made general. And as the former owes its generality not to its being the sign of an abstract or general line, but of all particular right lines that may possibly exist, so the latter must be thought to derive its generality from the same cause, namely, the various particular lines which it indifferently denotes.

(13) To give the reader a yet clearer view of the nature of abstract ideas, and the uses they are thought necessary to, I shall add one more passage out of the *Essay on Human Understanding*, which is as follows:

> *Abstract ideas* are not so obvious or easy to children or the yet unexercised mind as particular ones. If they seem so to grown men it is only because by constant and familiar use they are made so. For, when we nicely reflect upon them, we shall find that general ideas are fictions and contrivances of the mind, that carry difficulty with them, and do not so easily offer themselves as we are apt to imagine. For example, does it not require some pains and skill to form the general idea of a triangle (which is yet none of the most abstract, comprehensive, and difficult); for it must be neither oblique nor rectangle, neither equilateral, equicrural, nor scalenon, but *all and none* of these at once? In effect, it is something imperfect that cannot exist, an idea wherein some parts of several different and *inconsistent* ideas are put together. It is true the mind in this imperfect state has need of such ideas and makes all the haste to them it can, for the convenience of communication and enlargement of knowledge to both which it is naturally very much inclined. But yet one has reason to suspect such ideas are marks of our imperfection. At least this is enough to show that the most abstract and general ideas are not those that the mind is first and most easily acquainted with, nor such as its earliest knowledge is conversant about.—Book IV, Chap. 7, sec. 9.

If any man has the faculty of framing in his mind such an idea of a triangle as is here described, it is in vain to pretend to dispute him out of it, nor would I go about it. All I desire is that the reader would fully and certainly inform himself whether he has such an idea or no. And this, methinks, can be no hard task for anyone to perform. What more easy than for anyone to look a little into his own thoughts, and there try whether he has, or can attain to have, an idea that shall correspond with the description that is here given of the general idea of a triangle, which is "neither oblique nor rectangle, equilateral, equicrural nor scalenon, but all and none of these at once"?

(14) Much is here said of the difficulty that abstract ideas carry with them, and the pains and skill requisite to the forming them. And it is on all hands agreed that there is need of great toil and labor of the mind to emancipate our thoughts from particular objects and raise them to those sublime speculations that are conversant about abstract ideas. From all which the natural consequence should seem to be, that so difficult a thing as the forming abstract ideas was not necessary for *communication,* which is so easy and familiar to all sorts of men. But, we are told, if they seem obvious and easy to grown men, "it is only because by constant and familiar use they are made so." Now, I would fain know at what time it is men are employed in surmounting that difficulty and furnishing themselves with those necessary helps for discourse. It cannot be when they are grown up, for then it seems they are not conscious of any such painstaking; it remains, therefore, to be the business of their childhood. And surely the great and multiplied labor of framing abstract notions will be found a hard task for that tender age. Is it not a hard thing to imagine that a couple of children cannot prate together of their sugar plums and rattles and the rest of their little trinkets till they have first tacked together numberless inconsistencies and so framed in their minds abstract general ideas and annexed them to every common name they make use of?

(15) Nor do I think them a whit more needful for the *enlargement of knowledge* than for *communication.* It is, I know, a point much insisted on, that all knowledge and demonstration are about universal notions, to which I fully agree; but then it does not appear to me that those notions are formed by abstraction in the manner premised—*universality,* so far as I can comprehend, not consisting in the absolute, positive nature or conception of any thing, but in the relation it bears to the particulars signified or represented by it; by virtue whereof it is that things, names, or notions, being in their own nature *particular,* are rendered *universal.* Thus, when I demonstrate any proposition concerning triangles, it is to be supposed that I have in view the universal idea of a triangle, which ought not to be understood as if I could frame

an idea of a triangle which was neither equilateral, nor scalenon, nor equicrural, but only that the particular triangle I consider, whether of this or that sort it matters not, does equally stand for and represent all rectilinear triangles whatsoever, and is in that sense *universal*. All which seems very plain and not to include any difficulty in it.

•   •   •   •   •   •   •   •   •   •   •   •

(18) I come now to consider the *source* of this prevailing notion [the doctrine of abstract ideas], and that seems to me to be language. And surely nothing of less extent than reason itself could have been the source of an opinion so universally received. The truth of this appears, as from other reasons, so also from the plain confession of the ablest patrons of abstract ideas, who acknowledge that they are made in order to naming; from which it is a clear consequence that if there had been no such thing as speech or universal signs there never had been any thought of abstraction. See Book III, Chap. 6, § 39, and elsewhere of the *Essay on Human Understanding*. Let us examine the manner wherein words have contributed to the origin of that mistake: First then, it is thought that every name has, or ought to have, one only precise and settled signification, which inclines men to think there are certain abstract, determinate ideas which constitute the true and only immediate signification of each general name; and that it is by the mediation of these abstract ideas that a general name comes to signify any particular thing. Whereas, in truth, there is no such thing as one precise and definite signification annexed to any general name, they all signifying indifferently a great number of particular ideas. All which does evidently follow from what has been already said, and will clearly appear to anyone by a little reflection. To this it will be objected that every name that has a definition is thereby restrained to one certain signification. For example, a "triangle" is defined to be "a plane surface comprehended by three right lines," by which that name is limited to denote one certain idea and no other. To which I answer that in the definition it is not said whether the surface be great or small, black or white, nor whether the sides are long or short, equal or unequal, nor with what angles they are inclined to each other; in all which there may

be great variety, and consequently there is no one settled idea which limits the signification of the word "triangle." It is one thing for to keep a name constantly to the same definition, and another to make it stand everywhere for the same idea; the one is necessary, the other useless and impracticable.

(19) But, to give a further account how words came to produce the doctrine of abstract ideas, it must be observed that it is a received opinion that language has no other end but the communicating of ideas, and that every significant name stands for an idea. This being so, and it being withal certain that names which yet are not thought altogether insignificant do not always mark out particular conceivable ideas, it is straightway concluded that they stand for abstract notions. That there are many names in use amongst speculative men which do not always suggest to others determinate, particular ideas is what nobody will deny. And a little attention will discover that it is not necessary (even in the strictest reasonings) that significant names which stand for ideas should, every time they are used, excite in the understandings the ideas they are made to stand for—in reading and discoursing, names being for the most part used as letters are in algebra, in which, though a particular quantity be marked by each letter, yet to proceed right it is not requisite that in every step each letter suggest to your thoughts that particular quantity it was appointed to stand for.

(20) Besides, the communicating of ideas marked by words is not the chief and only end of language, as is commonly supposed. There are other ends, as the raising of some passion, the exciting to or deterring from an action, the putting the mind in some particular disposition—to which the former is in many cases barely subservient, and sometimes entirely omitted, when these can be obtained without it, as I think does not unfrequently happen in the familiar use of language. I entreat the reader to reflect with himself and see if it does not often happen, either in hearing or reading a discourse, that the passions of fear, love, hatred, admiration, disdain, and the like, arise immediately in his mind upon the perception of certain words, without any ideas coming between. At first, indeed, the words might have occasioned ideas that were fit to produce those emotions; but, if I mistake not, it will be

found that, when language is once grown familiar, the hearing of the sounds or sight of the characters is oft immediately attended with those passions which at first were wont to be produced by the intervention of ideas that are now quite omitted. May we not, for example, be affected with the promise of a *good thing,* though we have not an idea of what it is? Or is not the being threatened with danger sufficient to excite a dread, though we think not of any particular evil likely to befall us, nor yet frame to ourselves an idea of danger in abstract? If anyone shall join ever so little reflection of his own to what has been said, I believe that it will evidently appear to him that general names are often used in the propriety of language without the speaker's designing them for marks of ideas in his own, which he would have them raise in the mind of the hearer. Even proper names themselves do not seem always spoken with a design to bring into our view the ideas of those individuals that are supposed to be marked by them. For example, when a Schoolman tells me, "Aristotle has said it," all I conceive he means by it is to dispose me to embrace his opinion with the deference and submission which custom has annexed to that name. And this effect may be so instantly produced in the minds of those who are accustomed to resign their judgment to the authority of that philosopher, as it is impossible any idea either of his person, writings, or reputation should go before. Innumerable examples of this kind may be given, but why should I insist on those things which everyone's experience will, I doubt not, plentifully suggest unto him?

(21) We have, I think, shown the impossibility of abstract ideas. We have considered what has been said for them by their ablest patrons, and endeavored to show they are of no use for those ends to which they are thought necessary. And lastly, we have traced them to the source from whence they flow, which appears to be language. It cannot be denied that words are of excellent use, in that by their means all that stock of knowledge which has been purchased by the joint labors of inquisitive men in all ages and nations may be drawn into the view and made the possession of one single person. But at the same time it must be owned that most parts of knowledge have been strangely perplexed and darkened by the abuse of words, and general ways of speech wherein they are

delivered. Since therefore words are so apt to impose on the understanding, whatever ideas I consider, I shall endeavor to take them bare and naked into my view, keeping out of my thoughts so far as I am able those names which long and constant use has so strictly united with them; from which I may expect to derive the following advantages:

(22) *First,* I shall be sure to get clear of all controversies purely verbal—the springing up of which weeds in almost all the sciences has been a main hindrance to the growth of true and sound knowledge. *Secondly,* this seems to be a sure way to extricate myself out of that fine and subtle net of *abstract ideas* which has so miserably perplexed and entangled the minds of men; and that with this peculiar circumstance, that by how much the finer and more curious was the wit of any man, by so much the deeper was he likely to be ensnared and faster held therein. *Thirdly,* so long as I confine my thoughts to my own ideas divested of words, I do not see how I can easily be mistaken. The objects I consider I clearly and adequately know. I cannot be deceived in thinking I have an idea which I have not. It is not possible for me to imagine that any of my own ideas are alike or unlike that are not truly so. To discern the agreements or disagreements there are between my ideas, to see what ideas are included in any compound idea and what not, there is nothing more requisite than an attentive perception of what passes in my own understanding.

(23) But the attainment of all these advantages does presuppose an entire deliverance from the deception of words, which I dare hardly promise myself—so difficult a thing it is to dissolve a union so early begun and confirmed by so long a habit as that betwixt words and ideas. Which difficulty seems to have been very much increased by the doctrine of *abstraction.* For so long as men thought abstract ideas were annexed to their words, it does not seem strange that they should use words for ideas—it being found an impracticable thing to lay aside the word and retain the *abstract* idea in the mind, which in itself was perfectly inconceivable. This seems to me the principal cause why those men who have so emphatically recommended to others the laying aside all use of words in their mediations, and contemplating their bare ideas, have yet failed to perform it themselves. Of late many have been very

sensible of the absurd opinions and insignificant disputes which grow out of the abuse of words. And, in order to remedy these evils, they advise well that we attend to the ideas signified and draw off our attention from the words which signify them. But, how good soever this advice may be they have given others, it is plain they could not have a due regard to it themselves so long as they thought the only immediate use of words was to signify ideas, and that the immediate signification of every general name was a determinate abstract idea.

(24) But, these being known to be mistakes, a man may with greater ease prevent his being imposed on by words. He that knows he has no other than *particular* ideas will not puzzle himself in vain to find out and conceive the *abstract* idea annexed to any name. And he that knows names do not always stand for ideas will spare himself the labor of looking for ideas where there are none to be had. It were, therefore, to be wished that everyone would use his utmost endeavors to obtain a clear view of the ideas he would consider, separating from them all that dress and encumbrance of words which so much contribute to blind the judgment and divide the attention. In vain do we extend our view into the heavens and pry into the entrails of the earth, in vain do we consult the writings of learned men and trace the dark footsteps of antiquity—we need only draw the curtain of words, to behold the fairest tree of knowledge, whose fruit is excellent and within the reach of our hand.

(25) Unless we take care to clear the first principles of knowledge from the embarrassment and delusion of words, we may make infinite reasonings upon them to no purpose; we may draw consequences from consequences, and be never the wiser. The further we go, we shall only lose ourselves the more irrecoverably, and be the deeper entangled in difficulties and mistakes. Whoever, therefore, designs to read the following sheets, I entreat him to make my words the occasion of his own thinking and endeavor to attain the same train of thoughts in reading that I had in writing them. By this means it will be easy for him to discover the truth or falsity of what I say. He will be out of all danger of being deceived by my words, and I do not see how he can be led into an error by considering his own naked, undisguised ideas.

Signs and Behavior
Situations

There is wide disagreement as to when something is a sign. Some persons would unhesitatingly say that blushing is a sign, others would not. There are mechanical dogs which will come out of their kennels if one claps one's hands loudly in their presence. Is such clapping a sign? Are clothes signs of the personality of those who wear them? Is music a sign of anything? Is a word such as "Go!" a sign in the same sense as is a green light on a street intersection? Are punctuation marks signs? Are dreams signs? Is the Parthenon a sign of Greek culture? Disagreements are widespread; they show that the term "sign" is both vague and ambiguous.

This disagreement extends to many other terms which are commonly used in describing sign processes. The terms "express," "understand," "refer," "meaning" would provide many instances. So would "communication" and "language." Do animals communicate? If so, do they have a language? Or do only men have language? Yes, run some answers; no, run others. We find the same diversity of replies if we ask whether thought or mind or consciousness is involved in a sign process; whether a poem "refers" to what it "expresses"; whether men can signify what cannot be experienced;

* From *Signs, Language and Behavior* (Englewood Cliffs, N.J.; Prentice-Hall, Inc., 1946), reprinted by permission of the publisher.

whether mathematical terms signify anything; whether language signs are preceded genetically by nonlanguage signs; whether the elements in an undeciphered "dead" language are signs.

In the face of such disagreements, it is not easy to find a starting point. If we are to seek for a formulation of the word "sign" in biological terms, the task is to isolate some distinctive kind of behavior which agrees fairly well with frequent usages of the term "sign." Since usage of the term is, however, not consistent, it cannot be demanded that the chosen behavioral formulation agree with all the various usages which are actually current. At some point the semiotician must say: "Henceforth we will recognize that anything which fulfills certain conditions is a sign. These conditions are selected in the light of current usages of the term 'sign,' but they may not fit in with all such usages. They do not therefore claim to be a statement of the way the term 'sign' is always used, but a statement of the conditions under which we will henceforth admit within semiotic that something is a sign."

Then from such a starting point a behavioral theory of signs will build up step by step a set of terms to talk about signs (taking account of current distinctions but attempting to reduce for scientific purposes their vagueness and ambiguity), and will endeavor to explain and predict sign phenomena on the basis of the general principles of behavior which underlie all behavior, and hence sign behavior. The aim is to take account of the distinctions and analyses which former investigators have made, but to ground these results whenever possible upon general behavior theory. In the nature of the case such a scientific semiotic will often deviate from current terminology, and can only be developed slowly and laboriously. It will often seem pedantic and less illuminating for many purposes than less scientific approaches—which therefore are to be encouraged in the light of the many problems and purposes which a treatment of signs aims to fulfill. It is not to be expected that all discussions of literary, religious, and logical signs can be translated at once with profit into a behavioral formulation. The present approach does not therefore wish to exclude other approaches to semiotic. But it does proceed upon the belief that basic progress in this complex field rests finally upon the development of a genuine science of signs, and that this development can be most profitably carried on by a biological orientation which places signs within the context of behavior.

2. PRELIMINARY ISOLATION OF SIGN BEHAVIOR

We shall begin by taking two examples of behavior to which the term "sign" is often applied both in common usage and in the writings of semioticians. Then a superficial analysis of these examples will disclose the features which a more technical formulation of the nature of a sign must embody. If both situations reveal certain common elements, then both may be called sign behavior; the differences in the two situations would then suggest differences between kinds of signs. If analysis shows too great differences, then the alternative would be to choose different terms to describe the two situations, and to adopt a narrower definition of "sign": in either case we would then be in a position to consider whether any additional phenomena are to be called signs, that is, whether the characterization of signs based upon the two examples in question is to be held as a basis for determining when something is a sign or whether it is to be expanded to include situations of a widely different sort.

The first example is drawn from experiments on dogs. If a hungry dog that goes to a certain place to obtain food when the food is seen or smelled, is trained in a certain way, it will learn to go to this place for food when a buzzer is sounded even though the food is not observed. In this case the dog is attentive to the buzzer but does not normally go to the buzzer itself; and if the food is not made available until some time after the buzzer has sounded, the dog may not go to the place in question until the time interval has elapsed. Many persons would say in such a situation that the buzzer sound is to the dog a sign of food at the given place, and in particular, a nonlanguage sign. If we abstract from the experimenter and his purposes in this example, and consider only the dog, the example approximates what have often been called "natural signs," as when a dark cloud is a sign of rain. It is in this way that we wish the experiment to be considered.

The second example is drawn from human behavior. A person on the way to a certain town is driving along a road; he is stopped by another person who says that the road is blocked some distance away by a landslide. The person who hears the sounds which are uttered does not continue to the point in question, but turns off on a side road and takes another route to his destination. It would be commonly said that the sounds made by the one person and heard by the other (and indeed by the utterer also) were signs to both of them of the obstacle on the road, and in particular were language signs, even though the actual responses of the two persons are very different.

Common to these two situations is the fact that both the dog and the person addressed behave in a way which satisfies a need— hunger in the one case, arrival at a certain town in the other. In each case the organisms have various ways of attaining their goals: when food is smelled the dog reacts differently than when the buzzer is sounded; when the obstacle is encountered the man reacts differently than when spoken to at a distance from the obstacle. Further, the buzzer is not responded to as food nor the spoken words as an obstacle; the dog may wait awhile before going for food and the man may continue to drive for a time down the blocked road before turning off to another road. And yet in some sense both the buzzer and the words control or direct the course of behavior toward a goal in a way similar to (though not identical with) the control which would be exercised by the food or the obstacle if these were present as stimuli: the buzzer determines the dog's behavior to be that of seeking food in a certain place at a certain time; the words determine the man's behavior to be that of getting to a certain town by avoiding a certain obstacle at a given place on a given road. The buzzer and the words are in some sense "substitutes" in the control of behavior for the control over behavior which would be exercised by what they signify if this was itself observed. The differences between nonlanguage and language signs remain for subsequent discussion.

It is clear at once that the formulation of "sign" frequent in early behavior theory is too simple: namely, it cannot be simply said that a sign is a substitute stimulus which calls out to itself the same response which would have been called out by something else had it been present. For the response to food is to food itself, while the response to the buzzer is not to it as if it were food; and the actual response to the situation in which the sign appears may be greatly different from the response to a situation where what is signified, and not the sign, is present. The dog, for instance, may salivate when the buzzer is sounded but it cannot actually eat unless food is present; the man may feel anxiety when he is addressed, but his turning off the road before reaching the obstacle is a very different response from that which he would make if he had gone directly to the place of blockage itself (and even more different from the behavior of the person who told him of the obstacle).

Nor can the difficulties in the earlier attempts to identify signs with any and all substitute stimuli be avoided by attempting to say that whatever influences a response with respect to what is not at the moment a stimulus is a sign. For example, a drug will influence the way an organism will respond to stimuli which later affect it, and yet it would be too great a departure from common usage to call such a drug a sign.

The difficulties in these formulations may perhaps be avoided if, as our examples suggest, signs are identified within goal-seeking behavior. So in the light of our analysis of what the two examples chosen as a point of reference have in common (and neglecting for the time being their differences) we arrive at the following preliminary formulation of at least one set of conditions under which something may be called a sign: *If something, A, controls behavior towards a goal in a way similar to (but not necessarily identical with) the way something else, B, would control behavior with respect to that goal in a situation in which it were observed, then A is a sign.*

The buzzer and the spoken sounds are then signs of food and obstacle because they control the course of behavior with respect to the goals of getting food and getting to a certain place in a way similar to the control which food and obstacle would exercise if they were observed. Whatever exercises this type of control in goal-seeking behavior is a sign. And goal-seeking behavior in which signs exercise control may be called *sign behavior.*

3. TOWARD PRECISION IN THE IDENTIFICATION OF SIGN BEHAVIOR

For many purposes the preceding account of a sign is adequate; it at least suggests a behavioral way of formulating what is commonly meant in saying that a sign "stands for" or "represents" something other than itself. But for more strictly scientific purposes a more exact formulation is required in order to clarify the notions of similarity of behavior and goal-seeking behavior. We might at this point simply leave it to the scientists in their field to state further refinements, and indeed anything we add is in the nature of the case tentative. But since our concern is to push semiotic as rapidly as possible in the direction of a natural science, the following suggestions are made.

Implicit in the preceding account are four concepts which need further clarification: preparatory-stimulus, disposition to respond, response-sequence, and behavior-family. When these notions are elucidated a more precise statement of a set of conditions sufficient for something to be called a sign can be given.

A *preparatory-stimulus* is any stimulus which influences a response to some other stimulus. Thus it has been found by O. H. Mowrer that the magnitude of the jump of a rat to a shock stimulus is increased if a tone sounds before the shock stimulus is encountered. Such a stimulus differs from other stimuli, say the shock, in that as a preparatory-stimulus it influences a response to something other than itself rather than causing a response to itself (it may of course also cause a response to itself, that is, not be merely or solely a preparatory-stimulus). By a *stimulus* is meant, following Clark L. Hull, any physical energy which acts upon a receptor of a living organism; the source of this energy will be called the *stimulus-object*. By a *response* is meant any action of a muscle or gland; hence there are reactions of an organism which are not necessarily responses. A preparatory-stimulus affects or causes a reaction in an organism, but, as Mowrer makes clear, it need not call out a response to itself, but only to some other stimulus. In the account toward which we are moving it is not held that all preparatory-stimuli are signs, but only that preparatory-stimuli which meet certain additional requirements are signs. That a preparatory-stimulus need not when presented call out a response makes intelligible the fact that a command to turn right at a certain place may produce at the time of utterance no overt, or as far as we know, "implicit" response of turning right, and yet may determine that the person commanded turns right when he reaches the place in question. A preparatory-stimulus does however cause some reaction in an organism, affects it in some way, and this leads to the introduction of the term "disposition to respond."

A *disposition to respond* to something in a certain way is a state of an organism at a given time which is such that under certain additional conditions the response in question takes place. These additional conditions may be very complex. An animal disposed to go to a certain place to obtain food may not go there even if food is observed—he may not be willing or able to swim across an intervening water barrier or to move if certain other animals are present as stimulus-objects. The complex of conditions also includes other states of the organism. The person commanded to turn at a certain corner may not turn even when the corner is reached: as he walked to the corner he may have come to believe that his informant was deliberately trying to misdirect him, so that confidence in one's informant may be at times a necessary condition for making a response to which one is disposed because of signs.

There may be dispositions to respond which are not caused by preparatory-stimuli, but every preparatory-stimulus causes a disposition to respond in a certain way to something else. Logically, therefore, "disposition to respond" is the more basic notion, and a preparatory-stimulus is a stimulus which causes a disposition to respond in a certain way to something else. And since not all preparatory-stimuli would normally be called signs, and not all dispositions to response which are caused by preparatory-stimuli are relevant to the delimitation of sign processes, additional criteria are involved; and to be in accord with our own preliminary formulation of sign behavior, these criteria must introduce the notion of behavior toward a goal.

A *response-sequence* is any sequence of consecutive responses whose first member is initiated by a stimulus-object and whose last member is a response to this stimulus-object as a goal-object, that is, to an object which partially or completely removes the state of the organism (the "need") which motivates the sequence of responses. Thus the series of responses of a hungry dog which sees a rabbit, runs after it, kills it, and so obtains food is a response-sequence. For the sight of the rabbit starts a series of responses to the rabbit in terms of which the rabbit is finally obtained as food. The intervening responses in the sequence can occur only if the environment provides the necessary stimuli for their release, and such sources of stimuli may be called *supporting stimulus-objects*. The terrain over which the dog runs in this case provides the support necessary for the responses of following the rabbit and tracking it down, while the rabbit provides the stimuli initiating and terminating the series of responses.

A *behavior-family* is any set of response-sequences which are initiated by similar stimulus-objects and which terminate in these objects as similar goal-objects for similar needs. Hence all the response-sequences which start from rabbits and eventuate in securing rabbits as food would constitute the rabbit-food behavior-family. A behavior-family may in an extreme case have only one member; no limit is set to the number of possible members. Behavior-families have various degrees of inclusiveness. All the objects which a dog eats would, for instance, determine an extensive "object-food" behavior-family which would include the rabbit-food behavior-family as a subordinate behavior-family.

In these terms it is possible to formulate more precisely a set of conditions sufficient for something to be a sign: *If anything, A, is a preparatory-stimulus which in the absence of stimulus-objects initiating response-sequences of a certain behavior-family causes a disposition in some organism to respond under certain conditions by response-sequences of this behavior-family, then A is a sign.*

According to these conditions, the buzzer is a sign to the dog since it disposes the animal to seek food in a certain place in the absence of direct stimulation from food objects at this place, and similarly, the spoken words are signs to the driver since they dispose him to response-sequences of avoiding an obstacle at a certain point on a certain road although the obstacle is not itself at the time of hearing the sounds a stimulus-object.

The merit of this formulation is that it does not require that the dog or the driver respond to the sign itself, the sign serving merely as a preparatory-stimulus for response to something else. Nor does it require that the dog or the driver finally respond overtly as they would if food or an obstacle had been stimulus-objects; it merely requires that if the animal makes the response-sequences which it is disposed to make when certain additional conditions are met (conditions of need and of supporting stimulus-objects) these response-sequences will be of the same behavior-family as those which the food or obstacle would have initiated. In this way the difficulties which earlier behavioral formulations of signs encountered are avoided. And yet objective behavioral criteria are furnished for determining whether something is or is not a sign. It is further believed that these criteria do not deviate from those which underlie certain common usages of the term "sign."

* * * * * * * * * * * *

6. THE BASIC TERMS OF SEMIOTIC

It is now possible to isolate the basic terms of semiotic, for such terms will simply refer to various discernible aspects of sign-behavior. The term *sign* has already been introduced, or to speak more exactly, a criterion has been given under which certain things are admitted to be signs—whether in the course of our inquiry other criteria will have to be given to isolate other classes of signs remains for the time being an open question. But we at least are able to say that if something is a preparatory-stimulus of the kind specified in our previous formulation it is a sign. And this is the necessary first step for building a science of signs. For it identifies a subject matter for such a science and permits the introduction of a number of other terms for talking about this subject matter. Such terms can be introduced in a number of ways; we propose the following method of building a language to talk about signs.

Any organism for which something is a sign will be called an *interpreter*. The disposition in an interpreter to respond, because of the sign, by response-sequences of some behavior-family will be called an *interpretant*. Anything which would permit the completion of the response-sequences to which the interpreter is disposed because of a sign will be called a *denotatum* of the sign. A sign will be said to *denote* a denotatum. Those conditions which are such that whatever fulfills them is a denotatum will be called a *significatum* of the sign. A sign will be said to *signify* a significatum; the phrase "to have signification" may be taken as synonymous with "to signify."

So in the example of the dog, the buzzer is the sign; the dog is the interpreter; the disposition to seek food at a certain place, when caused by the buzzer, is the interpretant; food in the place sought which permits the completion of the response-sequences to which the dog is disposed is a denotatum and is denoted by the buzzer; the condition of being an edible object (perhaps of a certain sort) in a given place is the significatum of the buzzer and is what the buzzer signifies.

In the case of the driver the words spoken to him are signs; the driver is the interpreter; his disposition to respond by avoiding a landslide at a certain place in the road is the interpretant; the landslide at that place is the denotatum; the conditions of being a landslide at that place is the significatum of the spoken words.

According to this usage of terms, while a sign must signify, it may or may not denote. The buzzer can signify to the dog food at a given place without there being food at the place in question, and the landslide signified by the spoken words may not in fact exist. Usually we start with signs which denote and then attempt to formulate the significatum of a sign by observing the properties of denotata. But it is possible at the higher levels of human sign behavior to determine by decision the significatum of a sign (to "lay down" the conditions under which the sign will denote), and in this case the problem is not what the sign signifies but whether or not it denotes anything. We encounter cases of this nature frequently in the more complex sign processes.

The relation between interpretant and significatum is worth noting. The interpretant, as a disposition to respond caused by a sign, answers to the behavioral side of the behavior-environment complex; the significatum, as the set of terminal conditions under which the response-sequences to which the organism is disposed can be completed, connects with the environmental side of the complex. Each therefore involves the other. A complete description of the interpretant would include a description of what the organism is disposed to act toward, and a formulation of the significatum is simply a formulation of what would permit the completion of the response to which the organism is disposed because of a sign. The distinction between behavior and environment need not of course coincide with the distinction between the organism and the nonorganic world, since an organism can respond to other organisms and to itself. It is because of this that parts of the organism, dreams, feelings, and even interpretants can be signified.

Under the present usage, a sign cannot signify or denote its own interpretant, though it may signify and denote the interpretants of other signs (as in the case of "interpretant" itself). The buzzer does not signify the dog's disposition to respond but signifies food at a given place and time. This usage is not the only possible one, and at no point is the language of semioticians more at variance. A merit of the present usage of "signify" is that it does not make the significatum of every term—such as "spiral nebula" or "atom" —include biological events, though it recognizes that there are no signs which signify without dispositions to respond (that is, without interpretants). And since with this usage a sign does not denote its significatum, the temptation is avoided to make the significatum into a special kind of thing—a temptation which seems to underlie the Platonic doctrine of Ideas and various philosophic doctrines of "subsistence."

The term "meaning" is not here included among the basic terms of semiotic. This term, useful enough at the level of everyday analysis, does not have the precision necessary for scientific analysis. Accounts of meaning usually throw a handful of putty at the target of sign phenomena, while a technical semiotic must provide us with words which are sharpened arrows. "Meaning" signifies any and all phases of sign processes (the status of being a sign, the interpretant, the fact of denoting, the significatum), and frequently suggests mental and valuational processes as well; hence it is desirable for semiotic to dispense with the term and to introduce special terms for the various factors which "meaning" fails to discriminate.

Since something is a sign, significatum, denotatum, interpreter, or interpretant only with respect to its occurrence in sign behavior, and since such constituents of sign processes are studied by other sciences in other connections, the basic terms of semiotic are statable in terms drawn from the biological and physical sciences—a point which will prove to be of central significance for understanding the relation of socio-humanistic studies to the natural sciences. Since the factors operative in sign processes are all either stimulus-objects or organic dispositions or actual responses, the basic terms of semiotic are all formulable in terms applicable to behavior as it occurs in an environment. Semiotic thus becomes a part of the empirical science of behavior, and can utilize whatever principles and predictions the general theory of behavior has attained or can attain.

The formulation in terms of other signs of what a sign signifies (the description of the conditions which something must fulfill to be a denotatum of the sign) will be called a *formulated significatum*. A formulated significatum is *designative* if it formulates the significatum of an existing sign, and is *prescriptive* if it formulates the significatum which a sign is henceforth to have—a distinction which the commonly employed term "semantic rule" fails to make. A sign may, of course, signify without there being a formulation of what it signifies. A recognition of this simple fact cuts the ground out from under the frequent insinuations that a sign is "without meaning" to a person or animal who cannot "tell what the sign means." For something to signify is a different thing from the often very difficult task of formulating what it signifies.

·   ·   ·   ·   ·   ·   ·   ·   ·   ·   ·   ·

MORITZ SCHLICK

Meaning and
Verification

I

Philosophical questions, as compared with ordinary scientific problems, are always strangely paradoxical. But it seems to be an especially strange paradox that the question concerning the meaning of a proposition should constitute a serious philosophical difficulty. For is it not the very nature and purpose of every proposition to express its own meaning? In fact, when we are confronted with a proposition (in a language familiar to us) we usually know its meaning immediately. If we do not, we can have it explained to us, but the explanation will consist of a new proposition; and if the new one is capable of expressing the meaning, why should not the original one be capable of it? So that a snippy person when asked what he meant by a certain statement might be perfectly justified in saying, "I meant exactly what I said!"

It is logically legitimate and actually the normal way in ordinary life and even in science to answer a question concerning the meaning of a proposition by simply repeating it either more distinctly or in slightly different words. Under what circumstances, then, can there be any sense in asking for the meaning of a statement which is well before our eyes or ears?

Evidently the only possibility is that we have not *understood* it.

---

* Reprinted from *The Philosophical Review* 45, 1936, by permission of Mrs. B. van de Velde-Schlick, A. M. Schlick, and the editors.

And in this case what is actually before our eyes or ears is nothing but a series of words which we are unable to handle; we do not know how to use it, how to "apply it to reality." Such a series of words is for us simply a complex of signs "without meaning," a mere sequel of sounds or a mere row of marks on paper, and we have no right to call it "a proposition" at all; we may perhaps speak of it as "a sentence."

If we adopt this terminology we can now easily get rid of our paradox by saying that we cannot inquire after the meaning of a proposition, but can ask about the meaning of a sentence, and that this amounts to asking, "What proposition does the sentence stand for?" And this question is answered either by a proposition in a language with which we are already perfectly familiar; or by indicating the logical rules which will make a proposition out of the sentence, that is, will tell us exactly in what circumstances the sentence is to be *used*. These two methods do not actually differ in principle; both of them give meaning to the sentence (transform it into a proposition) by locating it, as it were, within the system of a definite language; the first method making use of a language which is already in our possession, the second one building it up for us. The first method represents the simplest kind of ordinary "translation"; the second one affords a deeper insight into the nature of meaning, and will have to be used in order to overcome philosophical difficulties connected with the understanding of sentences.

The source of these difficulties is to be found in the fact that very often we do not know how to handle our own words; we speak or write without having first agreed upon a definite logical grammar which will constitute the signification of our terms. We commit the mistake of thinking that we know the meaning of a sentence (*i.e.,* understand it as a proposition) if we are familiar with all the words occurring in it. But this is not sufficient. It will not lead to confusion or error as long as we remain in the domain of everyday life by which our words have been formed and to which they are adapted, but it will become fatal the moment we try to think about abstract problems by means of the same terms without carefully fixing their signification for the new purpose. For every word has a definite signification only within a definite context into which it has been fitted; in any other context it will have no meaning unless we provide new rules for the use of the word in the new case, and this may be done, at least in principle, quite arbitrarily.

Let us consider an example. If a friend should say to me, "Take me to a country where the sky is three times as blue as in England!" I should not know how to fulfill his wish; his phrase would appear nonsensical to me, because the word "blue" is used in a way which is not provided for by the rules of our language. The combination of a numeral and the name of a color does not occur in it; therefore my friend's sentence has no meaning, although its exterior linguistic form is that of a command or a wish. But he can, of course, give it a meaning. If I ask him, "What do you mean by three times as blue?" he can arbitrarily indicate certain definite physical circumstances concerning the serenity of the sky which he wants his phrase to be the description of. And then, perhaps, I shall be able to follow his directions; his wish will have become meaningful for me.

Thus, whenever we ask about a sentence, "What does it mean?," what we expect is instruction as to the circumstances in which the sentence is to be used; we want a description of the conditions under which the sentence will form a *true* proposition, and of those which will make it *false*. The meaning of a word or a combination of words is, in this way, determined by a set of rules which regulate their use and which, following Wittgenstein, we may call the rules of their *grammar*, taking this word in its widest sense.

(If the preceding remarks about meaning are as correct as I am convinced they are, this will, to a large measure, be due to conversations with Wittgenstein which have greatly influenced my own views about these matters. I can hardly exaggerate my indebtedness to this philosopher. I do not wish to impute to him any responsibility for the contents of this article, but I have reason to hope that he will agree with the main substance of it.)

Stating the meaning of a sentence amounts to stating the rules according to which the sentence is to be used, and this is the same as stating the way in which it can be verified (or falsified). The meaning of a proposition is the method of its verification.

The "grammatical" rules will partly consist of ordinary definitions, that is, explanations of words by means of other words, partly of what are called "ostensive" definitions, that is, explanations by means of a procedure which puts the words to actual use. The simplest form of an ostensive definition is a pointing gesture combined with the pronouncing of the word, as when we teach a child the signification of the sound "blue" by showing a blue object. But in most cases the ostensive definition is of a more complicated form; we cannot point to an object corresponding to words like "because" "immediate," "chance," "again," and so forth. In these cases we require the presence of certain complex situations, and the meaning of the words is defined by the way we use them in these different situations.

It is clear that in order to understand a verbal definition we must know the signification of the explaining words beforehand, and that the only explanation which can work without any previous knowledge is the ostensive definition. We conclude that there is no way of understanding any meaning without ultimate reference to ostensive definitions, and this means, in an obvious sense, reference to "experience" or "possibility of verification."

This is the situation, and nothing seems to me simpler or less questionable. It is this situation and nothing else that we describe when we affirm that the meaning of a proposition can be given only by giving the rules of its verification in experience. (The addition, "in experience," is really superfluous, as no other kind of verification has been defined.)

This view has been called the "experimental theory of meaning"; but it certainly is no theory at all, for the term "theory" is used for a set of hypotheses about a certain subject matter, and there are no hypotheses involved in our view, which proposes to be nothing but a simple statement of the way in which meaning is *actually* assigned to propositions, both in everyday life and in science. There has never been any other way, and it would be a grave error to suppose that we believe we have discovered a new conception of meaning which is contrary to common opinion and which we want to introduce into philosophy. On the contrary, our conception is not only entirely in agreement with, but even derived from, common sense and scientific procedure. Although our criterion of meaning has always been employed in practice, it has very rarely been formulated in the past, and this is perhaps the only excuse for the attempts of so many philosophers to deny its feasibility.

The most famous case of an explicit formulation of our criterion is Einstein's answer to the question, What do we mean when we speak of two events at distant places happening simultaneously? This answer consisted in a description of an experimental method by which the simultaneity of such events was actually ascertained. Einstein's philosophical opponents maintained—and some of them still maintain—that they knew the meaning of the above question independently of any method of verification. All I am trying to do is to stick consistently to Einstein's position and to admit no exceptions from it. (Professor Bridgman's book on *The Logic of Modern Physics* is an admirable attempt to carry out this program for all concepts of physics.) I am not writing for those who think that Einstein's philosophical opponents were right.

II

Professor C. I. Lewis, in a remarkable address on "Experience and Meaning" (published in *The Philosophical Review*, March 1934), has justly stated that the view developed above (he speaks of it as the "empirical-meaning requirement") forms the basis of the whole philosophy of what has been called the "logical positivism of the Viennese Circle." He criticizes this basis as inadequate chiefly on the ground that its acceptance would impose certain limitations upon "significant philosophic discussion" which, at some points, would make such discussion altogether impossible and, at other points, restrict it to an intolerable extent.

Feeling responsible as I do for certain features of the Viennese philosophy (which I should prefer to call Consistent Empiricism), and being of the opinion that it really does not impose any restrictions upon significant philosophizing at all, I shall try to examine Professor Lewis' chief arguments and point out why I think that they do not endanger our position—at least as far as I can answer for it myself. All of my own arguments will be derived from the statements made in section I.

Professor Lewis describes the empirical-meaning requirement as demanding "that any concept put forward or any proposition asserted shall have a definite denotation; that it shall be intelligible not only verbally and logically but in the further sense that one can specify those empirical items which would determine the applicability of the concept or constitute the verification of the proposition" (*loc. cit.*). Here it seems to me that there is no justification for the words "but in the *further* sense . . .", *i.e.*, for the distinction of two (or three?) senses of intelligibility. The remarks in section I show that, according to our opinion, "verbal and logical" understanding *consists in* knowing how the proposition in question could be verified. For, unless we mean by "verbal understanding" that we know how the words are actually used, the term could hardly mean anything but a shadowy feeling of being acquainted with the words, and in a philosophical discussion it does not seem advisable to call such a feeling "understanding." Similarly, I should not advise that we speak of a sentence as being "logically intelligible" when we just feel convinced that its exterior form is that of a proper proposition (if, *e.g.*, it has the form, substantive —copula—adjective, and therefore appears to predicate a property of a thing). For it seems to me that by such a phrase we want to say much *more*, namely, that we are completely aware of the whole grammar of the sentence, that is, that we know exactly the circumstances to which it is fitted. Thus knowledge of how a proposition is verified is not anything over and above its verbal and logical understanding, but is identical with it. It seems to me, therefore, that when we demand that a proposition be verifiable we are not adding a new requirement but are simply formulating the conditions which have actually always been acknowledged as necessary for meaning and intelligibility.

The mere statement that no sentence has meaning unless we are able to indicate a way of testing its truth or falsity is not very useful if we do not explain very carefully the signification of the phrases "method of testing" and "verifiability." Professor Lewis is quite right when he asks for such an explanation. He himself suggests some ways in which it might be given, and I am glad to say that his suggestions appear to me to be in perfect agreement with my own views and those of my philosophical friends. It will be easy to show that there is no serious divergence between the point of view of the pragmatist as Professor Lewis conceives it and that of the Viennese Empiricist. And if in some special questions they arrive at different conclusions, it may be hoped that a careful examination will bridge the difference.

How do we define verifiability?

In the first place I should like to point out that when we say that "a proposition has meaning only if it is verifiable" we are not saying ". . . if it is *verified.*" This simple remark does away with one of the chief objections; the "here and now predicament," as Professor Lewis calls it, does not exist any more. We fall into the snares of this predicament only if we regard verification itself as the criterion of meaning, instead of "possibility of verification" (= verifiability); this would indeed lead to a "reduction to absurdity of meaning." Obviously the predicament arises through some fallacy by which these two notions are confounded. I do not know if Russell's statement, "Empirical knowledge is confined to what we actually observe" (quoted by Professor Lewis, *loc. cit.*), must be interpreted as containing this fallacy, but it would certainly be worth while to discover its genesis.

Let us consider the following argument which Professor Lewis discusses, but which he does not want to impute to anyone:

> Suppose it maintained that no issue is meaningful unless it can be put to the test of decisive verification. And no verification can take place except in the immediately present experience of the subject. Then nothing can be meant except what is actually present in the experience in which that meaning is entertained.

This argument has the form of a conclusion drawn from two premisses. Let us for the moment asume the second premiss to be meaningful and true. You will observe that even then the conclusion does *not* follow. For the first premiss assures us that the issue has meaning if it *can* be verified; the verification does not have to take place, and therefore it is quite irrelevant whether it can take place in the future or in the present only. Apart from this, the second premiss is, of course, nonsensical; for what fact could possibly be described by the sentence "verification can take place only in present experience"? Is not verifying an act or process like hearing or feeling bored? Might we not just as well say that

I can hear or feel bored only in the present moment? And what could I mean by this? The particular nonsense involved in such phrases will become clearer when we speak of the "egocentric predicament" later on; at present we are content to know that our empirical-meaning postulate has nothing whatever to do with the now-predicament. "Verifiable" does not even mean "verifiable here now"; much less does it mean "being verified now."

Perhaps it will be thought that the only way of making sure of the verifiability of a proposition would consist in its actual verification. But we shall soon see that this is not the case.

There seems to be a great temptation to connect meaning and the "immediately given" in the wrong way; and some of the Viennese positivists may have yielded to this temptation, thereby getting dangerously near to the fallacy we have just been describing. Parts of Carnap's *Der Logische Aufbau der Welt*, for instance, might be interpreted as implying that a proposition about future events did not really refer to the future at all but asserted only the present existence of certain expectations (and, similarly, speaking about the past would really mean speaking about present memories). But it is certain that the author of that book does not hold such a view now, and that it cannot be regarded as a teaching of the new positivism. On the contrary, we have pointed out from the beginning that our definition of meaning does not imply such absurd consequences, and when someone asked, "But how can you verify a proposition about a future event?", we replied, "Why, for instance, by waiting for it to happen! 'Waiting' is a perfectly legitimate method of verification."

Thus I think that everybody—including the Consistent Empiricist—agrees that it would be nonsense to say, "We can mean nothing but the immediately given." If in this sentence we replace the word "mean" by the word "know" we arrive at a statement similar to Bertrand Russell's mentioned above. The temptation to formulate phrases of this sort arises, I believe, from a certain ambiguity of the verb "to know" which is the source of many metaphysical troubles and to which, therefore, I have often had to call attention on other occasions (see, *e.g., Allgemeine Erkenntnislehre* 2nd ed. 1925, § 12). In the first place the word may stand simply for "being aware of a datum," that is, for the mere presence of a feeling, a color, a sound, and so forth; and if the word "knowledge" is taken in this sense the assertion "Empirical knowledge is confined to what we actually observe" does not say anything at all, but is a mere tautology. (This case, I think, would correspond to what Professor Lewis calls "identity-theories" of the "knowledge-relation." Such theories, resting on a tautology of this kind, would be empty verbiage without significance.)

In the second place the word "knowledge" may be used in one of the significant meanings which it has in science and ordinary life; and in this case Russell's assertion would obviously (as Professor Lewis remarked) be false. Russell himself, as is well known, distinguishes between "knowledge by acquaintance" and "knowledge by description," but perhaps it should be noted that this distinction does not entirely coincide with the one we have been insisting upon just now.

III

Verifiability means possibility of verification. Professor Lewis justly remarks that to "omit all examination of the wide range of significance which could attach to "possible verification," would be to leave the whole conception rather obscure" (*loc. cit.*). For our purpose it suffices to distinguish between two of the many ways in which the word "possibility" is used. We shall call them "empirical possibility" and "logical possibility." Professor Lewis describes two meanings of "verifiability" which correspond exactly to this difference; he is fully aware of it, and there is hardly anything left for me to do but carefully to work out the distinction and show its bearing upon our issue.

I propose to call "empirically possible" anything that does not contradict the laws of nature. This is, I think, the largest sense in which we may speak of empirical possibility; we do not restrict the term to happenings which are not only in accordance with the laws of nature but also with the actual state of the universe (where "actual" might refer to the present moment of our own lives, or to the condition of human beings on this planet, and so forth). If we chose the latter definition (which seems to have been in

Professor Lewis' mind when he spoke of "possible experience as conditioned by the actual," *loc. cit.*) we should not get the sharp boundaries we need for our present purpose. So "empirical possibility" is to mean "compatibility with natural laws."

Now, since we cannot boast of a complete and sure knowledge of nature's laws, it is evident that we can never assert with certainty the empirical possibility of any fact, and here we may be permitted to speak of *degrees* of possibility. Is it possible for me to lift this book? Surely!—This table? I think so!—This billiard table? I don't think so!—This automobile? Certainly not!—It is clear that in these cases the answer is given by *experience*, as the result of experiments performed in the past. Any judgment about empirical possibility is based on experience and will often be rather uncertain; there will be no sharp boundary between possibility and impossibility.

Is the possibility of verification which we insist upon of this empirical sort? In that case there would be different degrees of verifiability, the question of meaning would be a matter of more or less, not a matter of yes or no. In many disputes concerning our issue it is the empirical possibility of verification which is discussed; the various examples of verifiability given by Professor Lewis, for example, are instances of different empirical circumstances in which the verification is carried out or prevented from being carried out. Many of those who refuse to accept our criterion of meaning seem to imagine that the procedure of its application in a special case is somewhat like this: A proposition is presented to us ready made, and in order to discover its meaning we have to try various methods of verifying or falsifying it, and if one of these methods works we have found the meaning of the proposition; but if not, we say it has no meaning. If we really had to proceed in this way, it is clear that the determination of meaning would be entirely a matter of experience, and that in many cases no sharp and ultimate decision could be obtained. How could we ever know that we had tried long enough, if none of our methods were successful? Might not future efforts disclose a meaning which we were unable to find before?

This whole conception is, of course, entirely erroneous. It speaks of meaning as if it were a kind of entity inherent in a sentence and hidden in it like a nut in its shell, so that the philosopher would have to crack the shell or sentence in order to reveal the nut or meaning. We know from our considerations in section I that a proposition cannot be given "ready made"; that meaning does not inhere in a sentence where it might be discovered, but that it must be bestowed upon it. And this is done by applying to the sentence the rules of the logical grammar of our language, as explained in section I. These rules are not facts of nature which could be "discovered," but they are prescriptions stipulated by acts of definition. And these definitions have to be known to those who pronounce the sentence in question and to those who hear or read it. Otherwise they are not confronted with any proposition at all, and there is nothing they could try to verify, because you can't verify or falsify a mere row of words. You cannot even start verifying before you know the meaning, that is, before you have established the possibility of verification.

In other words, the possibility of verification which is relevant to meaning cannot be of the empirical sort; it cannot be established *post festum*. You have to be sure of it before you can consider the empirical circumstances and investigate whether or no or under what conditions they will permit of verification. The empirical circumstances are all-important when you want to know if a proposition is *true* (which is the concern of the scientist), but they can have no influence on the *meaning* of the proposition (which is the concern of the philosopher). Professor Lewis has seen and expressed this very clearly (*loc. cit.*), and our Vienna positivism, as far as I can answer for it, is in complete agreement with him on this point. It must be emphasized that when we speak of verifiability we mean *logical* possibility of verification, and nothing but this.

I call a fact or a process "logically possible" if it can be *described*, that is, if the sentence which is supposed to describe it obeys the rules of grammar we have stipulated for our language. (I am expressing myself rather incorrectly. A fact which could not be described would, of course, not be any fact at all; *any* fact is logically possible. But I think my meaning will be understood.) Take some examples. The sentences, "My friend died the day after tomorrow"; "The lady wore a dark red dress which was bright green"; "The campanile is 100 feet and 150 feet high"; "The child was naked, but wore a long white nightgown," obviously violate the rules which, in ordinary English, govern the use of the words occurring in the sentences. They do not describe any facts at all; they are meaningless, because they represent *logical* impossibilities.

It is of the greatest importance (not only for our present issue but for philosophical problems in general) to see that whenever we speak of logical impossibility we are referring to a discrepancy between the definitions of our terms and the way in which we use them. We must avoid the severe mistake committed by some of the former Empiricists like Mill and Spencer, who regarded logical principles (*e.g.*, the Law of Contradiction) as laws of nature governing the psychological process of thinking. The nonsensical statements alluded to above do not correspond to thoughts which, by a sort of psychological experiment, we find ourselves unable to think; they do not correspond to any thoughts at all. When we hear the words, "A tower which is both 100 feet and 150 feet high," the image of two towers of different heights may be in our mind, and we may find it psychologically (empirically) impossible to combine the two pictures into one image, but it is not this fact which is denoted by the words "logical impossibility." The height of a tower cannot be 100 feet and 150 feet at the same time; a child cannot be naked and dressed at the same time—not because we are unable to imagine it, but because our definitions of "height," of the numerals, of the terms "naked" and "dressed," are not compatible with the particular combinations of those words in our examples. "They are not compatible with such combinations" means that the rules of our language have not provided any use for such combinations; they do not describe any fact. We could change these rules, of course, and thereby arrange a meaning for the terms "both red and green," "both naked and dressed"; but if we decide to stick to the ordinary definitions (which reveal themselves in the way we actually use our words) we have decided to regard those combined terms as meaningless, that is, not to use them as the description of *any* fact. Whatever fact we may or may not imagine, if the word "naked" (or "red") occurs in its description we have decided that the word "dressed" (or "green") cannot be put in its place in the same description. If we do not follow this rule it means that we want to introduce a new definition of the words, or that we don't mind using words without meaning and like to indulge in nonsense. (I am far from condemning this attitude under all circumstances; on certain occasions—as in *Alice in Wonderland*—it may be the only sensible attitude and far more delightful than any treatise on Logic. But in such a treatise we have a right to expect a different attitude.)

The result of our considerations is this: Verifiability, which is the sufficient and necessary condition of meaning, is a possibility of the logical order; it is created by constructing the sentence in accordance with the rules by which its terms are defined. The only case in which verification is (logically) impossible is the case where you have *made* it impossible by not setting any rules for its verification. Grammatical rules are not found anywhere in nature, but are made by man and are, in principle, arbitrary; so you cannot give meaning to a sentence by *discovering* a method of verifying it, but only by *stipulating* how it *shall* be done. Thus logical possibility or impossibility of verification is always *self-imposed*. If we utter a sentence without meaning it is always *our own fault*.

The tremendous philosophic importance of this last remark will be realized when we consider that what we said about the meaning of *assertions* applies also to the meaning of *questions*. There are, of course, many questions which can never be answered by human beings. But the impossibility of finding the answer may be of two different kinds. If it is merely empirical in the sense defined, if it is due to the chance circumstances to which our human existence is confined, there may be reason to lament our fate and the weakness of our physical and mental powers, but the problem could never be said to be absolutely insoluble, and there would always be some hope, at least for future generations. For the empirical circumstances may alter, human facilities may develop, and even the laws of nature may change (perhaps even suddenly and in such a way that the universe would be thrown open to much more extended investigation). A problem of this kind might be called practically unanswerable or technically unanswerable, and might cause the scientist great trouble, but the philosopher, who is concerned with general principles only, would not feel terribly excited about it.

But what about those questions for which it is *logically* impossible to find an answer? Such problems would remain insoluble under all imaginable circumstances; they would confront us with a definite hopeless *Ignorabimus;* and it is of the greatest importance for the philosopher to know whether there are any such issues. Now it is easy to see from what has been said before that this calamity could happen only if the question itself had no meaning. It would not be a genuine question at all, but a mere row of words with a question-mark at the end. We must say that a question is meaningful, if we can *understand* it, that is, if we are able to decide for any given proposition whether, if true, it would be an answer to our question. And if this is so, the actual decision could only be prevented by empirical circumstances, which means that it would not be *logically* impossible. Hence no meaningful problem can be insoluble in *principle*. If in any case we find an answer to be logically impossible we know that we really have not been asking anything, that what sounded like a question was actually a nonsensical combination of words. A genuine question is one for which an answer is logically possible. This is one of the most characteristic results of our empiricism. It means that in principle there are no limits to our knowledge. The boundaries which must be acknowledged are of an empirical nature and, therefore, never ultimate; they can be pushed back further and further; there is no unfathomable mystery in the world.

The dividing line between logical possibility and impossibility of verification is absolutely sharp and distinct; there is no gradual transition between meaning and nonsense. For either you have given the grammatical rules for verification, or you have not; *tertium non datur.*

Empirical possibility is determined by the laws of nature, but meaning and verifiability are entirely independent of them. Everything that I can describe or define is logically possible—and definitions are in no way bound up with natural laws. The proposition "Rivers flow uphill" is meaningful, but happens to be false because the fact it describes is *physically* impossible. It will not deprive a proposition of its meaning if the conditions which I stipulate for its verification are incompatible with the laws of nature; I may prescribe conditions, for instance, which could be fulfilled only if the velocity of light were greater than it actually is, or if the Law of Conservation of Energy did not hold, and so forth.

An opponent of our view might find a dangerous paradox or even a contradiction in the preceding explanations, because on the one hand we insisted so strongly on what has been called the "*empirical-meaning requirement*," and on the other hand we assert most emphatically that meaning and verifiability do not depend on any empirical conditions whatever, but are determined by purely logical possibilities. The opponent will object: if meaning is a matter of experience, how can it be a matter of definition and logic?

In reality there is no contradiction or difficulty. The word "experience" is ambiguous. Firstly, it may be a name for any so-called "immediate data"—which is a comparatively modern use of the word—and secondly we can use it in the sense in which we speak, for example, of an "experienced traveler," meaning a man who has not only seen a great deal but also knows how to profit from it for his actions. It is in this second sense (by the way, the sense the word has in Hume's and Kant's philosophy) that verifiability must be declared to be independent of experience. The possibility of verification does not rest on any "experiential truth," on a law of nature or any other true general proposition, but is determined solely by our definitions, by the rules which have been fixed for our language, or which we can fix arbitrarily at any moment. All of these rules ultimately point to ostensive definitions, as we have explained, and through them verifiability is linked to *experience* in the *first* sense of the word. No rule of expression presupposes any law or regularity in the world (which is the condition of "experience" as Hume and Kant use the word), but it does presuppose data and situations, to which names can be attached. The rules of language are rules of the application of language; so there must be something to which it can be applied. Expressibility and verifiability are one and the same thing. There is no antagonism between logic and experience. Not only can the logician be an empiricist at the same time; he *must* be one if he wants to understand what he himself is doing.

. . . .

RULON WELLS

Meaning and Use

1. RUSSELL AND WITTGENSTEIN

Many ideas stemming from Bertrand Russell are of great value for linguistics; then why has their diffusion hardly begun to take place? Less from sheer ignorance of the ideas than from unawareness that they are relevant. If a popular cliché can be trusted, technical results need to be "translated" in order to become available to the layman. But here it's not hard words that are the obstacle; in the last analysis it is the very peculiar relationship between science and philosophy.

In the present paper we shall have under consideration a body of writings by men who have aimed at philosophy but have contributed to science on the way. From their own point of view their contributions to science are incidental. But our point of view is the reverse of theirs. We are called upon, not merely to excerpt their ideas but to adapt them. A subtle difference?—but big enough to have preserved the said ideas nearly intact. A chemical analogy suggests itself in preference to a mechanical one. Philosophical and scientific aspects of their work are chemically combined, not mechanically mixed; no mere screen, no dipper, no magnet will separate them. I hope that my meaning will become clearer later on than it can be here.

* Reprinted from *Word* 10 (1954), by permission of the author and the editor.

Within the Russellian movement three reasonably distinct main branches may be noted. In order of their appearance they are: (1) The approach of Russell himself, formulated in the first quarter of this century. (2) Logical positivism, deeply indebted to Wittgenstein's *Tractatus Logico-Philosophicus* (1922) and taking shape as a self-conscious, self-named group a little before 1930. (3) A movement centering about Wittgenstein after he had accepted a call to Cambridge in 1929 and had rejected many of his own earlier doctrines. (As early as 1914 Russell began acknowledging "the benefit of vitally important discoveries, not yet published, by my friend Mr. Ludwig Wittgenstein"—(1914), p. vii. Thus Wittgenstein has played a major part in all three branches of the Russellian movement.) As Wittgenstein published practically nothing in this period, his ideas were disseminated—apart from his personal teaching—only through the writings of his disciples, John Wisdom and others, and through the private circulation of various unpublished lecture notes.

After the Second World War leadership in the Wittgenstein movement, and thereby in British philosophy in general, shifted to Oxford, where a remarkable quickening had taken place. Ideas of Wittgenstein's were joined there to the somewhat divergent ideas of Gilbert Ryle and others, and a group of thinkers with sufficient consensus to warrant being called a school has emerged. The name that has become current for these Oxford philosophers and for others, wherever situated, of closely related views, is "the philosophy of ordinary language." There are writers such as John Wisdom and C. L. Stevenson, considerably influenced by Wittgenstein but to whose thought the term "philosophy of ordinary language," in the technical sense that is in process of growing up, might not be applied. I will bypass such questions of detail by speaking, usually, of "Wittgensteinians."

Wittgenstein retired from Cambridge in 1949 and died in 1951. *Philosophical Investigations* was published in 1953. For obituary notices see Anonymous (1951) and Ryle (1951a); for reminiscences see Russell (1951), Wisdom (1952), and Moore (1954). Ryle (1951b) is a popular discussion. Journal publications by Wittgensteinians are principally to be found in the volumes for the past decade of

Mind, Analysis, Proceedings of the Aristotelian Society, Aristotelian Society Supplementary Volumes, and *Philosophical Review.*

In what follows I shall give few direct quotations. References are made less for the assignment of credit than to guide the interested reader. The "chemical" job of isolating the scientifically interesting aspects of the movement and showing how they might be developed is so intricate that it is not worth while to retrace the steps here. For present purposes, it is only the end result that matters.

The whole Russellian movement will not be under discussion, but (primarily) only the third or later-Wittgenstein branch. Since this is the most recently developed branch, and for that very reason the least widely known, the decision to concentrate on it seems reasonable. But the choice does require us, for example, to pass over the important Chapter VII, "Analysis of conversational language," of Reichenbach (1947), which belongs to the second or logical positivist branch.

2. THE DYADIC CONCEPTION OF MEANING

The best way to bring out Wittgenstein's novelty is by comparisons. Beginning with a half-historical survey of varying conceptions of the sign, we will move on (Sections 3 and 4) to Bloomfield's view of meaning, which is superficially similar to Wittgenstein's but significantly different, and will end the preliminaries with some account (Section 5) of Russell's program and his solutions.

The most obvious way to conceive meaning is to conceive it as a dyadic relation between a sign and an object. So natural, so appealing, this conception has cropped up again and again. Even sophisticated thinkers have bent their ingenious efforts to preserving it. A rival account, and one that is rather popular today, recognizes three factors: sign, object, and user. But a moment's thought will prove that even this triadic conception is not exact. For instance, we would need to mention the time of signification: A is a sign of B to C at time D; at another time, it may be a sign to B of something different, or may not be a sign to B at all. Further, this triadic conception could be modified by speaking not (with

Morris) of the user, but (with Peirce) of the interpretant, that is, of the thought or mental effect *in* the interpreter or user. If we do this, and consider interpretants as individual acts, then the time reference is already implicit and it would be redundant to mention it again. If we consider interpretants as kinds of acts, then the time must be specified. Thus there can be different versions of the triadic conception, some more exact than others.

The modern triadic conception has been given two applications. First, it underlies the argument for the view that "the linguistic sign is arbitrary." Consequently, the moderns who accept it are taking sides on the ancient *physei-thesei* controversy. Second, and in consequence of the first, it has been used (above all by C. K. Ogden) to refute word magic, that is, the doctrine of an intrinsic identity between linguistic sign and its object. For if there is no intrinsic connection at all, there cannot be an intrinsic connection of identity.

Ogden and Richards—to this extent resembling Aristotle—analyze the triadic relation as a conjunction of two dyads: one holding between sign and interpretant, the other between interpretant and object. This analysis enables them, or at least encourages them, to treat the resulting dyads as varieties of the cause-effect or stimulus-response relation. Odgen and Richards are closer to Bloomfield's position than he (1933, p. 515) gives them credit for.

The preceding paragraphs have been arranged around the problem, What variables or factors does signification involve? The only one on which there has been agreement is the sign (vehicle, *significant*) itself. As to the nature of the object, opinions have been too numerous to mention. Everyone recognizes that one and the same sign may have more than one sense; and nominalistic philosophers hold that every fresh instance of a sign involves a new meaning of it. But leaving aside both these considerations, there is the distinction of denotation and connotation to reckon with. We can prove rigorously that *some* such distinction is needed; for there are pairs of expressions that apply to the same objects but that differ in objective meaning somehow or other. Besides, "No one with a respect for sense would dream of pointing to someone . . . and saying . . . 'the meaning of yonder phrase is suffering from influenza' " (Ryle 1932, p. 25; *cf.* 1949, pp. 70, 73–74). Quine in his address to linguists (1953, p. 47; *cf.* 9, 21, and 130) makes the point by distinguishing meaning from reference. And years ago Gardiner stressed the distinction of meaning from thing-meant (Ullmann 1951, pp. 33fn., 70). The simple dyadic conception of meaning leaves this distinction betwen different kinds of "objects" out of account just as much as it leaves the interpreter.

The number of theories of meaning is vast; so is their variety. Semanticists have been groping in a labyrinth. But there is a cheering thought. To get out of the maze is not our sole wish; we want to *explore* the maze too. We want to understand it, become intimately familiar with it, know all its ins and outs. What we would welcome is not so much a thread of Ariadne as a flash-light.

Let us feel around in one of the darkest alleys again, the dyadic theory of meaning. One kind of sign, the symbol in one sense of the word, is a surrogate for its object. The conscious dreaming of a journey substitutes for the unconscious thought of death; the mathematician's square-root sign stands for the words "that (positive) number whose square is——." Some philosophers have tried to handle all signification by bringing it under the idea of surrogation. Another version of the dyadic, single-object conception tries to assimilate all meaning or signifying to naming. Russell tried to do this too, and his and Wittgenstein's big discoveries came from their perception of the difficulties. If we hold that all expressions are really names, then the first difficulty is that we must explain why some expressions are obviously names whereas others appear not to be. A century ago people were willing to say that whereas "John" names a person, "or" and "not" name thoughts in the mind. But this half-hearted view opens up a new approach. Why not unify our account by making *all* words name something mental? To avoid this absurdity Russell (1940) introduces a distinction between two *kinds* of meaning: expression and indication. Every sign that indicates, also expresses; but some signs that express don't indicate anything. Logical words like "or" and "not" express a state of mind but do not indicate any objective state of affairs, unless a state of mind itself is being talked about. Since indication is virtu-ally the same as the old relation of naming, Russell has abandoned the dyadic single-object doctrine by recognizing that a sign may have two "objects" simultaneously—that which it indicates and that which it expresses.

Now although what a sign indicates corresponds to what it denotes, what it expresses does not coincide with what it connotes. The reason is that connotation as logicians understand it is something objective, not something mental. Or at least this is what one school of thought maintains. Expression, on the other hand, is more like the interpretant of sign–object–interpretant theories.

Here we have an example of the difference between philosophy and science. The philosopher ponders such questions as whether we need to recognize extramental objective connotations or whether we can consider that they are abstractions created by the mind and existing only in it. The scientist on the other hand would be only too glad to hurry right past this question, if someone can show him how to do it. This problem of autonomy will occupy us in the next section. Here it may be remarked that Wittgenstein's slogan, "Don't look for the meaning, look for the use," virtually offers the scientist the help he is looking for.

3. BLOOMFIELD AND AUTONOMY

Among the notable and distinctive features of science—and one that sets it in contrast with philosophy—is its policy, "Divide and conquer." The piecemeal method (Russell) of considering problems in isolation is one secret of its success; but it is a policy that only makes sense as a deduction from a higher one, namely, the overarching conception of scientific results as tentative.

Wherever possible, we would like to apply the "Divide and conquer" policy in the following way. We would like the several sciences to be so related that each one shall be able to profit by relevant advances in the others, and yet not be held back by their difficulties. This scheme for letting a science eat its cake and have it too can be put into practice to whatever extent we can establish a twofold relationship: (1) autonomy and (2) reducibility.

(1) The concepts and propositions of one field are autonomous from those of another when changes in the latter do not require changes in the former. Autonomy of A from B is the more advisable, the more likely it is that B will undergo change.

(2) The concepts and propositions of one field are reducible to those of another if they can be reinterpreted, in a regular and systematic manner, as concepts and propositions of the latter. Descartes's analytic geometry reduces geometry to algebra; Whitehead and Russell's *Principia Mathematica* reduces arithmetic and algebra to the logic of classes and relations. Instances from empirical science have only recently been worked out. A number of them are very beautifully discussed in Woodger (1952).

(Reducibility is what the logical positivists have called "unity of laws," in contrast to the weaker relationship of "unity of language." See papers by Feigl and by Carnap in Feigl-Sellars, 1949, pp. 22–23, 421–22, and 510–14. We might say that reducibility of A to B permits A to be "hooked up" or "plugged into" B, and autonomy from B permits A to be "unhooked" or "unplugged.")

These abstract remarks can be immediately applied to semantics. The science of psychology and the nonscientific field of philosophy are the two areas or inquiries upon which it is most often proposed to make semantics depend. Dependence on psychology makes semantics full of vicissitudes; dependence on philosophy splits it into perennially surviving camps. It should be autonomous from both for the same reason that the Civil Service should be autonomous from elected parties.

Proposals to reduce semantics to something else have vastly exceeded proposals to make it autonomous. Bloomfield (1933 and earlier papers) is among the latter few. He states his view as an approval of Delbrück; but he and not Delbrück deserves the major credit because Delbrück's position would scarcely be known without Bloomfield and because he shows more elaborately how to carry out the program. Hjelmslev too has stressed the importance of autonomy.

As history proves, it is hard to keep the two stresses in balance. Few thinkers have seen that the *twofold* relation is needed. And neither of the two relations can be achieved by an automatic method. Autonomy admits of degrees; and there is autonomy by abstraction and autonomy by fiction. Autonomy by abstraction simply ignores those facts from another domain whose description would require alien concepts and propositions. Autonomy by fiction, on the other hand, is used where facts belonging to another domain

are used and are described in a manner convenient to the borrow-
ing science, but without commitment to the belief that the science
in whose domain these facts belong will accept that manner of description. (For instance, a semantical account of the temporal process of interpretation may break up this process into stages; but
these stages will be fictive in that admittedly the science of psychology, to whom the proper description of this process belongs,
may not recognize these same stages as psychological realities.)

There is a paradox in Bloomfield's actual position which recent
criticism has pointed up. (See Schlauch 1946, Basilius 1952, Olmsted
1952, Fries 1954.) Bloomfield tells linguists to steer clear of psychology by being mechanists. But there are three points we must make
in reply. (1) The advice to steer clear of psychology, that is, to au-
tonomize, is good advice even if the proposed way of doing it is
poor and is inconsistent with the advice itself. (2) In addition to
overstressing autonomy at the expense of reducibility (see above),
Bloomfield is only acquainted with autonomy by abstraction and
not with autonomy by fiction. Thus he cuts off linguistics (including semantics) from one of the means of following his own advice.
(3) In diagnosing the conflict between mentalism and mechanism
he mislocates the issue and thus plants his germ of truth in the
sand of confusion.

The second and third points need to be elaborated, because it is
there that Bloomfield fails where Wittgenstein succeeds.

The day of scientific semantics is far off—this is the tenor of
Bloomfield (1933)—for two reasons. First, semantics when it *is* reduced to psychology must be reduced to a mechanistic, not to a
mentalistic psychology. Second, Bloomfield evidently has the conception that this mechanistic psychology will itself be reduced to
physiology, including neurology. (It is this conception of psychology
as reduced that identifies him with the era of Watson and Weiss
rather than with that of Hull.) Autonomy of linguistics from psychology, and of psychology from physiology, is something to be put
up with, endured; it is a stopgap, a makeshift. (The semantical techniques available at the present time are, for the most part, "makeshift devices" (1933) p. 140.) In this frame of mind one can have no
very great enthusiasm for devising such makeshifts.

To set things to rights we need a better understanding of the mentalism–mechanism issue. In rejecting mentalism Bloomfield has only one argument: that mentalistic explanations are tautologous, circular, empty. And he goes on to identify, in effect, three contrasts: mentalistic versus mechanistic, philosophical versus scientific, and empty versus significant. But he is doubly mistaken: not all mentalistic statements are empty, and not all empty statements are mentalistic.

We may make the idea of emptiness more precise by following up Bloomfield's remark that an explanatory statement of the form "B because A" is empty when B is the only evidence for A. For example, it would be empty to say "He ran because he was frightened" if the only evidence for his being frightened was that he ran. For in that case the statement that he was frightened "adds nothing" to the statement that he ran.

Presumably this is offered as a necessary as well as a sufficient condition for emptiness; that is, an explanatory statement is empty under this condition and not otherwise. Thus we can expand the remark in the preceding paragraph to read: An explanatory statement of the form "B because A" is empty when and only when B is the only evidence for A. This remark and the phrase about "adding nothing" are the clues we have to follow up.

The barest tautology would be of this form: "B because B." If on the other hand we say "B because B and A" or "B and A, therefore B," where A is something not implied by B, then we have added something. "B because B and A" is no longer a tautology, because B is not the only evidence for B and A. A is also evidence for it, so that we are equally justified in asserting, "A because B and A."

This will be sufficient to establish our present point: that tautologies in Bloomfield's sense are seldom met with—or never. "He ran because he was frightened" is not such a tautology, for there *is* other evidence for his fright in addition to his running. His running may be the most obvious and most near-at-hand evidence, and it may even be the only actual evidence known to us; but it is not the only possible evidence, that is, not the only fact that would count as evidence. What I am saying here is only a commonplace of current philosophy of science.

Sometimes language deceives us. Consider for example the explanation, "Wolves are fierce because it is their nature to be fierce." Someone with a tough mind might inform us that this really means, "Wolves are fierce because wolves are fierce." But even if so, the latter statement is not a tautology; translation into a symbolic language would make us realize that it is best taken as meaning "This wolf is fierce because all wolves are fierce, and that wolf is fierce because all wolves are fierce, and the other wolf is fierce because all wolves are fierce, and so forth."

There are further problems involved, which we need not go into, such as the relation of "description" to "explanation." Bloomfield would probably say that even though he had inadequately characterized "tautology," he would still want to rule out as idle statements like "This wolf is fierce because all wolves are fierce." Now as it happens, what he seems to want has been shown by recent philosophy of science to be hopeless. What he wants, in principle, is to dispense with all "constructs" and "intervening variables," and to correlate observables directly with observables.

Seeing that the hopelessness of this widespread dream was not shown until the mid thirties, and is still not common knowledge (see Stevenson, 1944, pp. 46–53 for a good discussion), we need not blame Bloomfield for ignorance. It is enough to recognize that what was plausible in his day is not now plausible two decades later.

The upshot of the last few paragraphs is the following. We cannot throw out mentalistic explanations on the ground of tautology, for tautology in what appears to be Bloomfield's sense is neither essential to them nor peculiar to them. In the second place, we cannot throw them out on the ground of using "constructs" either, because the present day view is that practically all science needs to make use of constructs. I conclude that whatever Bloomfield's valid point may have been, we cannot accept his formulation of it.

Actually, it is not difficult (with the help of present-day insights) to state Bloomfield's point more aptly. "Avoid tautological explanations; be sure to state your explanations fully and precisely enough so that others can tell whether they are tautological or not; and avoid making use of 'dispositions to respond' and other constructs *whenever possible.*" This is still good advice.

As remarked some paragraphs earlier, Bloomfield identifies three contrasts: (1) mentalistic *vs.* mechanistic, (2) empty *vs.* significant, and (3) philosophical *vs.* scientific. The independence of the first two has now been shown. The third is also independent of the first two. The reasons for holding this view are deliberately excluded from the scope of the present paper; but it may be remarked in passing that it is to Wittgenstein that the world is indebted for them.

4. MILL, BLOOMFIELD, AND CIRCUMSTANCES

John Stuart Mill's "methods of experimental inquiry" are well-known—too well known, indeed, since the time used for their teaching might better be spent on more up-to-date techniques. Mill states his "Method of Agreement" as follows (*Logic* III, viii.1): "If two or more instances of the phenomenon under investigation have only one circumstance in common, the circumstance in which alone all the instances agree, is the cause (or effect) of the given phenomenon."

Now the concept of stimulus and response is simply this conception of cause and effect, applied to psychology. And Bloomfield undertakes to reduce the semantical concept of meaning to the psychological concept of stimulus and response. Knowing these two facts, we can *predict* that he will define meaning in more or less the following way: the meaning of a linguistic form is "the situation in which the speaker utters it and the response which it calls forth in the hearer" (1933, p. 139; *cf.* 1926, § 6; Bloch and Trager 1942 Section 1.2(2); Harris 1940 p. 227). I lay stress on the point that Bloomfield's definition, not in detail but in general, is a simple consequence (whether consciously or unwittingly so does not matter) of applying to this particular subject matter the general conception of cause formulated by Mill; for we may then expect that any difficulties in Mill's conception will be matched by difficulties in Bloomfield's. Now in Mill the principal difficulties concern (1) the plurality or unicity of causes and (2) the notion of "circumstance."

(1) Mill speaks of "the circumstance in which alone all the instances agree." But is there any guarantee that there is such a circumstance? What if we find a number of instances of a phenome-

non without *any* obvious circumstance in common? In that case we invent or postulate some nonphenomenal circumstance, thus preserving by postulation the unicity of causes. Analogously, Bloomfield speaks (1933, p. 141) of "the . . . features . . . which are common to all the situations that call forth the utterance of the linguistic form"; and to guarantee that there are such features we may have to postulate unobservables.

The problem becomes acute in connection with displaced speech. It is Bloomfield's merit to have played up the difficulties of this phenomenon, and a proof of his honesty that he acknowledges the difficulties to be greatest for his own kind of explanation. The discussion in (1933, pp. 141–44), suggests that he thinks the answer will be found in "obscure internal stimuli" (143). In addition to the prying question whether "obscure" means "hard to observe" or "impossible to observe (unobservable)," there is a deeper objection. If we are entitled to invoke obscure internal stimuli to handle displaced speech, why not handle *all* speech by this means? Why not say that the feature common to all utterances of "Oh, look! There's an apple" is one of these obscure internal stimuli, which, therefore, by Bloomfield's definition, is the meaning of that sequence of sentences? And this question shows us that Bloomfield's definition has simply failed to capture the ordinary meaning of "meaning."

(2) There is another side of the coin. If we refuse to posit nonphenomenal causes, we may not find common "circumstances" or "features." On the other hand, if we admit just any complex of phenomena, we will have too many common circumstances rather than too few. If we accept Russellian logic, we can prove a priori that for any class of phenomena there is a property (circumstance, feature) common to all of them and peculiar to them. And in any case it is usually not hard, given such a class, to find some feature —not at all far-fetched—some feature of spatial position, or the fact of their all occurring within a certain time period, and so forth, that is common to them all. So if Mill's methods are ever to be applicable, "circumstance" must mean *"relevant* circumstance."

This now standard criticism has its counterpart for Bloomfield. If we merely define the meaning of an utterance as the feature common to all (and only?) the occasions on which it is uttered, we may find, instead of the one feature we want, either none or several —too few or too many. Some further limitation must be imposed. If a common sense notion of what makes a feature is to be used, at least that notion should be examined. In applying the notion of a relevant feature we should not flop from the demands of an impossibly rigorous theory to the flaccid sanctions of common sense.

It is at this point Wittgenstein comes to our aid.

5. RUSSELL

Nearly fifty years ago Russell published "that paradigm of philosophy" (Ramsey, 1931, p. 263), the theory of descriptions. By a "description" or more precisely a "singular description" or "definite description" he meant an expression of the form "the so-and-so," provided it be used to refer to one and only one thing (as in "the author of *Waverley*") and not to a kind (as in "the elephant is a pachyderm"). His analysis led him to four closely related ideas:

(1) Every proposition has a logical form, and it may also have constituents arranged in this form. There can be two propositions with the same form but different constituents; also, two propositions with the same constituents but different forms.

(2) There may be a discrepancy between the apparent logical form of a proposition and its real logical form. In that case, the apparent logical form is created by a sentence which faultily expresses that proposition.

(3) In particular, propositions containing singular descriptions appear to have the same logical form as propositions containing genuine proper names (*e.g.* "The wall I am looking at is yellow" seems to have the same logical form as "That is yellow"). Furthermore, those expressions that are commonly taken to be proper names do not satisfy the logician's definition of "proper name," but they function rather as substitutes for descriptions. (*E.g.* "Homer" functions as a substitute for "the man who was called 'Homer.'") Finally, to complete the paradox, the words that do satisfy the logician's definition of "proper name" are words such as "I," "this," "here," "now," which are traditionally classed as pronouns and adverbs.

(4) By a technique called "definition in use" or "contextual definition" it is possible to replace any sentence containing a singular description by a different sentence, expressing the same proposition, but which expresses that same proposition aptly, because its apparent logical form coincides with the real logical form of the proposition it is expressing.

Thesis (4) is put forward in Russell (1905); (3) in the same place and more elaborately in Russell (1911); (1) in Whitehead and Russell (1910) and more elaborately later; (2) is the latest to crystallize —there are hints in Whitehead and Russell (1910) pp. 2 (3) and 31 middle—but it is paraphrased by Wittgenstein (1922) 4.0031: "Russell's merit is to have shown that the apparent logical form of the proposition [translate: 'sentence'—RW] need not be its real form." Then it is fully worked out, with examples, by Stebbing (1930, pp. 35, 79, 126ff., 139), Ryle (1932), and Kneale (1936). Flew (1951, p. 7) calls this thesis (2) that "which is most central and most fundamental to . . . the dominant tendency in modern British philosophizing."

The technique of thesis (4) is of vast though unexploited significance for scientific semantics; but we shall not take it up in the present paper. (1) and (3) will also have to be set aside. It is (2) and the developments from it that concern us.

The contrast of apparent and real logical form immediately suggests two programs, one analytic and one constructive. On the analytic side, let us consider every expression in our ordinary natural languages, and, in every case where apparent and real logical form are not the same, replace the expression by another expression, synonymous with it, whose apparent and real forms *are* the same. (If the synonymous expression is a paraphrase of the original, and therefore belongs to the same language, all the better.) On the constructive side, let us try to build an ideal language in which there is never any discrepancy between apparent and real logical form.

Russell himself and the logical positivists went ahead with both programs, attaching particular importance to the second. Ordinary language because of its vagueness, ambiguity, and extensive use of ellipsis will often fail to provide a perfect paraphrase for a faulty expression, and thus we must have recourse to an artificial language in any case. The Wittgensteinians, on the other hand (the third of the three branches mentioned in Section 1), accepted the first program but rejected the second. They did so because of a new insight that Russell had overlooked.

Consider the two statements, "Tame tigers growl" and "Tame tigers exist." These two expressions look alike, in that their grammar is the same: A plural noun phrase is followed by a verb. But semantically they are vastly different. The second can be paraphrased "There are tame tigers," but the first cannot be paraphrased in any similar way. It makes sense to say that tame tigers growl, eat, and so forth, but not that tame tigers exist, eat, and so forth. When one falls into the language-trap of assimilating "exist" to "growl," the result is the Ontological Argument for the existence of God. In breaking away from this trap, the first reaction is to say as Kant did that existence is not a predicate (unlike growling). But this is only a first step, for it still speaks as though there were something called "existence." It is more straightforward to treat the matter quite linguistically and say that the *word* "exists" simply does not work like the word "growls."

Russell paraphrases "Tame tigers growl" first as "All tame tigers growl" and then, more analytically, as "All things that are tame tigers growl." "Tame tigers exist" he paraphrases as "There are tame tigers." So far the Wittgensteinians would agree with him. But in going further and holding that the final paraphrases more accurately represent the real logical form, he makes a metaphysical commitment which they regard as unnecessary. For purposes of explaining how language works, there is no need to decide which of various synonymous expressions captures the real logical form; not even any need to suppose that there is a real form to be captured. It is sufficient to point out two things: (a) that an expression A can sometimes be paraphrased by an expression B that is of an apparently very different grammar; and (b) that there can be another expression C, apparently similar in grammar to A, but not admitting of the same kind of paraphrase. In both cases, we do not compare the expression with reality but with other expressions.

This retreat from metaphysics marks the transition from Russell to Wittgenstein.

6. WITTGENSTEIN

Wittgenstein has avoided slogans and generalities, but Wisdom (1953, p. 117) has offered this epitome: "Don't look for the meaning, look for the use."

We can see two of Russell's ideas converging and developing into this formula. One is the idea that singular descriptions have no meaning but do have use, because they *contribute* to meaning (Russell, 1938, p. x). The other is that we exhibit the use of an expression by seeing how it can be paraphrased, what kinds of reasoning it can be used in, under what circumstances it is used, and so on. The formula does not mean that no expression has meaning; it means that meaning is a special kind of use, and that every expression has use even if it has no meaning. This will be illustrated by examples. The formula tells us not to force all uses into the mold of meaning.

Now we begin to make contact with the historical remarks in Section 2. Wittgenstein is offering a way out of the dyadic conception of meaning. His way will be interesting if, and only if, he can tell us or teach us *how* to determine uses.

Probably the best expository method at this point is to give a number of examples and then see what will emerge from an inductive study of them.

I will select for this purpose a number of English adjectives, and discuss the different "uses" that adjectives may have and the techniques by which these differences are brought to light. I assemble under this heading a number of examples that have been separately discussed by various Russellians and Wittgensteinians. In general, the examples that are simple and also scientifically interesting are not the ones of greatest importance for philosophy, so this selection cannot give any inkling of why the Wittgensteinian approach should be creating such excitement among philosophers.

Let us consider the following groups of adjectives: (1) All, some, no; (2) One, ten; (3) Big, little; (4) Numerous; (5) Grey, sweet, loud; (6) Former, future; (7) Apparent, real; (8) Spoiled, addled.

We may as well begin with a classic passage from *Through the Looking-Glass:*

"Who did you pass on the road?" the King went on, holding out his hand to the messenger for some hay.

"Nobody," said the messenger.

"Quite right," said the King: "this young lady saw him too. So of course Nobody walks slower than you."

"I do my best," the messenger said in a sullen tone. "I'm sure nobody walks much faster than I do."

"He can't do that," said the King, "or else he'd have been here first."

Flew (1951, p. 8) comments thus: "When they ['philosophers'] have talked of misunderstanding the logic of our language [cf. Wittgenstein, 1922, 4.003] they have been alluding to the mistakes made by people who are misled by grammatical similarities or dissimilarities into overlooking logical dissimilarities or similarities. Such is the mistake of the King who treats 'Nobody' as if it had the logic of 'Somebody,' as if 'Nobody' referred to somebody, albeit a rather insubstantial somebody." Actually, it would be more accurate to describe the mistake as supposing that the word "nobody" is an ordinary proper name, like "Alice." For even if in the above passage we replaced "nobody" by "somebody," there would still be the same fallacy: the conjunction of "Somebody walks slower than you" and "Somebody walks much faster than you" does not entail "Somebody walks both slower and much faster than you," although the conjunction of "Alice walks slower than you" and "Alice walks much faster than you" does entail "Alice walks both slower and much faster than you." The Wittgensteinians refer to this as a difference between the "logic" of "somebody" and of "nobody," on the one hand, and of "Alice" on the other. Or as a difference between the way the former two expressions work, and the way the latter works. Or as a difference in "grammar."

It is important to notice that both the word "logic" and the word "grammar" are used by the Wittgensteinians in a broader sense than is usual. It is natural to call the above-discussed difference a difference in logic, but not to call it a difference in grammar. Elsewhere, for example, in group (5), we shall come across differences that it would be natural to call differences in grammar, but not in logic. Thus we have to inquire why, in the hands of Wittgenstein, the meanings of the two words have converged.

One difference of "logic" or "grammar," and an obvious one, between "some" and "no," is that from "He saw Alice" one may infer "He saw somebody," but not "He saw nobody." On the other hand there are features of logic or grammar that they share, for example, that from "He saw somebody" one may infer "Somebody was seen by him," and that similarly from "He saw nobody" one may infer "Nobody was seen by him."

The difference between "all" and "every" seems quite trivial, and merely grammatical in the narrowest sense. When a noun has both a singular and a plural, "all" takes the plural and "every" takes the singular—without further difference in meaning. "All persons are here," "Every person is here," "Everybody is here" have the same meaning—are interchangeable.

But compare the difference between "every" and "all" with the difference between "one" and "ten." "One," like "every," takes the singular, and "ten," like "all," takes the plural. But the parallel ends there. We could cut short discussion by the dictum that "one" just doesn't mean the same thing as "ten," or we could give evidence for our claim by such consideration as the following:

(A) Every person is here; therefore, all persons are here
(B) One person is here; therefore, ten persons are here

(A) would be accepted as a valid inference, but (B) would not.

"One" and "ten" raise a difficult problem. We have a deep-seated feeling that they belong together, but it is not easy to justify it in detail. There is no trouble about finding features that they share; for example, one can say—truly or falsely, but at least not nonsensically—"One and one make twenty," "Ten and ten make twenty," whereas it would be nonsensical to say "Some and some make twenty" or "Big and big make twenty." There is no trouble about finding features that unite "one" and "ten" and that separate them both from "some" and from "big"; the problem is to show that these features are fundamental. This is something that we have to pass over in the present paper.

"Big" and "little" seem like typical adjectives; so do "grey," "sweet," "loud." Yet there is an important difference between "little" and "grey," for example. It is a difference of logic, rather than of grammar, in the ordinary sense of these words. Namely, we can argue: "An elephant is an animal; therefore a grey elephant is a grey animal," but we cannot similarly argue: "An elephant is an animal; therefore a little elephant is a little animal." The linguist must face the problem, *Just how* shall this difference be described?, but in any case there it is.

Wittgenstein would call this difference a difference in logic, in grammar, or in logical grammar. Thus, "grammar" in his sense encompasses meaning and semantics in the ordinary sense.

The adjectives "big" and "little" enable us to make a simple point about the relationship between meaning, use, and grammar. These two words (and pairs of antonyms in general) would be said to have different meanings but the same grammar (or the same logic). Presumably they would be said to have different uses.

"Grey," "sweet," and "loud" raise two other problems. A cloud would be called grey but not sweet or loud, a grapefruit sweet or sweet-tasting but not grey-tasting nor loud, a noise loud and sweet but not grey. To this extent "grey," "sweet," and "loud" have different logics. (1) But we find ourselves inclined to say that a sweet noise is not sweet *in the same sense* as a sweet grapefruit; what shall we say about this inclination? (2) If we distinguish two senses of "sweet," then the three terms "grey," "sweet" (as applied to flavors), and "loud" are mutually exclusive: there is nothing to which two of them apply. Now although this difference in logic would be granted, we all feel that it is comparatively minor, in contrast to the "logical" features that they have in common. I refer to the fact that they are all names of sense-qualities. The problem, then, is this: On what grounds can we justify the classification of some resemblances or differences of logic as major, and others as minor?

The logic of "numerous" includes some features that it shares with "all," "ten," and "big." To put it in terms that a linguist would use, there are linguistic environments in which all of these words can occur. Of the peculiarities of the word, some are such as familiar linguistic means would bring to light—for example, that none of the other three words can replace "numerous" in "Enemies of the people are growing more numerous by the minute"; others require techniques of inference such as the following: From "Enemies of the people are big" one can infer "Some enemies of the people are big," but one cannot infer "Some enemies of the people are numerous" from "Enemies of the people are numerous." (This is one aspect of the traditional distinction in logic between distributive and collective terms.)

So far we have two kinds of facts about "numerous": (1) Grammatical facts in the formal linguistic sense. (2) Facts of inference. In addition there are two other kinds of facts: (3) Facts of paraphrase or synonymy: our sample sentence is synonymous with "The number of enemies of the people is increasing by the minute." (4) Facts of circumstances of use.

The fourth class is the one about which we have said the least. It is here that semantics in the ordinary sense is taken into account. *When* do we use the word "numerous"?

It is easy and uninteresting to answer that we say the so-and-so's are numerous when we believe that there are a lot of so-and-so's. It is equally easy, and still more uninteresting, to answer that we say it when our neural system is in a certain state. Between these two extremes the approach of Wittgenstein gives us a sensible, helpful answer. (See end of Section 4.)

First, we may point out the difference between uttering and asserting. We assert "Enemies of the people are numerous" when we make this a self-contained utterance; we utter it without asserting it when we say "If enemies of the people are numerous, then we are in peril," or "It isn't true that enemies of the people are numerous" or "He says that enemies of the people are numerous," and so forth. To classify the circumstances under which we can utter something without asserting it is one of the numerous jobs of detail that remains to be done.

Second, we may note the different ways in which something can be asserted: as a lie, as a joke, as an exaggeration, as a sober truth, and so forth. Another job of classification. (Wittgensteinians have spent a great deal of effort on this job, but without much success so far.)

Third, we may look into the circumstances under which people assert, as a sober truth, that enemies of the people are numerous. Perhaps the most striking facts are that the word "numerous" is used (1) relatively and (2) vaguely. (1) In a country of a million people ten enemies would not be numerous, whereas in a page of 300 words ten misprints would be more than enough to be numerous. This relativity is like that of "big" and "little": there must be some class of things to which implicit or explicit reference must be made. (2) Once the reference class is established, there is still vagueness. In a country of a million people, ten enemies would not be numerous and 100,000 enemies would be numerous, but where is the dividing line? There is none; there is no "line"; instead, there is a border "area," itself vaguely delimited, about which people are uncertain. The linguistic display of uncertainty when dealing with this area is instructive. Sometimes people hedge: Suppose that 5,000 is within this area: "So there are 5,000 enemies of the people in our country? Well, then, they're not so very numerous. And yet when you think about it that *is* quite a lot, isn't it?" Or they qualify: "5,000 enemies? That's relatively numerous." Or, and most interesting of all, they simply withdraw the word: "Are enemies of the people numerous in our country? Well, there are about 5,000 of them." This fact of withdrawal is one of the most distinctive marks of ordinary language, as contrasted with the artificial languages of the symbolic logician: the fact of including expressions which are clearly applicable in some cases, clearly inapplicable in others, simply not used in others; and in still other cases, used but withdrawn if challenged, and replaced by something more precise.

"Former" and "future." "The former mayor" looks like "the big mayor," but whereas a big mayor is a mayor, a former mayor is not a mayor. Linguistically we describe "former" as a back-formation: "He is the former mayor" can be paraphrased, "He was formerly the mayor." "Prince Charles is the future king" means the same as "Prince Charles will be the king." This is an obvious remark.

"Apparent" and "real." These words are back-formations just like "former" and "future," but the fact has been pretty universally overlooked. As a result, we often speak as though there were two classes of everything—the apparent ones and the real ones. It does not concern us here to trace the consequences for metaphysics, but we may remark on the complication caused by the fact that "real" in another sense contrasts with "spurious" or "fake" and is synonymous with "genuine," and in yet a third sense means "par excellence" as in "he's a real patriot."

"Spoiled," "addled." "In glossing a word," Quine writes (1953, p. 58), "we have so frequently to content ourselves with a lame partial synonym plus stage directions. Thus in glossing 'addled' we say 'spoiled' and add 'said of an egg.' " Stevenson (1944, p. 82) has distinguished these two techniques of glossing as defining versus characterizing—a distinction that plays a great part in his theory of emotive meaning.

We have now considered a miscellaneous sample of English adjectives and seen some of the semantically useful things that can be said about them. The techniques illustrated need to be systematized and, very likely, supplemented. Much of the help that the Wittgensteinians give can be found elsewhere, even in traditional writers. And it may be that much of what is new in Wittgensteinianism is mistaken. For instance, its broadened use of the terms "logic" and "grammar" in such a way as to make logic and grammar coincide has yet to be justified. Still and all, its impact will be refreshing. In my judgement its biggest contribution to linguistics is the help it gives us in treating meaning practically and autonomously, and at the same time in a way that does not preclude the hope of eventual reduction.

BIBLIOGRAPHY

Anonymous. Obituary. Dr. L. Wittgenstein, The London *Times,* May 2, 1951.

Basilius, H. "Neo-Humboldtian Ethnolinguistics," *Word* 1952, *8,* 95–105.

Bloch, B., and G. L. Trager (1942). *Outline of Linguistic Analysis,* Baltimore.

Bloomfield, L. "A Set of Postulates for the Science of Language," *Language* 1926, *2,* 153–64; reprinted in *International Journal of American Linguistics* 1949, *15,* 195–202.

Bloomfield, L. (1933). *Language,* New York.

Feigl, H., and W. Sellars (1949). *Readings in Philosophical Analysis,* New York.

Flew, A., ed. (1951). *Essays on Logic and Language,* Oxford.

Fries, C. C. "Meaning and Linguistic Analysis," *Language* 1954, *30,* 57–68.

Harris, Z. S. "Review of Louis Gray, Foundations of Language," *Language* 1940, *16,* 216–31.

Kneale, W. (1936). "Is Existence a Predicate?" reprinted in Feigl and Sellars (1949) pp. 29–43.

Moore, G. E. "Wittgenstein's lectures in 1930–33," *Mind* 1954, *63*, 1–15, 289–316.

Olmsted, D. L. (1952). "Some Psychological Assumptions in Linguistics," Talk to the Yale Linguistic Club, January 14, 1952.

Quine, W. V. (1953). *From a Logical Point of View*, Cambridge, Massachusetts.

Ramsey, F. P. (1931). *The Foundations of Mathematics*, London.

Reinchenbach, H. (1947). *Elements of Symbolic Logic*, New York.

Russell, B. (1905). "On Denoting," reprinted in Feigl and Sellars (1949) pp. 103–15, 289–316.

Russell, B. (1911). "Knowledge by Acquaintance and Knowledge by Description," reprinted in B. Russell, *Mysticism and Logic* (New York, 1918) pp. 209–32.

Russell, B. (1914). *Our Knowledge of the External World*, Chicago.

Russell, B. (1938). *The Principles of Mathematics* (Second Edition), New York.

Russell, B. (1940). *Inquiry into Meaning and Truth*, New York.

Russell, B. "Ludwig Wittgenstein," *Mind* 1951, *60*, 297.

Ryle, G. (1932). "Systematically Misleading Expressions," reprinted in *Flew* (1951) pp. 11–36.

Ryle, G. Review of Carnap, "Meaning and Necessity," *Philosophy* 1949, *24*, 69–76.

Ryle, G. Obituary. "Ludwig Wittgenstein," *Mind* 1951a, *60*, 295–6.

Ryle, G. "Ludwig Wittgenstein," *Analysis* 1951b, *12*, 1–9.

Schlauch, M. "Early Behaviorist Psychology and Contemporary Linguistics," *Word* 1946, *2*, 25–36.

Stebbing, L. S. (1930). *A Modern Introduction to Logic*, London.

Stevenson, C. L. (1944). *Ethics and Language*, New Haven.

Ullmann, S. (1951). *The Principles of Semantics*, Glasgow.

Whitehead, A. N., and B. Russell (1910). *Principia Mathematica*, Vol. I (Second Edition 1925), Cambridge, England.

Wisdom, J. "Ludwig Wittgenstein," 1934–1937, *Mind* 1952, *61*, 258–60.

Wisdom, J. (1953). *Philosophy and Psycho-analysis*, Oxford.

Wittgenstein, L. (1922). *Tractatus Logico-Philosophicus*, New York.

Wittgenstein, L. (1953). *Philosophical Investigations*, Oxford.

Woodger, J. H. (1952). *Biology and Language*, Cambridge, England.

The Meaning of a Word

I

I begin, then, with some remarks about "the meaning of a word." I think many persons now see all or part of what I shall say: but not all do, and there is a tendency to forget it, or to get it slightly wrong. In so far as I am merely flogging the converted, I apologize to them.

A preliminary remark. It may justly be urged that, properly speaking, what alone has meaning is a *sentence*. Of course, we can speak quite properly of, for example, "looking up the meaning of a word" in a dictionary. Nevertheless, it appears that the sense in which a word or a phrase "has a meaning" is derivative from the sense in which a sentence "has a meaning": to say a word or a phrase "has a meaning" is to say that there are sentences in which it occurs which "have meanings": and to know the meaning which the word or phrase has, is to know the meanings of sentences in which it occurs. All the dictionary can do when we "look up the meaning of a word" is to suggest aids to the understanding of sentences in which it occurs. Hence it appears correct to say that what "has meaning" in the primary sense is the sentence. And older philosophers who discussed the problem of "the meaning of words" tend to fall into *special* errors, avoided by more recent philoso-

* Reprinted from *Philosophical Papers* (Oxford: Clarendon Press, 1961) by permission of the publisher.

phers, who discuss rather the parallel problem of "the meaning of sentences." Nevertheless, if we are on our guard, we perhaps need not fall into these special errors, and I propose to overlook them at present.

There are many sorts of sentence in which the words "the meaning of the word so-and-so" are found, for example, "He does not know, or understand, the meaning of the word *handsaw*": "I shall have to explain to her the meaning of the word *pikestaff*": and so on. I intend to consider primarily the common question, "What is the meaning of *so-and-so?*" or "What is the meaning of *the word so-and-so?*"

Suppose that in ordinary life I am asked: "What is the meaning of the word *racy?*" There are two sorts of thing I may do in response: I may reply *in words,* trying to describe what raciness is and what it is not, to give examples of sentences in which one might use the word *racy,* and of others in which one should not. Let us call this *sort* of thing "explaining the syntactics" of the word "racy" in the English language. On the other hand, I might do what we may call "demonstrating the semantics" of the word, by getting the questioner to *imagine,* or even actually to *experience,* situations which we should describe correctly by means of sentences containing the words "racy," "raciness," and so forth, and again other situations where we should *not* use these words. This is, of course, a simple case: but perhaps the same two *sorts* of procedure would be gone through in the case of at least most ordinary words. And in the same way, if I wished to find out "whether he understands the meaning of the word *racy,*" I should test him at some length in these two ways (which perhaps could not be entirely divorced from each other).

Having asked in this way, and answered, "What is the meaning of (the word) 'rat'?," "What is the meaning of (the word) 'cat'?," "What is the meaning of (the word) 'mat'?," and so on, we then try, being philosophers, to ask the further *general* question, "What is the meaning of a word?" But there is something spurious about this question. We do not intend to mean by it a certain question which would be perfectly all right, namely, "What is the meaning of (the word) 'word'?": *that* would be no more general than is asking the meaning of the word "rat," and would be answered in a precisely similar way. No: we want to ask rather, "What is the meaning of a-word-in-general?" or "of *any* word"—not meaning "any" word *you like to choose,* but rather *no particular* word *at all,* just "any word." Now if we pause even for a moment to reflect, this is a perfectly absurd question to be trying to ask. I can only answer a question of the form "What is the meaning of '*x*'?" if "*x*" is some *particular* word you are asking about. This supposed *general* question is really just a spurious question of a type which commonly arises in philosophy. We may call it the fallacy of asking about "Nothing-in-particular" which is a practice decried by the plain man, but by the philosopher called "generalizing" and regarded with some complacency. Many other examples of the fallacy can be found: take, for example, the case of "reality"—we try to pass from such questions as "How would you distinguish a real rat from an imaginary rat?" to "What is a real thing?," a question which merely gives rise to nonsense.

We may expose the error in our present case thus. Instead of asking "What is the meaning of (the word) 'rat'?" we might clearly have asked "What is a 'rat'?" and so on. But if our questions have been put in *that* form, it becomes very difficult to formulate any *general* question which could impose on us for a moment. Perhaps "What is anything?"? Few philosophers, if perhaps not none, have been foolhardy enough to pose such a question. In the same way, we should not perhaps be tempted to generalize such a question as "Does he know the meaning of (the word) 'rat'?" "Does he know the meaning of a word?" would be silly.

Faced with the nonsense question "What is the meaning of a word?," and perhaps dimly recognizing it to be nonsense, we are nevertheless not inclined to give it up. Instead, we transform it in a curious and noteworthy manner. Up to now, we had been asking *"What-is-the-meaning-of* (the word) 'rat'?," and so forth; and ultimately *"What-is-the-meaning-of* a word?" But now, being baffled, we change so to speak, the hyphenation, and ask "What is *the-meaning-of-a-word?"* or sometimes, "What is the 'meaning' of a word?" (1. 22): I shall refer, for brevity's sake, only to the other (1. 21). It is easy to see how very different this question is from the other. At once a crowd of traditional and reassuring answers present themselves: "a concept," "an idea," "an image," "a class of similar sensa," and so forth. All of which are equally spurious answers to a pseudoquestion. Plunging ahead, however, or rather retracing our steps, we now proceed to ask such questions as "What is the-meaning-of-(the-word) 'rat'?" which is as spurious as "What-is-the-meaning-of (the word) 'rat'?" was genuine. And again we answer "the idea of a rat" and so forth. How quaint this procedure is, may be seen in the following way. Supposing a plain man puzzled, were to ask me "What is the meaning of (the word) 'muggy'?," and I were to answer, "The idea or concept of 'mugginess'" or "The class of sensa of which it is correct to say 'This is muggy'": the man would stare at me as at an imbecile. And that is sufficiently unusual for me to conclude that that was not at all the sort of answer he expected: nor, in plain English, *can* that question *ever* require that sort of answer.

To show up this pseudoquestion, let us take a parallel case, where perhaps no one has yet been deluded, though they well might be. Suppose that I ask "What is the point of doing so-and-so?" For example, I ask Old Father William "What is the point of standing on one's head?" He replies in the way we know. Then I follow this up with "What is the point of balancing an eel on the end of one's nose?" And he explains. Now suppose I ask as my third question "What is the point of doing *anything*—not anything *in particular*, but just *anything*?" Old Father Willliam would no doubt kick me downstairs without the option. But lesser men, raising this same question and finding no answer, would very likely commit suicide or join the Church. (Luckily, in the case of "What is the meaning of a word?" the effects are less serious, amounting only to the writing of books.) On the other hand, more adventurous intellects would no doubt take to asking "What is the-point-of-doing-a-thing?" or "What is the 'point' of doing a thing?": and then later "What is the-point-of-eating-suet?" and so on. Thus we should discover a whole new universe of a kind of entity called "points," not previously suspected of existence.

To make the matter clearer, let us consider another case which is precisely *unlike* the case of "What is the meaning of?" I can ask not only the question, "What is the square root of four?," of eight, and so on, but also "What is the square root of a number?": which is either nonsense or equivalent to "What is the 'square root' of a number?" I then give a definition of the "square root" of a number, such that, for any given number x, "the square root of x" is a definite description of another number y. This differs from our case in that "the meaning of p" is not a definite description of any entity.

The general questions which we want to ask about "meaning" are best phrased as, "What-is-the-meaning-of (the phrase) 'what-is-the-meaning-of (the word) "x"?'?" The *sort* of answer we should get to these quite sensible questions is that with which I began this discussion: namely, that when I am asked "What-is-the-meaning-of (the word) 'x'?," I naturally reply by explaining its syntactics and demonstrating its semantics.

All this must seem very obvious, but I wish to point out that it is fatally easy to forget it: no doubt I shall do so myself many times in the course of this paper. Even those who see pretty clearly that "concepts," "abstract ideas," and so on are fictitious entities, which we owe in part to asking questions about "the meaning of a word," nevertheless themselves think that there *is something* which is "the meaning of a word." Thus Mr. Hampshire[1] attacks to some purpose the theory that there is such a thing as "*the* meaning of a word": what *he* thinks is wrong is the belief that there is a *single* thing called *the* meaning: "concepts" are nonsense, and no single particular "image" can be *the* meaning of a general word. So, he goes on to say, the meaning of a word must really be "a *class* of similar particular ideas." "If we are asked 'What does this mean?' we point to (!) a class of particular ideas." But a "class of particular ideas" is every bit as fictitious an entity as a "concept" or "abstract idea." In the same way Mr. C. W. Morris (in the *Encyclopaedia of Unified Science*) attacks, to some purpose, those who think of "a meaning" as a definite something which is "simply located" somewhere: what *he* thinks is wrong is that people think of "a meaning" as a kind of entity which can be described wholly without reference to the total activity of "semiosis." Well and good. Yet he himself makes some of the crudest possible remarks about "the

---

[1] "Ideas, Propositions and Signs," in the *Proceedings of the Aristotelian Society*, 1939–40.

designatum" of a word: every sign has a designatum, which is not a particular thing but a *kind* of object or *class* of object. Now this is quite as fictitious an entity as any "Platonic idea": and is due to precisely the same fallacy of looking for "the meaning (or designatum) of a word."

Why are we tempted to slip back in this way? Perhaps there are two main reasons. First, there is the curious belief that all words are *names*, that is, in effect *proper* names, and therefore stand for something or designate it in the way that a proper name does. But this view that general names "have denotation" in the same way that proper names do, is quite as odd as the view that proper names "have connotation" in the same way that general names do, which is commonly recognized to lead to error. Secondly, we are afflicted by a more common malady, which is this. When we have given an analysis of a certain sentence, containing a word or phrase "*x*," we often feel inclined to ask, of our analysis, "What *in it*, is '*x*'?" For example, we give an analysis of "The State owns this land." in sentences about individual men, their relations and transactions: and then at last we feel inclined to ask: well now, *what*, in all that, *is* the State? And we might answer: the State *is* a collection of individual men united in a certain manner. Or again, when we have analysed the statement "trees can exist unperceived" into statements about sensing sensa, we still tend to feel uneasy unless we can say *something "really does"* "exist unperceived": hence theories about "sensibilia" and what not. So in our present case, having given all that is required, namely an account of "What-is-the-meaning-of 'What-is-the-meaning-of (the word) "*x*"?'" we *still* feel tempted, wrongly supposing our original sentence to contain a constituent "the-meaning-of (the-word)-'*x*'," to ask "Well now, as it turns out, what *is* the meaning of the word '*x*,' after all?" And we answer, "a class of similar particular ideas" and what not.

Of course, all my account of our motives in this matter may be only a convenient didactic schema: I do not think it is—but I recognize that one should not impute motives, least of all rational motives. Anyhow, what I claim is clear, is that there is *no* simple and handy appendage of a word called "the meaning of (the word) '*x*'."

II

I now pass on to the first of the two points which need now a careful scrutiny if we are no longer to be imposed upon by that convenient phrase "the meaning of a word." What I shall say here is, I know, not as clear as it should be.

Constantly we ask the question, "Is *y* the meaning, or *part* of the meaning, or *contained* in the meaning, of *x?*—or is it *not?*" A favourite way of putting the question is to ask, "Is the judgement '*x* is *y*' analytic or synthetic?" Clearly, we suppose, *y* *must* be *either* a part of the meaning of *x*, or not any part of it. And, if *y* *is* a part of the meaning of *x*, to say "*x* is not *y*" will be self-contradictory: while if it is *not* a part of the meaning of *x*, to say "*x* is not *y*" will present no difficulty—such a state of affairs will be readily "conceivable." This seems to be the merest common sense. And no doubt it *would* be the merest common sense *if* "meanings" were things in some ordinary sense which contained parts in some ordinary sense. But they are *not*. Unfortunately, many philosophers who know they are not, still speak as though *y* must either be or not be "part of the meaning" of *x*. But this is the point: *if* "explaining the meaning of a word" is really the complicated sort of affair that we have seen it to be, and *if* there is really nothing to call "the meaning of a word"—*then* phrases like "part of the meaning of the word *x*" are completely undefined; it is left hanging in the air, we do not know what it means at all. *We are using a working-model which fails to fit the facts that we really wish to talk about.* When we consider what we really do want to talk about, and not the working-model, what would really be meant at all by a judgement being "analytic or synthetic"? We simply do not know. Of course, we feel inclined to say "I can easily produce examples of analytic and synthetic judgements; for instance, I should confidently say 'Being a professor is *not* part of the meaning of being a man' and so forth." "A is A is analytic." Yes, but it is when we are required to give a *general definition* of what we mean by "analytic" or "synthetic," and when we are required to justify our dogma that *every* judgement is either analytic or synthetic, that we find we have, in fact, nothing to fall back upon *except our working-model*. From the start, it is clear that our working-model fails to do justice, for example, to the distinction between syntactics and semantics: for instance, talking about the contradictory of every sentence having to be either self-contradictory or not so, is to talk as though all sentences which we are prohibited from saying were sentences which offended against *syntactical* rules, and could be formally reduced to verbal self-contradictions. But this overlooks all semantical considerations, which philosophers are sadly prone to do. Let us consider two cases of some things which we simply *cannot say:* although they are *not* "self-contradictory" and although —and this of course is where many will have axes to grind—we cannot possibly be tempted to say that we have "synthetic *a priori*" knowledge of their contradictions.

Let us begin with a case which, being about *sentences* rather than *words,* is not quite in point, but which may encourage us. Take the well-known sentence "The cat is on the mat, and I do not believe it." That seems absurd. On the other hand "The cat is on the mat, and I believe it" seems trivial. If we were to adopt a customary dichotomy, and to say *either* a proposition p implies another proposition $r,$ *or* p is perfectly compatible with not-r, we should at once in our present case be tempted to say that "The cat is on the mat" *implies* "I believe it": hence both the triviality of adding "and I believe it" and the absurdity of adding "and I do not believe it." But of course "the cat is on the mat" does *not* imply "Austin believes the cat is on the mat": nor even "the speaker believes the cat is on the mat"—for the speaker may be lying. The doctrine which is produced in this case is, that not p indeed, but *asserting* p implies "I (who assert p) believe $p.$" And here "implies" must be given a special sense: for of course it is not that "I assert p" implies (in the ordinary sense) "I believe $p,$" for I may be lying. It is the sort of sense in which by asking a question I "imply" that I do not know the answer to it. By asserting p I *give it to be understood* that I believe $p.$

Now the reason why I cannot say "The cat is on the mat and I do not believe it" is not that it offends against syntactics in the sense of being in some way "self-contradictory." What prevents my saying it, is rather some semantic convention (implicit, of course), about the way we use words *in situations.* What precisely is the account to be given in this case we need not ask. Let us rather notice one significant feature of it. Whereas "*p* and I believe it" is somehow trivial, and "*p* and I do not believe it" is somehow nonsense, a third sentence "*p* and *I might not have* believed it" makes perfectly good sense. Let us call these three sentences Q, not Q, and "might not Q." Now what prohibits us from saying "*p*" implies "I believe *p*" in the ordinary sense of "implies," is precisely shown by this fact: that although not-Q is (*somehow*) absurd, "might not Q" is not at all absurd. For in ordinary cases of implication, not merely is not Q absurd, but "might not Q" is *also* absurd: for example, "triangles are figures and triangles have no shape" is no more absurd than "triangles are figures and triangles might have had no shape." Consideration of the sentence "might not Q" will afford a rough test as to whether *p* "implies" *r* in the *ordinary* sense, or in the special sense, of "implies."

Bearing this in mind, let us now consider a sentence which, as I claim, cannot possibly be classified as *either* "analytic" *or* "synthetic." I refer to the sentence, "This *x* exists," where *x* is a sensum, for example, "This noise exists." In endeavouring to classify it, one party would point to the triviality of "This noise exists," and to the absurdity of "This noise does not exist." They would say, therefore, that *existence* is "part of the meaning of" *this*. But another party would point out, that "This noise might not have existed" makes perfectly good sense. *They* would say, therefore, that *existence* cannot be "part of the meaning of" *this*.

Both parties, as we are now in a position to see, would be correct in their *arguments*, but incorrect in their *conclusions*. What seems to be true is that *using the word "this"* (not: the word "this") *gives it to be understood that* the sensum referred to "exists."

Perhaps, historically, this fact about the sentence-trio, "This noise exists," "This noise does not exist," and "This noise might not have existed," was pointed out before any philosopher had had time to pronounce that "This noise exists" is analytic, or is synthetic. But such a pronouncement might well have been made: and *to this day*, even when the fact has been pointed out, many philosophers *worry* about the case, supposing the sentence *must* be one or the other but painfully aware of the difficulties in choosing either. I wish to point out that consideration of the analogy between this case and the other, should cure us once and for all of this bogy, and of insisting on classifying sentences as *either* analytic *or* synthetic. It may encourage us to consider again what the facts in their actual complexity really are. (One thing it suggests is a reconsideration of "Caesar is bald" and similar propositions: but I cannot go into that.)

So far, however, we have scarcely begun in earnest: we have merely felt that initial trepidation, experienced when the firm ground of prejudice begins to slip away beneath the feet. Perhaps there are other cases, or other sorts of cases, where it will not be possible to say either that *y* is a "part of the meaning" of *x* or that it is not, without being misleading.

Suppose we take the case of "being thought good by me" and "being approved of by me." Are we to rush at this with the dichotomy: *either* "being approved of by me" *is* part of the meaning of "being thought good by me" *or* it is *not?* Is it *obvious* that "I think *x* good but I do not approve of it" is self-contradictory? Of course it is not *verbally* self-contradictory. That it either is or is not "really" self-contradictory would seem to be difficult to establish. Of course, we think, it must be one or the other—only "it's difficult to decide *which*": or "it depends on how you use the words." But are those really the difficulties which baffle us? Of course, *if* it were certain that every sentence *must* be either analytic or synthetic, those *must* be the difficulties. But then, it is not certain: no account even of what the distinction means, is given except by reference to our shabby working-model. I suggest that "I think *x* good but I do not approve of it" may very well be neither self-contradictory nor yet "perfectly good sense" in the way in which "I think *x* exciting but I do not approve of it" *is* "perfectly good sense."

Perhaps this example does not strike you as awkward. It cannot be expected that all examples will appeal equally to all hearers. Let us take some others. Is "What is good ought to exist" analytic or synthetic? According to Moore's theory, this must be "synthetic": yet he constantly in *Principia Ethica* takes its truth for granted. And that illustrates one of the main drawbacks of insisting on saying that a sentence *must* be either analytic or synthetic: you are almost certain to have left on your hands some general sentences which are certainly not analytic but which you find it difficult to conceive being false: i.e. you are landed with "synthetic *a priori* knowledge." Take that sentence of ill fame "Pink is more like red than black." It is rash to pronounce this "synthetic *a priori* knowledge" on the ground that "being more like red than black" is not "part of the meaning" or "part of the definition" of "pink" and that it is not "conceivable" that pink should be more like black than red: I dare say, so far as those phrases have any clear meaning, that it *is not:* but the question is: *is* the thing therefore "synthetic" *a priori* knowledge?

Or, again, take some examples from Berkeley: is *extended* "part of the meaning" of *coloured* or of *shaped,* or *shaped* "part of the meaning" of *extended?* Is "est sed non percipitur" self-contradictory (when said of a sensum), or is it not? When we worry thus, is it not worth considering the possibility that we are oversimplifying?

What we are to say in these cases, what even the possibilities are, I do not at present clearly see. (1) Evidently, we must throw away the old working-model as soon as we take account even of the existence of a distinction between syntactics and semantics. (2) But evidently also, our *new* working-model, the supposed "ideal" language, is in many ways a most inadequate model of any *actual* language: its careful separation of syntactics from semantics, its lists of explicitly formulated rules and conventions, and its careful delimitation of their spheres of operation—all are misleading. An *actual* language has few, if any, explicit conventions, no sharp limits to the spheres of operation of rules, no rigid separation of what is syntactical and what semantical. (3) Finally, I think I can see that there are difficulties about our powers of imagination, and about the curious way in which it is enslaved by words.

To encourage ourselves in the belief that this sort of consideration may play havoc with the distinction "analytic or synthetic," let us consider a similar and more familiar case. It seems, does it not, perfectly obvious that every proposition must have a contradictory? Yet it does not turn out so. Suppose that I live in harmony and friendship for four years with a cat: and then it delivers a philippic. We ask ourselves, perhaps, "Is it a real cat? or is it *not* a real cat?" "Either it *is,* or it *is not,* but we cannot be sure which." Now actually, that is not so: *neither* "It is a real cat" *nor* "it is not a real cat" fits the facts semantically: each is designed for other situations than this one: you could not say the former of something which delivers philippics, nor yet the latter of something which has behaved as this has for four years. There are similar difficulties about choosing between "This *is* a hallucination" and "This is *not* a hallucination." With sound instinct, the plain man turns in such cases to Watson and says "Well now, *what would you say?*" "How would you *describe* it? The difficulty is just that: there is *no* short description which is not misleading: the only thing to do, and that can easily be done, is to set out the description of the facts at length. Ordinary language breaks down in extraordinary cases. (In such cases, the cause of the breakdown is semantical.) Now no doubt an *ideal* language would *not* break down, whatever happened. In doing physics, for example, where our language is tightened up in order precisely to describe complicated and unusual cases concisely, we *prepare linguistically for the worst.* In ordinary language we do not: *words fail us.* If we talk as though an ordinary must be like an ideal language, we shall misrepresent the facts.

Consider now "being extended" and "being shaped." In ordinary life we never get into a situation where we learn to say that anything is extended but not shaped nor conversely. We have all learned to use, and have used, the words only in cases where it is correct to use both. Supposing now someone says "*x* is extended but has no shape." Somehow we cannot see what this "could mean" —there are no semantic conventions, explicit or implicit, to cover this case: yet it is not prohibited in any way—there are no limiting rules about what we might or might not say *in extraordinary cases.* It is not *merely* the difficulty of imagining or experiencing extraordinary cases, either, which causes worry. There is this too: we can only describe what it is we are trying to imagine, by means of words which precisely describe and evoke the *ordinary* case, which we are trying to think away. Ordinary language *blinkers* the already feeble imagination. It would be difficult, in this way, if I were to say "Can I think of a case where a man would be neither at home nor not at home?" This is inhibiting, because I think of the *ordinary* case where I ask "Is he at home?" and get the answer, "No": when certainly he is not at home. But supposing I happen *first* to think of the situation when I call on him just after he has died: then I see at once it would be wrong to say either. So in our case, the only thing to do is to imagine or experience all kinds of odd situations, and then suddenly round on oneself and ask: there, *now* would I say that, being extended it must be shaped? A new idiom might in odd cases be demanded.

I should like to say, in concluding this section, that in the course of stressing that we must pay attention to the facts of *actual* language, what we can and cannot say, and *precisely* why, another and converse point takes shape. Although it will not do to force actual language to accord with some preconceived model: it *equally* will not do, having discovered the facts about "ordinary usage," *to rest content* with that, as though there were nothing more to be discussed and discovered. There may be plenty that might happen and does happen which would need new and better language to describe it in. Very often philosophers are only engaged on this task, when they seem to be perversely using words in a way which makes no sense according to "ordinary usage." There may be extraordinary facts, even about our everyday experience, which plain men and plain language overlook.

JOHN R. SEARLE

Meaning and Speech Acts

~~~~~~

I

A common pattern of philosophical analysis in recent years has been
to show that a certain word is associated with certain kinds of
speech acts. It is said that the word in question is *used* to perform
certain kinds of speech acts, or that the word *functions* to perform
those kinds of speech acts. Moreover the statement that a word is
used to perform certain kinds of speech acts is taken by the philosophers who say this sort of thing to be a statement about the meaning of the word and hence to be part of a philosophical analysis or
explication of the word.

Here are some examples of this pattern of analysis: R. M. Hare
in *The Language of Morals* says "The primary function of the
word 'good' is to commend." [1] He also says the word "good" has
"commendatory meaning," and he says further that it has "evalua-
tive meaning." His remarks about the meaning of "good" thus asso-
ciate it with two types of speech acts, commending and evaluating,
and these remarks about meaning are based on his remarks to the
effect that "good" is used to, or functions to, commend.

P. F. Strawson in his article "Truth" says of the word "true" that

* Reprinted from *The Philosophical Review* 71, 1962, by permission of the
author and editors.
[1] Oxford, 1952, p. 127.

in using it "we are confirming, underwriting, admitting, agreeing with, what somebody has said." [2] In this connection he also mentions certain other speech acts, among them endorsing and conceding. That he takes these remarks about the use of the word to be relevant to the problem of the meaning of the word is at least suggested by his earlier remarks to the effect that the problem of how the word is used is the same problem as "the philosophical problem of truth." [3]

These are two obvious examples of the sort of analysis I have in mind, but the pattern which they exemplify is widely employed. This pattern of analysis involves at least the following: It is claimed in discussing a word W that

(1) W is used to perform speech act or acts A.
(2) The statement (1) tells us the meaning or at least part of the meaning of W.

How shall we construe these theses? Since (2) tells us that (1) is a fact about the meaning of W, it is tempting to construe (1) as saying:

(3) If W occurs in a sentence S and has its literal meaning in S, then characteristically in the utterance of S one performs A.

The difficulty though is that this thesis is very easily refuted, for if it is part of the meaning of W that any speaker who utters a sentence containing it, where its occurrence is literal, is characteristically performing act A, then in order to refute the thesis we need only to find contexts where the occurrence of W is literal and the speech act A could not be performed. And this is not hard to do. For example, let us substitute "good" for W and "commend" for A; then even if in uttering "This is a good car" one is commending the car, obviously one is not commending anything in the utterance of the interrogative form "Is this a good car?" [4] But perhaps this is not a serious counterexample, for someone defending the original analysis could simply argue that just as the sentence "This is a good

[2] *Philosophy and Analysis,* ed. by Margaret Macdonald (Oxford, 1954), p. 272.

[3] *Ibid.,* pp. 260–61.

[4] For a similar argument see Paul Ziff, *Semantic Analysis* (Ithaca, N.Y., 1960), p. 228.

car" has in part the force of "I commend this car," so "Is this a good car?" (addressed to a hearer) has in part the force of "Do *you* commend this car?" That is, the alleged counterexample is only a counterexample to (1) and (2) if we take them as implying (3). But instances of (1) such as " 'Good' is used to commend" should not be taken as saying what amounts to an instance of (3): "For *every* sentence S in which 'good' occurs in its literal meaning, an utterance of S is characteristically a *performance* of the act of commendation" (that would be, so to speak, a philistine interpretation), but rather it should be taken as:

(4) If *W* (*e.g.* "good") occurs in a sentence *S* and has its literal meaning in *S,* then characteristically when one utters *S,* speech act *A* (*e.g. commendation*) is *in the offing.* If *S* is a simple indicative sentence (*e.g.* "This is good"), it is performed; if *S* is interrogative, it is (perhaps) elicited and so on through other forms.

Now this I sincerely believe to be a more sympathetic interpretation of what linguistic philosophers must mean when they say that a word *W* is used to perform speech act *A,* and consequently I do not think they would regard the interrogative counterexamples as very troubling. Nonetheless I believe that counterexamples can be produced even to (4), counterexamples which may well prove decisive against these theories, at least as they were originally intended, and I now propose to do this using "good" as an example.

It is alleged that in saying, for example, "This is a good car" I am uttering something which has at least in part the same use as, or the same function as, or the same force as "I commend this car." This, I take it, is a reasonable interpretation of the remark "Good is used to commend," for a paradigm expression used to commend is "commend," or rather "I commend." Hence to say "good" is used to commend is to say "good" is used something like "I commend."

Let me just add parenthetically here that of course "commend" is being used to do the work of many other verbs, and it will not bear the burden. It would be more plausible and still in the spirit of the analysis to say not just " 'Good' is used to commend," but " 'Good' is used to commend, praise, express approval, express satisfaction, express appreciation, recommend, and so forth," depending on the context of the utterance. So in the future let us take this expanded version to be the one under discussion and henceforth when we say "commend" we mean "commend, and so forth."

Consider the following examples:

(1) If this is a good electric blanket, then perhaps we ought to buy it for Aunt Nellie.
(2) I wonder if it is a good electric blanket.
(3) I don't know whether it is a good electric blanket.
(4) Let us hope it is a good electric blanket.

In utterances of each of these one can suppose the occurrence of "good" to be quite literal, and yet in utterances of none of them are the speech acts of commendation, and so forth, performed; nor are such speech acts even in the offing in the way they might be supposed to be in the offing for utterances of the interrogative form "Is this a good electric blanket?"

That is, even if we agreed—and it is not at all clear that we would—that "Is this a good electric blanket?" had in part the force of or use of or function of "Do you commend this electric blanket?" still the above do not have the force or use or function of:

(1a) If I commend this electric blanket, then perhaps we ought to buy it for Aunt Nellie.
(2a) I wonder if I commend this electric blanket.
(3a) I don't know whether I commend this electric blanket.
(4a) Let us hope I commend this electric blanket.

We began by considering a similarity of function between expressions like "I commend this electric blanket" and "This is a good electric blanket." But this similarity of function is not preserved through the permutations of linguistic context in which each of these expressions can be placed without alteration of the literal meanings of the component words. What is hypothesized in the utterance of a hypothetical of the form "If I commend this, then so and so" is the performance of the action which is *performed* in the utterance of the categorical indicative "I commend this." But what is hypothesized in the utterance of a sentence of the form "If this is good, then so and so" is not the performance of the action which it is alleged we perform in the utterance of the categorical indicative "This is good," for indeed no act or action is here hypothesized at all.

In short, no matter how we try to construe the statement "The word 'good' is used to commend," as long as we take it as telling us about the meaning of the word "good," it seems to collapse in the face of such counterexamples as (1)–(4), for these are literal occurrences of the word, and the speech acts of commendation, and so forth, are not in the offing. And this thesis collapses in a way in which the thesis "'Commend' is used to commend" does not collapse.

I hope this point is completely clear. If someone tells me something about the *meaning* of a word, then presumably what he tells me should hold true generally of occurrences of the word where it has that literal meaning. If we construe "'Good' is used to commend" as telling us something about the meaning of "good," then even under our expanded sympathetic interpretation (4) it does not hold for all literal occurrences of "good." So it seems it must be defective in some respect.

The argument I am using seems to work against any identification of the meaning of a word (which is not a speech-act word like "commend" or "confirm" nor an interjection) with some speech act or range of speech acts. Thus even if "p is true" means something like "I confirm p," still "If p is true, then q is true" does not mean anything at all like "If I confirm p, then I confirm q." So this pattern of philosophical analysis seems to fail.

One of the original grounds for the views I am discussing was an apparent analogy between the use of such philosophically troubling words as "true," "good," and "know" and certain so-called performative verbs, for example, "confirm," "commend," and "guarantee." What I am arguing is that the analogy fails to hold for the sort of examples I have provided. So the sense in which "true" is used to confirm, "good" to commend, and "know" to guarantee seems to be quite different from the sense in which "confirm" is used to confirm, "commend" to commend, and "guarantee" to guarantee.

Nonetheless it seems to me there is something true and important in the results produced by the pattern of analysis I have discussed, and I now wish to try to uncover it. (A clue that "good" is tied to certain speech acts is provided by the fact that in nonphilosophical contexts it and certain other words are called terms of praise, suggesting a connection between these words and the speech act of praising.) The first step in my strategy will be to examine how the views in question were arrived at in order that we may see at which point the argument went wrong.

II

Many philosophers believe that the meaning of a word is its use, or is at any rate somehow connected with its use. This is taken to be both the germ of a theory of meaning and a methodological principle of philosophical analysis. As a methodological principle its application consists in transforming any question of the form "What does W mean?" into "How is W used?" But the difficulty with this transformation is that the philosophers who employ it almost invariably confine their discussion of the use of W to the use of sentences of a simple indicative kind which contain W. The transformation occurs as follows: The question

(1) What does W mean?

is taken as equivalent to the question

(2) How is W used?

which is then tacitly interpreted to mean

(3) How is W used in simple categorical indicative sentences of the form, e.g., "This is W"?

and that is then taken to be the same question as

(4) How are these sentences containing W used?

and that is taken to mean

(5) What speech acts does the speaker perform in uttering these sentences?

It seems to me the philosophers under discussion offer correct answers to (5) but not necessarily to (1). They take their answers to (5) to be answers to (1) because they suppose that (1) and (2) are the same, and they then tacitly interpret (2) so that it generates (3), (4), and (5). But my argument is that their correct answers to (5) cannot be correct answers to (1), and my counterexamples are designed to show that they fail as answers to (1) because the words they are analyzing have literal occurrence where the speech acts which they allege the words are used to perform are not even in the offing. My diagnosis of their mistake is to show that when they say that W is used to perform speech act A they are not answering the question they take themselves to be answering. The association of non-speech-act words with certain speech acts must seem puzzling in any case since the unit of the speech act is not the word but the sentence.

Another way to put this is as follows. To point out the association between "good" and commendation is not to answer the question "What does 'good' mean?" but the question "What is it to call something good?" Thus the old philosophical question "What is it for something to be good?" has been confused with the question "What is it to call something good?" The assumption that these two questions are the same is one of the most common mistakes in contemporary philosophy; it is a mistake arising from a particular interpretation of the view that the meaning of a word is its use.

We are now in a position to see why my examples are counterexamples to the original thesis. The conclusion, " 'Good' is used to commend," was arrived at *via* a study of what act is performed when something is called good. But in my examples nothing is *called* good. Rather in their utterances it is hypothesized that something is good, the hope is expressed that something is good, and so on.

If we had simply said "To call something good is to commend it," my examples would not be counterexamples to the thesis, for, hypothesizing, for example, that something gets called good is no doubt hypothesizing that it gets commended and so on through the other examples. But, to repeat, the mistake is to suppose that an analysis of calling something good gives us an analysis of "good." This is a mistake because any analysis of "good" must allow for the fact that the word makes the same contribution to different speech acts, not all of which will be instances of calling something good. "Good" means the same whether I ask if something is good, hypothesize that it is good, or just assert that it is good. But only in the last does it (can it) have what has been called its commendatory function.

So far then I have argued that the pattern of philosophical analysis which consists in saying of a word W (where W is not a speech-act word or an interjection) that it is used to perform a speech act A does not give us the sort of information about the meaning of W that Hare, Strawson, and others have supposed. But I have also argued that it does tell us something true and important, namely that in calling something W one characteristically performs speech act or acts A. Or, to put it another way, in asserting that something is W one is characteristically performing act or acts A.

In a paper of this sort one might just stop there—but from what I have said I am left with a residual problem to which I should like to sketch the outlines of a solution.

III

The problem is this: How can it be both the case that it is a non-contingent fact that calling something good is commending it, and so forth, and yet this noncontingent fact does not give us the sort of information about the meaning of "good" that Hare and others seem to have supposed. That is, I take it that it is not just a contingent fact that calling something good is praising it or commending it, and so forth. It is not, for example, like the fact that calling someone a Communist agent in present day Michigan is insulting or denigrating him. This is a fact about the political attitudes of contemporary Michiganiens and might not hold, say, for employees of the Soviet Embassy in Washington.

But if it is some sort of necessary fact that calling something good is commending it, then must not this be a necessary fact about the concept *good;* and if that is so must not this fact tell us at least part of the meaning of "good"? A similar problem could be posed about "true," "know," and so on.

What I have said previously I have tried to make a completely general thesis about a whole pattern of analysis in contemporary philosophy; what I am going to say now just concerns the word "good."

First I wish to distinguish two classes of speech-act verbs: In group X I include such verbs as:

grade
evaluate
assess
judge
rate
rank
appraise.

In group Y I include such verbs as:

commend
praise
laud
extol
express approval
express satisfaction
recommend.

These two classes are sometimes lumped together, but I think it is clear that they are different. I may evaluate something favorably or unfavorably, but I cannot extol it unfavorably. I may grade it as excellent or bad, but I cannot praise it as bad. Members of group Y thus stand to members of group X in a relation something like the relation of determinate to determinable. To praise something is often or perhaps even characteristically to offer an assessment of it. But not just any kind of assessment, rather a favorable assessment. But not all assessments are favorable.

For the purpose of performing acts in the determinable range—assessing, grading, and so forth,—there is, depending on the subject matter, a range of terms one can use. Thus, for example, in grading students we use the letters A, B, C, D, and F. One of the most common of these grading labels—as J. O. Urmson calls them[5] —is "good." Other common grading labels are "excellent," "bad," "fair," "poor," and "indifferent." Giving an assessment will characteristically involve among other things assigning a grading label, and conversely assigning one of these will characteristically be giving an assessment, evaluation, and so forth. And the term assigned will indicate the kind of assessment made, favorable or unfavorable, high or low, and so on.

[5] "On Grading," *Logic and Language*, ed. by A. G. N. Flew, 2nd ser. (New York, 1953).

The reason that it is a noncontingent fact that calling something good is commending, and so forth, is this: to call it good is to assign it a rank in the scale of assessment, or evaluation, but to assign it a rank in this scale is not merely to assess or evaluate it; it is to give a particular kind of evaluation of it. In the case of "good" it is to give it a fairly high or favorable evaluation. But giving a high evaluation is characteristically, as I have already suggested, commending or praising, and so forth—which of these it is depends on the situation in which the utterance is made.

So the quasi-necessary truth that calling something good is commending it does not tell us about the meaning of "good" but tells us about the way the word is embedded in the institutions in group X and the relations between those institutions and the speech acts in group Y. The connection between the meaning of "good" and the speech act of commendation, and so forth, though a "necessary" one, is thus a connection at one remove.

Well, what does "good" mean anyhow? Anything like a complete answer to this question is beyond the scope of this paper. As Wittgenstein suggested,[6] it has like "game," a family of meanings. Prominent among them is: meets the criteria or standards of assessment or evaluation. Some other members of the family are: satisfies certain interests; and even: satisfies certain needs or fulfills certain purposes. (These are not unrelated; that we have the criteria of assessment we do will depend on such things as our interests.) Hare has seen that *saying* that something meets the criteria or standards of evaluation or assessment is giving an evaluation or assessment of a certain kind, that is, commendatory.

But the incorrect inference that the meaning of "good" is therefore somehow explicable in terms of commendation prevents us from seeing what I have been trying to emphasize, that "good" means the same whether I am expressing a doubt as to whether something is good, or asking if it is good, or saying that it is good. For that reason the question "What is it to call something good?" is a different question from "What is the meaning of 'good'?"—and in that sense there is more to meaning than use.

[6] *Philosophical Investigations,* par. 77, Part I.

CHARLES C. FRIES

Meaning and Linguistic
Analysis

Many who have read the materials of present-day American linguists
and have listened to their discussions have gained the impression
that these linguists have cast out "meaning" altogether.[1] The two
statements following are typical.

> Certain leading linguists especially in America find it possible to ex-
> clude the study of what they call "meaning" from scientific linguistics,
> but only by deliberately excluding anything, in the nature of mind,
> thought, idea, concept. "Mentalism" is taboo.[2]

> A general characteristic of the methodology of descriptive linguistics,
> as practised by American linguists today, is the effort to analyze lin-
> guistic structure without reference to meaning.[3]

* Reprinted from *Language* 30, 1954, by permission of Mrs. Fries and the
editor.

[1] When I set out to challenge anew the conventional uses of meaning as the
basic tool of analysis in sentence structure and syntax—the area of linguistic
study in which it has had its strongest hold—I felt very keenly an obligation to
state as fully and as accurately as I could just what uses I did make of meaning in my procedures. This paper represents the result. Although the materials
presented here use general terms, I should like to point out that my experience
has dealt primarily with English. This statement of the principles and assumptions that have underlain and guided my studies of English may not have
equal relevance to the problems presented by other languages.

[2] J. R. Firth, "General Linguistics and Descriptive Grammar," *Transactions
of the Philological Society*, 1950.82 (London, 1951).

[3] John B. Carroll, *A Survey of Linguistics and Related Disciplines*, 15 (Cambridge, Mass., 1950).

One can point to a variety of quotations from the writings of our American linguists, that seem to substantiate the views that these linguists not only condemn the "use of meaning" in linguistic analysis (as indicated in the quotation from Carroll), but (as indicated in the quotation from Firth) even refuse to treat "meaning."

Concerning the supposed refusal to treat "meaning," quotations such as the following have sometimes been offered in evidence.

The situations which prompt people to utter speech include every object and happening in the universe. In order to give a scientifically accurate definition of meaning for every form of a language, we should have to have a scientifically accurate knowledge of everything in the speakers' world. The actual extent of human knowledge is very small, compared to this.

The statement of meanings is therefore the weak point in language-study, and will remain so until human knowledge advances very far beyond its present state.

The signals can be analyzed but not the things signaled about. This reinforces the principle that linguistic study must always start from the phonetic form and not from meaning. . . . The meanings . . . could be analyzed or systematically listed only by a well-nigh omniscient observer.[4]

Concerning the alleged condemnation of the "use of meaning" in linguistic analysis the evidence usually consists of quotations like the following.

Theoretically it would be possible to arrive at the phonemic system of a dialect entirely on the basis of phonetics and distribution, without any appeal to meaning—provided that in the utterance of the dialect not all the possible combinations of phonemes actually occurred.

. . . our approach differs in some respects from Bloomfield's—chiefly in that Bloomfield invokes meaning as a fundamental criterion . . .[5]

In the present state of morphemic analysis it is often convenient to use the meanings of utterance fractions as a general guide and short-cut to the identification of morphemes. This is especially so in the case of languages that are more or less well known to the analyst,

[4] Leonard Bloomfield, *Language*, pp. 139, 140, 162 (New York, 1933).

[5] Bernard Bloch, "A Set of Postulates for Phonemic Analysis," *Lg.* 24.5 note 8, 24.6 (1948).

and has been true for most morphemic work done up to now. When we are confronted, however, with a language that we know little about in terms of the relations of the linguistic behavior, it becomes clear that meaning can be of little help as a guide. The theoretical basis of analysis then becomes evident: it consists of the recognition of the recurrences and distributions of similar patterns and sequences. The analyst must therefore constantly keep in mind this theoretical basis, and must be aware that his hunches about what goes with what are really short-cut conclusions about distributional facts.[6]

In exact descriptive linguistic work . . . considerations of meaning can only be used heuristically, as a source of hints, and the determining criteria will always have to be stated in distributional terms. The methods presented in the preceding chapters offer distributional investigations as alternatives to meaning considerations.[7]

Some who are counted among our linguistic scholars have so vigorously condemned all "uses of meaning" that for many linguistic students the word *meaning* itself has almost become anathema.

On the other hand, those who oppose the recent developments in the methods of linguistic study nearly all assume, as a matter of course, that all use of every type of meaning has been rigidly excluded from the linguistic studies made in accord with these methods, and often make that assumed fact the basis of their opposition and criticism.

Sometimes it is insisted that the so-called "repudiation of meaning" in the work of American linguists stems from Leonard Bloomfield. This view rests not upon what Bloomfield has said about meaning (which seems to have been overlooked) but upon inferences drawn from a somewhat superficial reading of his discussions of mentalism and mechanism. Thus concerning Bloomfield there have been such assertions as the following.

Mechanists cannot successfully speak of meaning because they undertake to ignore certain phases of human response.

The mechanist cannot consider the ethnologic features of meaning, such as connotative colorings or social levels.

[6] George Trager and Henry Lee Smith, Jr., *An Outline of English Structure*, p. 54 (Oklahoma, 1951).

[7] Zellig S. Harris, *Methods in Structural Linguistics*, p. 365, note 6 (Chicago, 1951).

The mechanists' definition of a plant-name . . . cannot . . . extend beyond the definition which appears in a handbook of botany: it cannot deal with ethnically conditioned features of meaning.

Bloomfield's physicalism (mechanism, anti-mentalism), as it is expressed in his linguistic writings, was not a philosophy of the universe nor a psychological system, but solely, as he insisted over and over again, a matter of the method of scientific descriptive statement:

> An individual may base himself upon a purely practical, an artistic, a religious, or a scientific acceptance of the universe, and that aspect which he takes as basic will transcend and include the others. The choice, at the present state of our knowledge, can be made only by an act of faith, and with this the issue of mentalism should not be confounded. It is the belief of the present writer that the scientific description of the universe, whatever this description may be worth, requires none of the mentalistic terms, because the gaps which these terms are intended to bridge exist only so long as language is left out of account.[8]

Bloomfield strove vigorously to avoid mentalistic terms (*concept, idea, etc.*) in the statement of his linguistic materials and believed that every truly "scientific statement is made in physical terms." [9] But his efforts to achieve statements in physical rather than "mentalistic" terms do not lead to the conclusion that he "ignores meaning" or that "he takes no account of meaning." He and many of his followers have pointed to certain uses of meaning in linguistic analysis as constituting unscientific procedures, but he and many of his followers have constantly insisted that meaning cannot be ignored. Pertinent quotations from Bloomfield's *Language* are abundant:

> Man utters many kinds of vocal noise and makes use of the variety; under certain types of stimuli he produces certain vocal sounds, and his fellows, hearing these same sounds, make the appropriate response. To put it briefly, in human speech, different sounds have

[8] Bloomfield, *Linguistic Aspects of Science*, p. 12 (Chicago, 1944).

[9] Bloomfield, "Language or Ideas?," *Language*, 12.92 note 6. Bloomfield followed Weiss in objecting to the term *behaviorism* and believed that *physicalism* indicated much better the essential quality of the kind of descriptive statements he sought.

different meanings. To study this coordination of certain sounds with certain meanings is to study language. (27)

The study of significant speech-sounds is phonology or practical phonetics. Phonology involves the consideration of meanings. (28)

Only two kinds of linguistic records are scientifically relevant. One is a mechanical record of the gross acoustic features, such as is produced in the phonetics laboratory. The other is a record in terms of phonemes, ignoring all features that are not distinctive in the language. Until our knowledge of acoustics has progressed far beyond its present state, only the latter kind of record can be used for any study that takes into consideration the meaning of what is spoken. (85)

It is important to remember that practical phonetics and phonology presuppose a knowledge of meaning: without this knowledge we could not ascertain the phonemic features. (137)

Only in this way will a proper analysis (that is, one which takes account of the meanings) lead to the ultimate constituent morphemes. (161)

Let me add to these quotations an excerpt from a letter dated 29 January 1945, written by Bloomfield to a friend of mine:

It has become painfully common to say that I, or rather, a whole group of language students of whom I am one, pay no attention to meaning or neglect it, or even that we undertake to study language without meaning, simply as meaningless sound. . . . It is not just a personal affair that is involved in the statements to which I have referred, but something which, if allowed to develop, will injure the progress of our science by setting up a fictitious contrast between students who consider meaning and students who neglect or ignore it. The latter class, so far as I know, does not exist.

With Bloomfield, no serious study of human language can or does ignore "meaning." It is my thesis here that on all levels of linguistic analysis certain features and types of meaning furnish a necessary portion of the apparatus used. In what I shall say, however, I do not mean to defend the common uses of meaning as the *basis* of analysis and classification, or as determining the content of linguistic definition and descriptive statement, though such uses have characterized much of the study of language since the time of the Greeks. The issue is not an opposition between *no* use of meaning whatever, and *any* and *all* uses of meaning.

With many others, I believe that certain uses of meaning in certain specific processes of linguistic analysis and in descriptive statement are unscientific, that is, that they do not lead to satisfactory, verifiable, and useful results. The more one works with the records of actual speech the more impossible it appears to describe the requirements of sentences (for example) in terms of meaning content. The definitive characteristics distinguishing those expressions which occur alone as separate utterances from those which occur only as parts of larger units are not matters of content or meaning, but matters of form, different from language to language. In the defining of "subjects" and "objects," of the "parts of speech," of "negation," we have not successfully approached the problems by seeking criteria of meaning content. Only as we have been able to find and to describe the contrastive formal characteristics have we been able to grasp grammatical structures in terms that make prediction possible. Structures do signal meanings, it is true, and these meanings must be described. But the meanings cannot serve successfully to identify and distinguish the structures. Not only does each structure usually signal several different meanings, but—what is more important—there is probably in present-day English no structural meaning that is not signaled by a variety of structures.[10]

This challenging of certain uses of meaning, as I have said, does not constitute a repudiation of all meaning in linguistic analysis. Meaning of some kind and of some degree always and inevitably constitutes part of the framework in which we operate. If that is so, then for clarity and understanding, as well as for rigorous procedure on each level of analysis, we must state as completely as

[10] The meaning "performer of the action" is one of the meanings signaled by the structure we call "subject." We cannot, however, expect to *define* the structure "subject" as "performer of the action," for this meaning is signaled by a variety of other structures that are not "subjects." For example, in each of the following sentences, the word *committee* has the meaning "performer of the action (of recommending)," but only in the first sentence is this word in the structure of "subject": *The committee recommended his promotion; His promotion was recommended by the committee; The recommendation of the committee was that he be promoted; The committee's recommendation was that he be promoted; The action of the recommending committee was that he be promoted.* The structure of "subject," on the other hand, signals at least five different meanings—four in addition to that of "performer"—each distinguished by special formal arrangements. See C. C. Fries, *The Structure of English,* pp. 176–83 (New York, 1952).

possible the precise uses of each type of meaning that our procedures require and assume.[11]

How much and just what of linguistic analysis can be accomplished without the use of any kind or degree of meaning at all? Certain meanings seem essential to making the very first step—the setting up of the material to be worked with, to be analyzed and described. There must be a "meaning frame" within which to operate. We must know or assume, for example, (a) that the sound sequences we attempt to analyze are indeed real language utterances and the utterances of a single language, not those of several languages—a dozen or a hundred; (b) something of the range of possibilities in human language behavior and the significance of certain techniques or methods of procedure for linguistic analysis; and (c) a practical control of a language (usually another language) in which to grasp and record the processes and the results of the analysis. (Many difficulties arise from the fact that often the language of the descriptive record of the analysis differs greatly in its range of meanings and way of grouping experience from that of the language being analyzed.)

Under (b), for example, we assume that all languages have some type of meaningful units—morphemes; that all languages have

[11] To accuse linguists of deliberately refusing to treat meaning at all is to ignore the facts. The number of thoroughly trained linguists is very small indeed, and, although there are more positions for such linguists in the academic world than there were twenty years ago, there are not enough such positions to support a sufficient number of linguists to carry on the linguistic studies that are needed in every part of the field. For the past twenty-five years the really live issues that have claimed the attention of linguists have centered about linguistic structure. The new views of the significance of structure and the success of new procedures of structural analysis applied to various aspects of language have aroused such enthusiasm that most linguists have devoted their studies to these matters. Although the present center of liveliest interest in linguistics is structure rather than meaning, some portions of the general problems of meaning have received attention. (See for example Bloomfield's *Linguistic Aspects of Science*, 1939; *Philosophical Aspects of Language*, 1942; "Language or Ideas?," *Lg.* 12.89–95 [1936]; "Meaning," *Monatshefte für deutschen Unterricht* 35.101–6 [1943].)

Even with respect to the lexicon, we should, for the record, note that the American linguists whose center of interest has been the English language have given constant support to the labors of those who have been struggling with the problems of producing the various period dictionaries proposed by Sir William Craigie. The *Oxford Dictionary* itself was an effort to apply practically what was at that time called the "new philological science."

bundles of contrasts of sound that function in separating or marking out or identifying these morphemes; that generally the lexical items have some contrastive formal features that make possible their classification into structurally functioning units; that all languages have formal arrangements of some sort of these structurally functioning units into contrastive patterns that have significance as structural signals of certain features of meaning; and that the linguistically significant patterns of structural arrangement are limited, much fewer than the total number of morphemes.

We must approach every linguistic analysis with a large body of "meaning" in hand. The question is not, then, whether we can dispense with all meaning in linguistic analysis but rather, more specifically, whether we can proceed with a valid and useful analysis without some knowledge or some control (*e.g.* through an informant) of the meanings of the language forms which we are analyzing.

In respect to this specific question, we must face the problem of distinguishing, with some precision if possible, several varieties of meaning. I do not refer especially to the tremendous diversity of meanings which attach to the word *meaning*[12] itself, although that diversity often prevents fruitful discussion. A few quotations will show a little of this diversity:

> The meaning of any sentence is what the speaker intends to be understood from it by the listener.[13]

> By the meaning of a proposition I mean . . . the ideas which are called to mind when it is asserted.[14]

> What we call the meaning of a proposition embraces every obvious necessary deduction from it.[15]

[12] See Leo Abraham, "What is the theory of meaning about?," *The Monist* 46.228–56 (1936). In this article are gathered more than fifty typical quotations from philosophical and psychological writers, in each of which the term *meaning* is used in a different sense. At the end of these quotations he concludes, "There is clearly nothing both common and peculiar either to all the various disparate senses, or to only the more familiar among them, which itself bears, or should bear, the name 'meaning' . . . A subject matter for the 'theory of meaning' cannot, accordingly, be obtained by abstraction from all or some of the entities revealed by the linguistic phenomenology of the term 'meaning.' "

[13] A. Gardiner, "The Definition of the Word and the Sentence," *British Journal of Psychology,* 1922.361.

[14] N. Campbell, *Physics: The Elements,* p. 132 (1920).

[15] C. S. Peirce, *Collected Papers,* 5.165 (1934).

Meaning is a relation between two associated ideas, one of which is appreciably more interesting than the other.[16]

To indicate the situation which verifies a proposition is to indicate what the proposition means.[17]

The meaning of anything whatsoever is identical with the set of expectations its presence arouses.[18]

Meaning is the fact of redintegrative sequence . . . the evocation of a total response by a partial stimulus.[19]

. . . the word "meaning" has established itself in philosophical discourse because it conveniently covers both reason and value.[20]

The meaning of certain irregularities in the motion of the moon is found in the slowing up of the motion of the earth around its axis.[21]

"Meaning" signifies any and all phases of sign-processes (the status of being a sign, the interpretant, the fact of denoting, the signification) and frequently suggests mental and valuational processes as well.[22]

We come then to the conclusion that meaning is practically everything. We always see the meaning as we look, think in meanings as we think, act in terms of meaning when we act. Apparently we are never directly conscious of anything but meanings.[23]

As speakers of English have employed it, the word *meaning* has thus represented a great range of content. In English usage the word *meaning* has signified such diverse matters as "the denotation of a name," "the connotation of a symbol," "the implications of a concept," "the neuro-muscular and glandular reactions produced by anything," "the place of anything in a system," "the practical consequences of anything," "the usefulness of anything," "that to which the interpreter of a symbol does refer," "that to which the interpreter of a symbol ought to be referring," "that to which the

[16] F. Anderson, "On the Nature of Meaning," *Journal of Philosophy*, 1933.212.

[17] A. J. Ayer, "Demonstration of the Impossibility of Metaphysics," *Mind*, 1934.333.

[18] C. W. Morris, "Pragmatism and Metaphysics," *Philosophical Review*, 1934.557.

[19] H. L. Hollingworth, "Meaning and the Psycho-physical Continuum," *Journal of Philosophy*, 1923.440.

[20] W. E. Hocking, *Philosophical Review*, 1928.142.

[21] M. R. Cohen, *Reason and Nature*, p. 107 (1931).

[22] C. W. Morris, *Signs, Language, and Behavior*, p. 19 (New York, 1946).

[23] W. B. Pillsbury, "Meaning and Image," *Psychological Review*, 1908.156.

user of a symbol wants the interpreter to infer," "any object of consciousness whatever." This great diversity of statement arises out of an attempt to describe the specific content of the situations in which the word *meaning* appears. Even more difficult and controversial has been the effort to classify and define the various kinds of meaning in terms of the meaning content of utterances in general. Often these various "meanings" are grouped under two general headings: (1) the scientific, descriptive, representative, referential, denotive, cognitive kind of meaning, and (2) the emotive, expressive, noncognitive kind of meaning.[24]

The following quotation summarizes a portion of an analysis of utterances in terms of meaning content.

> Thus in the case of certain sorts of indicative, interrogative, imperative, and optative sentence-utterances . . . it seems possible to distinguish a number of factors, each of which may be and has been referred to as the meaning or part of the meaning of the utterance. These are: (1) the primary conceptual content symbolized, *i.e.* presented and evoked; (2) the propositional attitude (with regard to this) expressed and evoked; (3) the secondary conceptual content presented and evoked; (4) the propositional attitudes (regarding this) expressed and evoked; (5) the emotions and conative attitudes expressed; (6) the emotional tone; (7) the emotions and attitudes revealed; (8) other kinds of effects; (9) the purpose.[25]

Let me turn away from these attempts to classify and describe the different kinds of meaning in terms of the meaning content itself to a classification based upon the kinds of signals a language uses in fulfilling its social function. I am concerned here solely with language as it provides a connection between two nervous systems. Such a use of language is not by any means limited to the communication

[24] C. L. Stevenson, *Ethics and Language*, p. 33 (New Haven, 1944): "The emotive meaning of a word is the power that the word acquires, on account of its history in emotional situations, to evoke or directly express attitudes, as distinct from describing or designing them." Id. 73: "The independence of emotive meaning can be roughly tested by comparing descriptive synonyms which are not emotive synonyms. Thus to whatever extent the laudatory strength of 'democracy' exceeds that of 'government where rule is by popular vote,' the emotive meaning of the former will be independent."

[25] William Fankena, "Cognitive and Noncognitive Aspects of Language," *Language and Symbolism* [unpublished tentative report] 5.27, 28 (1952).

of knowledge; but it provides for all the ways in which the members of a group interact.

A well-known diagram (slightly modified) will furnish a simplified frame for some comments concerning my use here of the term *meaning* as it applies to language content. This diagram must not be taken as implying any psychological theory whatever.

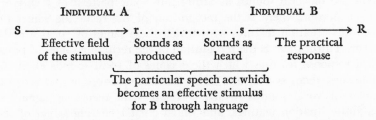

The speech act consists of both r, the succession of sound waves as produced by individual A, and s, the succession of sound waves as heard by individual B. Broadly speaking, there never is or can be an exact repetition of any particular succession of sound waves as produced and as heard: precise measurements and accurate recordings always reveal some differences. But in a linguistic community two or more physically different speech acts may fit into a single functioning pattern and thus may be functionally the "same." [26] Basically, then, the material that constitutes language must be recurring "sames" of speech acts. The sum of the speech acts of a community does not, however, constitute its language. Only as sequences of vocal sounds are grasped or recognized[27] as fitting into

[26] These "sames" must not be taken as the engineer's "norms" with margins of tolerance—statistical norms clustering around averages; see Martin Joos, Language design, *Journal of the Acoustical Society* 22.701–8 (1950). They are "sames" as the various types of "strike" in baseball are functionally the same; see Fries, *The Structure of English*, pp. 60–61.

[27] I take *recognition* here to mean not a conscious act of identification, but rather an automatic conditioned response connecting the patterns of vocal sound with recurrent features of experience. Recognition is itself a "meaning" response. I am assuming that every kind of meaning has this kind of process. On every level, it seems to me, shapes, colors, sizes, smells, tastes have meaning only as they fit into patterns that connect them in some way with recurring features of experience. When stimuli do not fit such patterns of recurring experience they are "meaningless," and confuse us. As a matter of fact it is usually the case that only features that do fit such patterns are reacted to at

recurring patterns do they become the stuff of language—only when they are correlated with recurring practical situations in man's experience and thus become the means of eliciting predictable responses.

The schematic formula above helps to direct attention to three aspects of meaning in language. First, there is the recognition of a sequence of vocal sounds as fitting into some pattern of recurring sames. Second, there is the recognition of the recurring sames of stimulus-situation features with which these sames of vocal sounds occur. Third, there is the recognition of the recurring sames of practical response features which these sames of vocal sounds elicit. A language, then, is a system of recurring sequences or patterns of sames of vocal sounds, which correlate with recurring sames of stimulus-situation features, and which elicit recurring sames of response features.[28]

In general, for linguists,[29] the "meanings" of an utterance consist of the correlating, regularly recurrent sames of the stimulus-situation features, and the regularly elicited recurring sames of response features.[30] These meanings are tied to the patterns of recurring

all; the others do not become effective features of stimuli. For adults there seems to be no such thing as "raw" observation unrelated to any pattern of experience.

[28] A linguistic community consists of those individuals that make the "same" regular and predictable responses to the "same" patterns of vocal sounds. The language function is fulfilled only in so far as it is possible to predict the response features that will regularly be elicited by the patterns of vocal sound. For the discussion here I am not concerned with what might be called "personal" meaning—the special nonrecurrent or not regularly recurring response features that mark individual differences.

[29] For many others the meaning of a text or a sequence of utterances has often been considered a function of (a) the "words" (as items of sound patterns which experience has connected in some way with reality), and (b) the "context." This context has included both the so-called "verbal context" or linguistic context (not specified further) and the "context of situation"—the circumstances in which the utterance occurs. Firth has pushed the analysis of "context" much farther in his dealing with "formal scatter" and "meaning by collocation." See his Modes of meaning, *Essays and Studies* (English Assn.) 1951.118–49, and General linguistics and descriptive grammar, *Transactions of the Philological Society*, 1951.85–87; *cf.* his earlier "Technique of Semantics," *Trans. Philol. Soc.* 1935.36–72, and "Personality and Language in Society," *Sociological Review*, 1950.

[30] In the study of the language records of a former time we have, because of the nature of the evidence, usually had to try to arrive at the meanings of the

sames of vocal sounds. In other words, the patterns of recurring sound sequences are the signals of the meanings. The meanings can be separated into various kinds or layers in accord with the several levels of patterns in the recurring sound sequences which do the signaling. Utterances will have then at least the following types or "modes" of meaning.

(a) There is the automatic recognition of the recurrent sames that constitute the lexical items. The lexical items selected for a particular utterance are distinguished from others that might have been selected by sharp patterns of sequences of sound contrasts. One layer of the meaning of the utterance is determined and signaled by the particular lexical items selected and thus recognized. This recognition covers both the identification of the item itself by its contrastive shape, and the situation and response features with which this shape correlates in the linguistic community. If the stress and intonation, as well as the social-cultural situation, are kept constant, the meaning of the utterance *The point of this pen is bent over* differs from that of each of the following only because the lexical items differ: *The point of this pin is bent over, The cover of this pan is bent over, The top of that pen was sent over.* One of the separable layers of the meanings signaled by our utterances is thus the lexical meanings.

One other feature of lexical meaning must be noted. In addition to the recognition of the shape or forms of the lexical item itself, identified by contrastive patterns of sound sequences, there is also the automatic (and sometimes more conscious) recognition of the distribution of each lexical item with "sets" of other lexical items as they occur in the complete utterance unit.[31] There is a "lexical scatter" as well as a "formal scatter." It is this recognition of the

---

language forms by connecting them with recurring elements of the situations in which they were used. In the study of living languages it is often possible to observe directly the responses which particular language forms elicit in a speech community. We assume that if a particular response regularly follows the utterance of a language pattern, then this pattern "means" this response. Upon such regular recurrences rests the kind of prediction that makes possible the social functioning of language.

[31] "Complete utterance unit" here means the total span of talk of one person in a single conversation or discourse.

particular set in which the lexical item occurs[32] that stimulates the selection of the specific "sense" in which that item is to be taken, the specific stimulus-response features for that utterance.

(b) In addition to the layer of lexical meaning there is the automatic recognition of the contrastive features of arrangement in which the lexical items occur.[33] These contrastive features of arrangement regularly correlate with and thus signal a second layer of meanings—structural meanings. The difference in meaning between the following sentences depends solely upon the contrastive features of arrangement, assuming that the stress and intonation as well as the social-cultural situation are kept constant: *There is a book on the table, Is there a book on the table.* Structural meanings are not vague matters of "context," so called. They are sharply defined and specifically signaled by a complex system of contrastive patterns.

Together, *lexical meanings* and *structural meanings* constitute the *linguistic meaning* of our utterances. Linguistic meaning thus consists of lexical meanings within a frame of structural meanings —that is, of the stimulus-response features that accompany contrastive structural arrangements of lexical items.

But the linguistic meaning is only part of the total meaning of our utterances. In addition to the regularly recurring responses to the lexical items and structural arrangements there are also throughout a linguistic community recurring responses to unique whole utterances or sequences of utterances. Rip Van Winkle's simple utterance, *I am a poor quiet man, a native of the place, and a loyal subject of the King, God bless him!,* almost caused a riot, not because of the linguistic meaning signaled by the lexical items

---

[32] As we record more specifically the details of the experience of language learning, we realize increasingly that we "learn" not only the shape of a lexical item and the recurrent stimulus-response features that correlate with it, but also the sets of other lexical items with which it usually occurs. Perhaps when psychologists explore the "free association" of words for an individual, they are really dealing with these sets of lexical distribution.

[33] In English the functioning units of the contrastive arrangements that signal meanings are not lexical items as such, but rather classes of these items. A variety of formal features make possible the classification of lexical items into a very small number of form classes, the member of which each function as structurally the same. Linguistic analysis must discover and describe these form classes as a means of dealing with the structures themselves.

and structures, but because the unique utterance as a whole, now, after the Revolution, meant to the group that he was a confessed enemy of the newly established government. The statement, *Bill Smith swam a hundred yards in forty-five seconds,* would have not only the linguistic meaning attaching to the lexical items and the structures, but also the significance of the unique utterance as a whole, that this man had achieved a new world record. The petulant child's insistence at bed-time that he is hungry often means to the mother simply that he is trying to delay the going to bed. Meanings such as these I call "social-cultural" meanings.[34] Linguistic meaning without social-cultural meaning constitutes what has been called "mere verbalism." The utterances of a language that function practically in a society therefore have both linguistic meaning and social-cultural meaning.

In general the meanings of the utterances are tied to formal patterns as signals.[35] In respect to linguistic meanings, I have assumed as a basis for study, that all the signals are formal features that can be described in physical terms of form, arrangement, and distribution. As I see it, the task of the linguistic analyst is to discover, test, and describe, in the system in which they occur, the formal features of utterances that operate as signals of meaning—specifically, (1) the contrastive features that constitute the recurrent sames of the forms of lexical units—the bundles of contrastive sound features by which morphemes are identified, (2) the contrastive markers by which structurally functioning groups of morphemes can be identified, and (3) the contrastive patterns that constitute the recurrent sames of the structural arrangements in which these structurally functioning classes of morphemes operate. In describing the results of the analysis, only verifiable physical terms of form, of arrangement, and of distribution are necessary. Whenever descrip-

---

[34] The term "social-cultural meaning" is not wholly satisfactory, but it is the best I have found to cover all the varieties of predictable meaning other than linguistic meaning. As indicated above, I have excluded from the discussion here the personal meaning of individual differences.

[35] This is true even of many of the varieties of social-cultural meaning—for example, the set of deviations from the norm of the sound segments that signal the meaning that a speaker is drunk, the whispering of an utterance that signals the meaning that the content of it is secret, and the unusual distribution that is the cue to a metaphor.

tive statements must depart from such formal matters, the fact is evidence of unsolved problems.

In the process of discovering just what formal features constitute the linguistic signals I can see no merit in denying ourselves access to any sources of suggestions concerning the nature of the materials that are significant. The more we know of the diverse characteristics of languages in general and of the processes that have marked language history, the more fruitfully prolific will be our suggestions. The less we know about language, the more frequently we may be led into blind alleys or follow the superstitions of the past.

In the process of testing these suggestions, however, and of proving the validity of our insights concerning the precise formal features that are significant, we need all the rigor that scientific procedure can offer. The real question centers upon the validity of the procedures through which we use techniques of distribution and of substitution. There must be some rigorous way of establishing "sameness" of frame and "sameness" of focus, as well as what constitutes "difference" in each case.

In carrying out these tasks certain uses of particular kinds of "meaning" within the utterance seem necessary and legitimate. (1) In testing the contrastive features that constitute the recurrent sames of lexical forms it is necessary to control in some way enough of the lexical meaning to determine whether forms showing certain differences of sound features are, for the particular language, "same" or "different." [36] (2) In testing the contrastive patterns that constitute the recurrent sames of structural arrangements it is necessary to control in some way enough of the structural meaning to determine whether particular variants are substitutable, leaving the arrangement the "same" for the language, or constitute such a change as to make the arrangement "different." Note that lexical meaning does not form part of the apparatus in which to test structural arrangements.

---

[36] Sometimes it is insisted that we use "differential" meaning, not "referential" meaning. Perhaps this statement means that the linguistic analyst seeks basically to establish the fact whether two instances differ in meaning content or not. He does not need to know what that content is or in what ways the two may differ. If they differ in meaning he assumes that there must be some difference in formal features, and sets out to find, prove, and describe that difference.

Social-cultural meanings which attach to the unique utterance as a whole or to a sequence of utterances do not seem to form any part of the frames in which to test either lexical forms or structural forms. Although a certain control of specific kinds of meaning seems to me essential for the various parts of linguistic analysis I should like to insist that as a general principle any use of meaning is unscientific whenever the fact of our knowing the meaning leads us to stop short of finding the precise formal signals that operate to convey that meaning.

JERROLD J. KATZ

The Semantic Component
of a Linguistic Description

I. INTRODUCTION[1]

The knowledge of linguistic structure one acquires in the transition from nonverbal infant to fluent speaker is the primary subject matter of an investigation of a particular natural language. Being in possession of such knowledge of a language L permits one to communicate with other speakers of L; and not being in possession of such knowledge of a language L prevents those who speak a different language from communicating with a normal monolingual speaker of L. We use the term "linguistic description" to refer to the linguist's theory about this knowledge.[2] We distinguish such a theory from an account of how knowledge of an language is acquired, on the one hand; and, on the other hand, we distinguish it from an account of how speakers employ their linguistic knowledge in actual communication. Whereas the former deals with the way in

* Reprinted from *Zeichen und System der Sprache* III; *Schriften zur Phonetik, Sprachwissenscheft und Kommunikationsforschung* 11 (Berlin: Akademie-Verlag, 1966) by permission of the author, editor, and publisher.

[1] This work was supported by the U.S. Army Signal Corps, the Air Force Office of Scientific Research, and the Office of Naval Research; in part by the National Science Foundation (Grant G-16526), the National Institutes of Health (Grant MH-04737-03), the National Aeronautics and Space Administration (Grant NsG-496); and in part by the U.S. Air Force (Electronic Systems Division) under contract AF 19(628)-2487.

[2] Katz, J. J., and Postal, P. *An Integrated Theory of Linguistic Descriptions,* M.I.T. Press, Cambridge, Massachusetts, 1964.

which innate dispositions and environmental factors combine to transform nonverbal infants into fluent speakers, the latter deals with the way in which knowledge of linguistic structure is put to use in actual speech situations to communicate thoughts, wishes, questions, feelings, and so forth.

A linguistic description has three components: a syntactic component, a semantic component, and a phonological component.[3] The syntactic component is, following Chomsky,[4] a system of formal rules which generates strings of minimally syntactically functioning elements—strings of formatives—together with a full analysis of their syntactic structure. We say nothing here about the character of the syntactic component, since it may be assumed that Chomsky's ideas are by now familiar to most linguists. The syntactic component is the generative source of a linguistic description, and the semantic and phonological components are purely interpretative systems without intrinsic generative capacity. The output of the syntactic component is, as is shown in Figure 1, the input to both the semantic and phonological components.

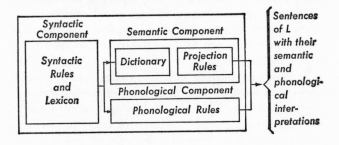

FIG. 1

The syntactic component enumerates the infinite set of abstract structures which represent the sentences of a language, while the semantic and phonological components operate as functions having these abstract structures as arguments and interpretations of them

[3] *Ibid.*
[4] Chomsky, N. *Syntactic Structures,* Mouton and Co., 's-Gravenhage, Second Printing (1962).

as values. Strings of formatives with their syntactic analysis, which comprise the output of the syntactic component, are formal objects, which are uninterpreted in terms of meaning and sound until they receive an interpretation by the operation of the semantic and phonological components. The phonological component interprets such formal objects as representations of stretches of vocal sound, while the semantic component interprets them as meaningful messages. That is, the phonological component provides a phonetic shape for a string of formatives it receives as input and the semantic component interprets such a string as that message which actual utterances having the phonetic shape assigned to that string convey to normal speakers in normal communication situations. The semantic and phonological components have no connection to each other: one is concerned with the sounds of speech while the other is concerned with the meanings imparted in speech. The absence of a connection between these components is the way in which the linguistic description represents the fact that the relation between meaning and sound is arbitrary.

A linguistic description is itself a component of a more general theory. This more general theory, which we will refer to as a "theory of linguistic communication," seeks to explain how speakers communicate in their language by hypothesizing that they possess the same knowledge of the linguistic structure of their language and common methods for putting such knowledge into operation. This explanation thus assumes that, as a result of having learned a language, both speaker and hearer are equipped with a mechanism, part of whose structure and principles of operation are correctly described by an optimal linguistic description, and with methods for putting such knowledge of linguistic structure to use. Linguistic communication is explained as a process in which the speaker uses his mechanism to encode a message in the form of an utterance which he articulates and in which the hearer uses his mechanism to decode this utterance to obtain the original message.

The whole process may be pictured as follows: the speaker, for reasons that are biographically relevant but linguistically not, chooses a message he wants to convey to the hearer. This may be some thought he wishes to exchange with him, some command he wants to give him, some question he needs to ask, and so forth.

This message is translated into syntactic form by the selection of a syntactic structure whose semantic interpretation is this message. This selection, which should not be thought of as a conscious choice on the part of the speaker, is governed by various considerations that have to do with the appropriateness of the forthcoming utterance to the circumstances that obtain. For example, syntactic structures which, though they bear the proper semantic interpretation, would yield utterances that are too long, too syntactically complicated, too pedantically sounding, and so forth, are rejected in favor of ones that are more suitable in these respects. Once a syntactic structure has been selected, the phonological component is utilized to convert this structure into a representation of vocal sound which serves as the basis for a signal to a device for speech articulation and an utterance of the appropriate syntactic form is vocalized. This utterance is transmitted to the auditory system of the hearer where it is converted into a signal which is decoded in the form of a phonetic shape. The syntactic component of the hearer's linguistic description is then utilized to recover the syntactic structure that the speaker originally selected to formalize his message. Once in possession of this structure, the hearer utilizes the semantic component to obtain its semantic interpretation, thereby representing to himself the same message that the speaker sought to communicate to him. Thus, an act of linguistic communication takes place.

This picture of what goes on in linguistic communication is obviously only the format for a full theory of linguistic communication. It gives no account of the methods by which the various components of the speaker's and hearer's linguistic knowledge are put to use in order to convert structures of one sort into structures of another. But, more significantly at this stage of research, it gives no account of the nature of the speaker's linguistic knowledge. Thus, for this model of communication to become an adequate theory of linguistic communication, it must first be elaborated and developed by the formulation of a precise specification of the internal structure of each of the three components of a linguistic description. This is the first step because a specification of the linguistic knowledge of a speaker is needed before we can make a serious attempt to say by what methods he puts this knowledge into operation.

But even without further elaboration and development, this model is important to have as an initial step toward the formulation of a fully precise theory of linguistic communication, primarily as a guide to successive steps of theory construction. For it sets forth in general form those features of the subject matter that a final theory must be able to explain and describes the pattern of such explanation. Every attempt at theory construction in linguistics starts with some model which guides successive steps and determines the pattern of explanation. Unfortunately, many linguists are content to leave their model unarticulated. The popular conception that a linguist begins his investigations in a theoretical vacuum and thus confronts his raw data without any biasing preconceptions, though it may appear more empirical and so more truly scientific, is only a pretense which must, in the end, harm the linguist who accepts it. The mistake in leaving one's theoretical jumping off point unarticulated is not only that then it serves less well as a guide to theory construction but that if some of the assumptions of the model that provides the conceptual framework must be revised in the light of further research it is thus harder to discover what assumptions are fallacious.

In this paper we are concerned with the task of specifying the internal structure of the semantic component of a linguistic description. Previous work in linguistics has given us a fairly precise account of the syntactic and the phonological components, but comparable achievements in the area of semantics have been conspicuously absent. To remedy this deficiency in linguistic theory and to take further steps toward a theory of linguistic communication, we shall try to formulate a conception of the semantic component that is not only adequate from the viewpoint of the facts about the semantics of natural languages but fits in with the generative conception of the syntactic and phonological components to form an adequate conception of the structure of a linguistic description of a natural language.

II. THE SEMANTIC COMPONENT

Given that a speaker and hearer communicate by employing mechanisms of linguistic communication to encode and decode messages, we start our attempt to formulate a conception of the semantic component by considering the observable semantic features of linguistic communication so that we may infer from them what must be the structure of the semantic component.

Before we examine these semantic features, we should say something about the nature of the inference from them to the structure of the mechanism responsible for them. First, the reason that such an inference is necessary is that we cannot obtain our knowledge of this mechanism directly. That is, we cannot look inside the speaker's and the hearer's heads to observe what happens when they successfully communicate, any more than a physicist can obtain his knowledge of quantum mechanics by direct observation of quantum phenomena. Like the physicist, the linguist is forced to resort to hypothesizing what the hidden phenomena must be in order for them to cause the observable phenomena. Thus, the linguist hypothesizes a mechanism with just the structure and principles of operation necessary to account for the behavior of speaker and hearer in communication. If the hypothesized mechanism accounts for this behavior in the simplest and most systematic way, then he may attribute the structure and principles of operation hypothesized in his theory to the actual mechanism of linguistic communication. This is the basis on which he can claim to have learned how this mechanism is structured and how it functions to achieve communication.

The primary semantic feature of linguistic communication is the ability of speakers to understand the meaning of indefinitely many utterances that they have never previously encountered. This feature of communication is so commonplace and so taken for granted in our daily use of language that it is often neither recognized nor accorded its proper theoretical significance. But if we consider for a moment what is involved in learning a foreign language, we will easily recognize the true theoretical significance of the speaker's ability to understand the meaning of utterances that are wholly novel to him. For we do not credit a person with mastery of a foreign language if he is able to comprehend only those sentences whose meaning he has been previously taught, any more than we credit animals with fluency in language when they respond appropriately to the verbal commands in which they have been drilled. Rather, the criterion of mastery of a language is whether a person can understand any sentence of the foreign language that he has never before been exposed to and that a speaker of that language would understand. The true theoretical significance of this ability is, then, that its performance is the test of linguistic fluency.

Chomsky and others who have been developing generative grammars have fully appreciated the significance of this feat of a speaker's.[5] This is why they require a grammar, that is, the syntactic and phonological components of a linguistic description, to be capable of generating an infinitely long list of sentences which, if extended sufficiently far, will include any string of formatives that is syntactically and phonologically well-formed in the language but will never include any string that is syntactically or phonologically ill-formed. Only grammars that meet this requirement can account for the syntactic and phonological aspects of the speaker's ability to understand novel sentences, since if the speaker's knowledge is not assumed to include such a grammar, there is no way to explain how he can apprehend the syntactic properties of novel sentences upon which an understanding of their meaning depends. But, even if we assume that a speaker's knowledge of his language includes syntactic and phonological components of the kind formulated by generative grammarians, on this assumption we can still only account for part of the knowledge that enables a speaker to accomplish the feat of understanding novel sentences. For an account of how a speaker grasps the syntactic and phonological structure of a novel sentence does not explain how he grasps its meaning. Described solely in terms of syntactic and phonological aspects of their structure, sentences are merely strings of formatives with labelled bracketings, together with a phonological interpretation. That is, sentences are formal objects, certain configurations of symbols, with certain pronunciations. Such objects can convey no more

---

[5] The significance lies in the fact that the linguist must account for the fact that the fluent speaker has acquired the means necessary for performing a task whose character compels us to admit that its performance results from the application of rules. Among the other reasons which compel us to make this admission is that cited by Miller, Pribram, and Galanter, *viz.* that the task of understanding any twenty word sentence is one a fluent speaker can perform, yet the number of twenty word sentences is 1030 while the number of seconds in a century is only 3.15 times 109. *Plans and the Structure of Behavior,* Miller, G. A., Pribram, K., and Galanter, E., Holt, New York (1960), pp. 146–47.

meaning than comparably structured strings of pronounceable nonsense terms.

Therefore, our problem in semantics is to account for whatever knowledge a speaker requires to perform the feat of understanding the meaning of novel sentences, short of his knowledge of syntax and phonology and those things upon which there is significant variation from one speaker to another.[6] To account for such knowledge, we must formulate a conception of the internal structure of the semantic component of a linguistic description on which this component is a system of recursive rules that function to assign a meaning to every string of formatives generated by the syntactic component. If a semantic component assigns the correct meaning to every sentence of a speaker's language, then, *a fortiori,* crediting the speaker with the knowledge represented in such recursive rules explains, *ceteris paribus,* how he is able to assign a meaning to any sentence he encounters for the first time.

Besides the feat of understanding novel sentences, there is another general feature of linguistic communication which indicates something about the manner in which the internal structure of the semantic component should be formulated. This is the compositional character of the process by which a speaker obtains the meaning of a sentence. That is, the meaning of any syntactically compound constituent is composed by putting together the meanings of the compound constituent's component parts. Therefore, in order for the semantic component to reconstruct the speaker's ability to understand sentences, the rules of the semantic component must project the meanings of a compound constituent from the meanings of the lower level constituents that make it up. Further, since, in any sentence, there are elements which have no internal syntactic structure, the morphemes, the speaker must be assumed to know their meanings without the aid of any device for compositionally constructing them. Hence, the semantic component must somehow contain a list of the morphemes and for each member of this list a representation of its meaning. Such knowledge will be recon-

---

[6] *Cf.* Katz, J. J., and Fodor, J. A. "The Structure of a Semantic Theory," *Language,* Vol. 40 (April–June 1963).

structed in a semantic component in the form of a dictionary. The rules, then, must operate on the entries of the dictionary for the morphemes in a sentence to project from them the meaning(s) of the whole sentence and each of its higher constituents.

Hence, a semantic component is based on the idea that the speaker's knowledge of the semantics of sentences of his language is knowledge of rules that apply to the meanings of syntactically elementary constituents, and then by further applications of such rules, to the combinations of meanings already effected by previous applications, until they ultimately produce a compound meaning for whole sentences and all their constituents. Basing a semantic component's internal structure on this idea is absolutely essential not only to explain the manner in which the speaker himself understands novel sentences but also to account for the fluent speaker's ability to understand new sentences in terms of what he has learned in learning his language. We can explain how a nonverbal infant becomes a fluent speaker on the basis of its exposure to a finite sample of sentences and nonsentences only if we hypothesize that acquiring the sort of knowledge of the semantics of a language that a speaker has is acquiring both the elementary meanings for the stock of morphemes that occur in the finite sample of sentences to which a child is exposed and also the recursive rules for compositionally projecting the meanings of sentences from such elementary meanings.

Since understanding the grammar of sentences underlies understanding their meaning, the semantic component must have the output of the syntactic component as its input. That is, the input to the semantic component is the set of strings of morphemes that the syntactic component marks as well-formed sentences of the language together with the syntactic description of each string in this set. The output of a semantic component is this set of strings with a semantic interpretation assigned to each member.

A semantic component has two subcomponents: a *dictionary* that associates an elementary meaning with every morpheme of the language and a set of *projection rules* that provides the combinatorial machinery for projecting the meaning of a whole sentence from the meanings of its components. The result of applying the projection rules to a sentence, that is, the output of the semantic component for that sentence, we call a *semantic interpretation* of that sentence. There are, therefore, three basic concepts to explain in order to provide a conception of the internal structure of a semantic component: *dictionary, projection rule,* and *semantic interpretation.*

The dictionary is a finite list of pairs called "dictionary entries." Each pair consists of a morpheme represented in the orthography employed by the grammar and a representation of its meaning in a certain normal form. The dictionary entry for a given morpheme is under the empirical constraint to represent every piece of semantic information about its meaning required by the projection rules to assign correct semantic interpretations to the sentences containing that morpheme. Thus, the normal form for dictionary entries must suffice to represent a full analysis of the meaning of morphemes.

The normal form for a dictionary entry is as follows: an entry consists of a set of finite sequences of symbols, each sequence consisting of an initial sequence of *syntactic markers,* followed by a sequence of *semantic markers,* and finally, a *selection restriction.* Dictionary entries may be represented in the form of tree diagrams, as illustrated in Figure 2, where each distinct path rooted at the

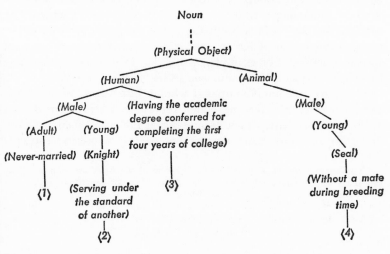

FIG. 2

formative is one full sequence of the set. Semantic markers are enclosed within parentheses, and selection restrictions are enclosed within angles. Syntactic markers are not enclosed at all, the dots under the syntactic marker Noun in Figure 2 indicate the possibility of further syntactic categorization, for example, into Common Noun, Count Noun, Animate Noun, and so forth.[7]

Each distinct path in such a tree represents a distinct sense of the morpheme which labels its root, and will be referred to a *reading*. The notion of a reading has an extension greater than that of the set of morphemes. The notion of *reading* will be employed to refer to the string of symbols which a semantic theory uses to represent one sense of any sequence of morphemes, that is, any expression, including a whole sentence. Thus, the notion of a reading of a constituent less than a whole sentence is intended as a formal reconstruction of the logician's and philosopher's notion of a concept, while the notion of a reading for a whole declarative sentence is intended as a formal reconstruction of their notion of a proposition or statement.

A morpheme, and likewise any sequence of formatives, with n distinct readings is represented as n-ways semantically ambiguous. In Figure 2, for example, "bachelor" is represented as four-ways semantically ambiguous, that is, as having four distinct senses. The syntactic markers, which originate in the grammar, serve to differentiate senses that differ in syntactic categorization or "part of speech function." For example, "store" has at least two senses, one in its function as a Noun and one in its function as a Verb.

Senses are not undifferentiated wholes, but rather, have a complex structure. The reading which represents a sense provides an analysis of that sense which decomposes it into its elementary parts and their relations. Semantic markers are the theoretical concepts

---

[7] Two comments on Figure 2. First, the word *bachelor*, though a noun, can select and exclude other nouns in various types of constructions, *e.g.*, in noun noun cases such as *He is my bachelor friend*, or in noun-in-apposition cases such as *Mr. Smith, the neighborhood bachelor, is here*. Thus, we must represent *bachelor* having a selection restriction for each sense; thus the terminal elements for each reading in Figure 2 is a selection restriction enclosed in angles.

Second, the particular selection restrictions are omitted because their inclusion would only complicate matters unnecessarily at this point. '

that a semantic theory uses to express the elementary parts of the meaning of a morpheme. Thus, the semantic markers appearing in a reading and their formal relations are intended to represent the structure of the unreducible meaning components of a sense. There is here a strong analogy to the manner in which a chemical formula for a molecule of a substance represents the atoms of various kinds and the bonds between them. The formula for the chemical compound alcohol given in Figure 3 represents the structure of an

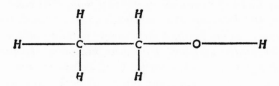

FIG. 3

alcohol molecule in a way analogous to the way in which the set of readings given in Figure 2 represents the structure of the meaning of "bachelor." Both representations exhibit the elements out of which the compound is formed and their relations. In the former case, the definition employs the chemical concepts of *hydrogen, carbon, oxygen,* and so forth, while in the latter, the definition employs the linguistic concepts of *Noun, human, male, young,* and so forth. This analogy points up one further thing. The names of the semantic markers used to represent the elementary meaning components of a sense are not to be identified with the corresponding English words, just as the names "hydrogen," "oxygen," "carbon" and "molecule" used to represent the chemical concepts of hydrogen, oxygen, carbon, and molecule are not to be identified with their corresponding English words. These semantic concepts are concepts of a scientific theory, just as these chemical concepts are concepts of a scientific theory. Only the former belong to the conceptual apparatus of linguistic theory while the latter belong to the conceptual apparatus of chemical theory.

Semantic markers are thus the concepts that enable us to formulate generalizations about the meaning of sets of linguistic constructions. In this respect they function somewhat like syntactic markers. The syntactic markers *S, NP,* and *VP* enable us to state the empirical generalization that any string of English formatives whose initial substring is a *NP* and whose remaining part is a *VP* is itself a *S*. Such generalizations are normally formulated as syntactic rules, that is, $S \rightarrow NP + VP$. Semantic markers also make it possible to state empirical generalizations, but such generalizations are not expressed in the form of rules. For example, the semantic marker (Human) enables us to express the generalization that the meanings of the expressions *bachelor, the man who lives next door, my sister's favorite classmate, the children,* and so forth, all have something semantic in common, which is not part of the meanings of the expressions, *the monkey, those nuts and bolts, the funny mole on his arm, earth,* and so forth. Further, the semantic marker (Male) enables us to express the empirical generalization that the members of the first set, though they have the aforementioned similarity in meaning, are not exactly the same in meaning, since only *bachelor, the man who lives next door, my uncle,* and so forth, have this semantic property. Thus, the mode of expressing such generalizations is to include the relevant semantic markers in the reading for the expressions whose relatedness one wishes to represent. The way in which the first generalization about the meanings of *bachelor, the man who lives next door, my sister's favorite classmate, children,* will be represented is by constructing the dictionary so that the readings for the lexical items *bachelor, man, classmate, child,* and so forth all contain an occurrence of the semantic marker (Human). Thus, including a semantic marker into a dictionary entry is formulating a semantic generalization.

Semantic ambiguity at the sentence level has its source in ambiguity at the dictionary level. A necessary but not sufficient condition for a sentence to be semantically ambiguous is that it contains at least one morpheme having two or more distinct readings in its dictionary entry. For example, the source of the semantic ambiguity of "There is no school any more" is the ambiguity between the sense on which "school" means session(s) of a teaching institution and the sense on which it means the physical schoolhouse itself. The presence of an ambiguous morpheme in a sentence is not a sufficient condition for that sentence to be semantically ambiguous because there may be other parts of the sentence which, by virtue of their meaning, prevent the ambiguous morpheme from contributing more than one of its senses to the meaning of the entire sentence. Thus, although as we have just seen, "school" is ambiguous at least two ways, the sentence "The school burned up" is not semantically ambiguous because the verb "burn up" permits its subject to bear only senses that contain the concept of a physical object as a part. This selection of some senses and exclusion of others is reconstructed in a semantic theory by the inclusion in a reading of what has been referred to above as a *selection restriction.*

Selection restrictions are formal devices which express a necessary and sufficient condition for the reading in which they appear to be combined with other readings by the application of a projection rule. Selection restrictions express a condition upon the content of a reading, in the form of a truth-functional compound of semantic markers. This condition is interpreted as permitting the reading containing the selection restriction to combine with another reading just in case that other reading contains the semantic markers necessary to satisfy the condition. For example, one reading in the dictionary for "honest" represents the sense "one who characteristically refuses to appropriate for himself what rightfully belongs to another and avoids lies and deception." Thus, the *reading* for this sense is given the selection restriction < (Human) & $\overline{\text{(Infant)}}$ > which asserts that an adjectival occurrence of "honest" bears this sense if and only if the reading for the noun that this occurrence of the adjective "honest" modifies contains the semantic marker (Human) but not (Infant). If the selection restriction in a reading is not satisfied by any reading with which it might combine (because these readings do not contain the necessary markers) and moreover, there are no other readings whose selection restrictions are satisfied by any of these readings, then there is no *derived reading* for the whole syntactic construction. This represents the fact that that construction is semantically anomalous. For example, the construction "honest geranium" is such that the reading for "geranium" lacks the semantic marker (Human) necessary for any sense of "honest" to apply, and thus this construction will be marked as semantically anomalous by a semantic component. "Honest baby" will be marked as semantically anomalous also, but in this case because the reading for the noun head of the construction has the semantic marker (Infant) which the selection restriction in the reading for the modifier precludes. Such constructions as "honest man," "honest group of friendly people," "farmer who is honest," and so forth will all be marked as nonanomalous constructions.

If the dictionary consisted of entries all of which were formulated exactly in the form of Figure 2, that is, if each entry *explicitly* contained every semantic marker that represents a component of the meaning of the morpheme, then the dictionary as a whole would contain an incredible amount of redundancy in the sense of having an extremely large number of unnecessary semantic markers. For instance, the semantic marker (Physical Object), which as we have seen above, appears in the entry for "bachelor," as well as in a very great many other entries, would occur redundantly in a large percentage of these cases. For it is a regularity that whenever either the semantic marker (Human) or (Animal) or (Artifact) or (Plant) or any one of a number of other semantic markers occur in a reading of an entry, the semantic marker (Physical Object) will appear in the reading also. Thus, if we take this regularity into account, the dictionary can be greatly economized by eliminating every occurrence of (Physical Object) where (Human), (Animal), (Artifact), (Plant), and so forth, occurs and by including, within the dictionary, a rule which expresses the regularity. This *implicitly* includes Physical Object in every entry which contains either (Human), (Animal), (Artifact), (Plant), and so forth. In the case of (Physical Object), the rule would be [(Human) v (Animal) v (Artifact) v . . . v (Plant)] →(Physical Object). Moreover, if we similarly capitalize on all other such regularities, the dictionary can be extensively economized. To effect such an economy, we propose rules of the form $F[(M_1), (M_2), \ldots, (M_k)] \rightarrow (M_{k+1})$, where "F" is some truth-function of the semantic markers $(M_1), (M_2), \ldots, (M_k)$. These rules state that if a reading contains semantic markers $F[M_1], (M_2), \ldots, (M_k)]$, then that reading also contains the semantic marker (M_{k+1}). These rules may be thought of as comprising a special component of the dictionary, which is now regarded as in maximally reduced form. Furthermore, such rules have an important theoretical interpretation in that they represent inclusion relations among the semantic categories of linguistic theory. For such a rule says that the categories represented by the semantic markers on its left-hand side are subcategories of, or are included in, the category represented by the semantic marker on its right-hand side. This permits us to empirically justify general statements about the category relations in languages on the grounds of the simplicity of the dictionaries for those languages.

These rules, which we refer to as "category inclusion rules" or "redundancy rules," and dictionary entries for morphemes written in maximally economical form, comprise the dictionary of a semantic component. The rules apply just after the rule (I), to be described shortly, applies. They operate on readings assigned by (I) to the terminal nodes of a P-marker and expand these readings at this point. We shall justify this ordering after we have discussed rule (I).

Up to this point, we have characterized only the notion of meaning as it applies to the morphemes of the language. The projection rules of a semantic theory characterize the remaining part of the notion of meaning by providing a recursive definition of the meaning of any syntactically well-formed sequences of morphemes. Thus, together with the dictionary, they provide a complete characterization of the notion of meaning. This characterization will be extensionally adequate in that it enables us to assign a meaning to every syntactically well-formed sequence of morphemes, that is, to every sentence of the language and every sentential constituent. That the projection rules must be formulated so that they do this is clearly a *desideratum* since, if the projection rules fail, the semantic theory fails to describe the language fully and so fails to explain how a speaker can understand the meaning of any sentence.

The projection rules operate on a sentence such as *The child likes hard candy* together with the description of its syntactic structure provided by the syntactic component in the form of a labelled tree diagram such as in Figure 4.

The dictionary rule (I) enables us to use the semantic information stored in the dictionary to determine the meaning of each of the morphemes in a sentence. This rule associates each morpheme in the sentence with all and only those readings from its dictionary entry that are compatible with the syntactic categorization the dictionary receives in the syntactic description of the sentence given by its P-marker. The rule (I) is as follows:

> Associate with the morpheme M in a P-marker all and only those readings in M's dictionary entry that syntactically categorize M in the same ways that M is categorized in that P-marker.

By iterated application of this rule each morpheme in a sentence is associated with a set of readings. For example, in the sentence "The child likes hard candy," "candy" is associated with a reading that represents the sense "confection made with a sweetening agent (usually sugar) and possibly fruits, nuts, chocolate, and so forth," but it does not receive the sense that "candy" has as an intransitive verb. If the sentence were instead "The fruits candy easily," then

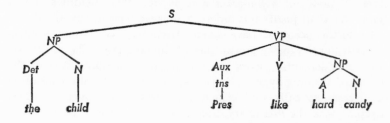

FIG. 4

the situation would be the other way around. But notice that, at this stage, the set of readings associated with the adjective "hard" contains not only a reading which represents the sense of "not easily penetrated" but also a reading which represents the sense "fit for physical exertion or endurance," which will have to be weeded out by the application of further projection rules.

After rule (I) has operated fully and each of the morphemes of the sentence has been associated with a set of readings from the dictionary, the category inclusion rules discussed just above operate. They expand these readings by introducing into a reading the semantic markers that appear on the right-hand side of every category inclusion rule whose left-hand side is satisfied by the semantic markers in the reading. Thus, for example, since the reading for "child" in the sentence of Figure 4 has the semantic marker (Human), the category inclusion rules will expand this reading by introducing, *inter alia,* the semantic marker (Physical Object). The reason why these rules must operate at this point in the semantic interpretation of a sentence is that the semantic markers that are introduced by them are needed in order that the operations of the further projections rules (which combine these readings to form derived readings for higher order constituents) have the information they require to determine whether selection restrictions are satisfied. For example, the semantic marker (Physical Object) is required in the reading for "child" in order that the selection restriction in the reading for the verb "hit" in a sentence such as "The child hit the ground with a thud" be satisfied and such a sentence be marked as nonanomalous and given its proper readings.

The other projection rules combine readings already associated with items in a tree diagram to form derived readings, which are then combined with other derived readings, and these with still others, until a set of derived readings which expresses the meaning of the whole sentence is associated with the top node labelled "S." The bracketing provided in the tree diagram specifies which readings a projection rule can combine, by bracketing together the sequences of morphemes whose associated readings are to be joined to form a derived reading. The projection rules proceed from the bottom of a labelled tree diagram combining readings to produce derived readings which are associated with the node of the tree which immediately dominates the nodes with which the readings that were combined are associated. Derived readings thus provide a characterization of the meaning of the sequence of formatives that is dominated by the node to which they have been assigned. In this manner, each constituent of a sentence is assigned a set of readings (readings from dictionary entries in the case of formatives and derived readings in the case of syntactically composite constituents), until the highest constituent, the whole sentence, is reached and assigned a set of derived readings.

An example of a projection rule which provides such derived readings is the following:

(R 1) Given two readings associated with nodes branching from the same node X, one of the form,

Sequence of morphemes $m_1 \rightarrow$ syntactic markers of head $\rightarrow (a_1)$ $\rightarrow (a_2) \rightarrow \ldots \rightarrow (a_n) < 1 >$

and the other of the form,

Sequence of morphemes $m_2 \rightarrow$ syntactic markers of modifier $\rightarrow$ $(b_1) \rightarrow (b_2) \rightarrow \ldots \rightarrow (b_n) < 2 >$

such that the string of semantic markers of the head has a substring which satisfies $< 2 >$, then there is a derived reading of the form,

Sequence of words $m_2 + m_1 \rightarrow X \rightarrow (a_1) \rightarrow (a_2) \rightarrow \ldots \rightarrow (a_n)$ $\rightarrow (b_1) \rightarrow (b_2) \rightarrow \ldots \rightarrow (b_n) < 1 >$

where any (b_i) is null just in case there is an (a_j) such that $(b_i) = (a_j)$

This derived reading is assigned to the set of readings associated with the node labelled X.

This projection rule operates on a pair of readings assigned to constituents that are related by the modifier-head relation, that is, to cases of adjective-noun modification, verb-adverb modification, adverb-adjective modification, and so forth. Since there is a different projection rule for each different way in which constituents can be grammatically related, there is a different projection rule for combining the readings of a verb and its object, a verb and its subject, and so on. Thus, the number of projection rules required in a semantic theory is dictated by the number of distinct grammatical relations defined in the syntactic component.

The projection rule given immediately above explicates the process of attribution in language, that is, the process whereby a new semantically significant unit is created by combining a modifier and head. In attribution, as is shown by the way this rule embeds the reading of the modifier into the reading of the head, the semantic properties of the new unit are those of the head except that the meaning of the new unit is more determinate than that of the head by virtue of the semantic information contributed by the meaning of modifier. The rule brings the selection restriction in the reading of the modifier into force by allowing the embedding just in case the reading of the head has the requisite semantic content. Finally, the erasure clause at the end of the rule avoids pointlessly duplicating semantic markers in the derived reading. Thus, for example it is unnecessary to include each of the semantic markers (Human) and (Female) twice in the derived reading for the compound "spinster aunt" just because the readings for both words contain occurrences of these semantic markers.

We now introduce the notion "semantically interpreted tree diagram T." We define this notion as a set of pairs, one member of which is a labelled node of the tree diagram T and the other member of which is a maximal set of readings, each reading in this set providing one of the meanings of the sequence of morphemes that is dominated by that labelled node. The set of readings for each node is maximal in the sense that every reading for the sequence of morphemes which can belong to the set (on the basis of the dictionary, the projection rules, and the syntactic structure represented in the tree diagram) is a member of the set, and every node of the tree diagram has a maximal set of readings assigned to it.

We can now explain the final notion that needs to be explained to define "semantic component," namely the notion "semantic interpretation of a sentence." A sentence has more than one description of its syntactic structure in case the sentence is syntactically ambiguous. Thus, Figure 5 below illustrates this situation:

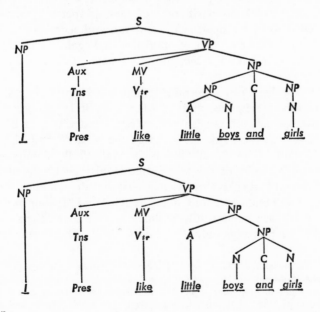

FIG. 5

We obviously want to construct the notion "semantic interpretation of a sentence" in such a way that the semantic interpretation of a syntactically ambiguous sentence like "I like little boys and girls" reflects the semantic structure of each and every semantically interpreted tree diagram corresponding to a term of the sentence's syntactic ambiguity. To accomplish this, we must first define the preliminary notion "semantic interpretation of a sentoid," where by *sentoid* we understand a P-marker or tree diagram assigning a sentence a syntactically unique bracketing structure.[8] Thus, by the concept "sentoid" is meant a syntactically unambiguous sentence, disambiguated by the tree diagram paired with it.

Since the semantic interpretations of sentences and sentoids produced as the output of a semantic component constitute the component's whole description of the semantics of a language, for a semantic component to be empirically adequate, these semantic interpretations must correctly predict and explain the semantic properties of every sentence of the language. Thus, we must now consider what semantic properties of sentences a speaker is able to detect. Once we know what some of these properties are, we will know what sort of properties of sentences and sentoids a semantic component must be capable of predicting and against what intuitive judgments of speakers a semantic component can be empirically tested.[9]

First, speakers can determine when a sentence or sentoid is semantically ambiguous, and in what ways it is ambiguous. For example, speakers of English will correctly judge that "I like civil engineers," "Is the bank the scene of the crime?," and "Find the seal as soon as you can!" are each semantically ambiguous by virtue, respectively, of the ambiguous words "civil," "bank," and "seal." Second, speakers can detect that certain sentences such as "There is an honest geranium in my garden" and "Is your insecticide a spinster?" are semantically anomalous and that others such as "There is a pretty geranium in my garden" and "Is your aunt a

---

[8] Cf. *An Integrated Theory of Linguistic Descriptions* for a detailed discussion of this notion.

[9] The semantic properties to be discussed immediately below are, of course, only some of those that must be successfully predicted. Others will be discussed in the next section.

spinster?" are not. Third, he can determine that certain sentences are paraphrases of each other, as are "Eyedoctors eye blonds," "Occulists eye blonds," and "Blonds are eyed by occulists," and that others are not paraphrases, as "Eyedoctors eye what gentleman prefer" is not a paraphrase of the aforementioned sentences.

The notion "semantic interpretation of a sentoid" must be defined in such a way that if a sentoid exhibits any of these semantic properties they can be marked as properties of the sentoid in terms of formal features of the semantically interpreted tree diagram for the sentoid. Thus, we define "semantic interpretation of the sentoids" to be (1) the tree diagram of the sentoid semantically interpreted by the operation of the projection rules and (2) the set of statements about s that follows from (1) and the definitions: Let "C" be any constituent of s, that is, the whole sentoid or any of its parts.

(D 1) C is *semantically anomalous* if and only if the set of readings associated with the node labelled "C" in its semantically interpreted tree diagram contains no readings, that is, is null.

(D 2) C is *semantically ambiguous n ways* if and only if the set of readings associated with the node labelled "C" in its semantically interpreted tree diagram contains n members, for n greater than 1.

(D 3) C is *semantically unambiguous* if and only if the set of readings associated with the node labelled "C" in its semantically interpreted tree diagram contains exactly one member.

(D 4) C_1 and C_2 are *synonyms on a reading* if and only if the set of readings associated with the node labelled "C_1" in its semantically interpreted tree diagram and the set of readings associated with the node labelled "C_2" in its semantically interpreted tree diagram have at least one member in common.

(D 5) C_1 and C_2 are *fully synonymous* if and only if the set of readings associated with the node labelled "C_1" in its semantically interpreted tree diagram and the set of readings associated with the node labelled "C_2" in its semantically interpreted tree diagram are identical.

Now we can define the notion "semantic interpretation of the sentence S" as (1) the set which contains the semantic interpretations for each sentoid of S and (2) the set of statements about S that follows from (1) and the schema: C is *fully P* if and only if in each semantic interpretation of a sentoid of S in (1) there is a statement that S is P with respect to that sentoid. For example, by this schema "Geraniums like little boys and girls" is marked as fully anomalous because it is anomalous on the readings for both sentoids.

Evaluating the adequacy of dictionary entries and readings for constituents is wholly a matter of determining how well they play their role within the framework of the overall semantic component. No dictionary entry or reading can be tested entirely on its own. If on the basis of (D1)–(D5) and the above schema the whole semantic component correctly predicts all the semantic properties of every sentence, then the dictionary and the projection rules (and the syntactic component) are all justified. If, on the other hand, the component makes false predictions, then, as in any scientific theory, deciding what is wrong is a question of deciding on systematic grounds what part(s) of the theory have been formulated incorrectly. Basically, however, the question of whether a dictionary entry adequately represents the meaning of a morpheme is a matter of how well that entry serves as a basis from which the projection rules can extrapolate the meaning of the infinitely many sentences containing that morpheme. The question of whether the false predictions are due to a falsely formulated dictionary entry rather than to an incorrectly formulated projection rule can be decided on the basis of whether the false predictions are confined to those sentences containing the particular morpheme or extend to every sentence that the projection rule plays a role in semantically interpreting including those that do not contain an occurrence of the morpheme in question. What changes in a dictionary entry should be made to prevent false predictions is a matter of making changes and trying out the new dictionary entries to determine which works best.

*   *   *   *   *   *   *   *   *   *   *   *

JOHN LYONS

Componential Analysis
and Universal Semantics

PRELIMINARY DISCUSSION

What is meant by the term "componential analysis" in semantics **is** best explained by means of a simple example—one that has often been used for this purpose by linguists. Consider the following sets of English words:

1. man   woman   child
2. bull   cow   calf
3. rooster   hen   chicken
4. drake   duck   duckling
5. stallion mare   foal
6. ram   ewe   lamb

On the basis of our intuitive appreciation of the sense of these words we can set up such proportional equations as the following:

man:woman:child::bull:cow:calf

This equation expresses the fact (and for the moment we may assume that it is a fact) that, from the semantic point of view, the words *man, woman* and *child,* on the one hand, and *bull, cow* and *calf,* on the other, all have something in common; furthermore,

* Reprinted from *Introduction to Theoretical Linguistics* (Cambridge, Cambridge University Press, 1968) by permission of the author and publisher.

that *bull* and *man* have something in common, which is not shared by either *cow* and *woman* or *calf* and *child;* that *cow* and *woman* have something in common, which is not shared by either *bull* and *man* or *calf* and *child;* that *calf* and *child* have something in common that is not shared by either *bull* and *man* or *cow* and *woman.* What these different groups of words have in common we will call a *semantic component.* (Other terms have also been used in the literature: "plereme," "sememe," "semantic marker," "semantic category," and so forth; references will be found in the notes.)

Let us now introduce some elementary arithmetical considerations. Given a numerical proportion (what the Greek mathematicians and grammarians called an "analogy": of the general form

a:b::c:d

where the first of the four expressions divided by the second is equal to the third divided by the fourth, we can factorize the proportion into what for the present purpose we may call its "components"; and we can then refer to each of the four expressions as the *product* of a pair of components. . . . For example, from the proportion

2:6::10:30

we can extract the components 1, 2, 3 and 10. The proportion can then be restated as

$$(2 \times 1):(2 \times 3)::(10 \times 1):(10 \times 3)$$

where 2 is analysed as the product of 2 and 1; 6 as the product of 2 and 3; and so on. In this instance, three of the components are *prime numbers,* 1, 2 and 3; the fourth, 10, is not. However, in the case of numerical proportions we can always discover whether a given number is a prime or not; and, if it is not, we can determine its *ultimate components*—the set of prime numbers in terms of which it can be factorized. For the present purpose, we may assume that the process of factorization rests upon the availability of all the relevant proportions. For instance, if we have available the further proportion 1:2::5:10, we could factorize 10 into the prime numbers 2 and 5; and we could then express our original proportion as

$$(2 \times 1):(2 \times 3)::((2 \times 5) \times 1):((2 \times 5) \times 3)$$

Each of the four expressions is now restated as the product of its ultimate components.

Let us now apply these considerations to the analysis of the English words given above. From the proportion *man:woman::bull: cow*, we can extract four components of sense: we will refer to these as (male), (female), (adult-human), (adult-bovine). At this stage of the analysis, if one were actually analysing the words on the basis of proportional equations, (adult-human) and (adult-bovine) would be regarded as single components. But as soon as we restate the proportion *man:woman:child::bull:cow:calf* as

> (male) × (adult-human):(female)
> > × (adult-human):(nonadult-human)
> ::(male) × (adult-bovine):(female)
> > × (adult-bovine):(nonadult-bovine)

we can extract the further components (adult) and (nonadult). No one of these components, it should be observed, is assumed to be an ultimate component (a "prime"): it is conceivable that, by bringing forward for comparison other words of English and setting up further proportions, we should be able to factorize (human) or (male) into "smaller" semantic components, just as we factorized 10 into 5 and 2. Eventually we might hope to describe the sense of all the words in the vocabulary in terms of their ultimate semantic components. Assuming that the proposed analysis of the few English words given above is correct as far as it goes (and we will presently consider what "correct" means here), we can say that the sense of *man* is the product of the components (male), (adult) and (human); that the sense of *mare* is the product of (female), (adult) and (equine); and so on.

The componential approach to semantics has a long history in linguistics, logic and philosophy. It is inherent in the traditional method of definition by dividing a genus into species and species into subspecies; and this method of definition is reflected in most of the dictionaries that have ever been compiled for particular languages, and in the organization of such works as *Roget's Thesaurus*. A number of attempts have been made in recent years to formalize these traditional principles of semantic analysis. We may begin by discussing some of the more important assumptions upon which current componential theories of semantics are based or with which they are frequently associated. The first is the assumption that the semantic components are language-independent, or universal.

THE ALLEGED UNIVERSALITY
OF SEMANTIC COMPONENTS

It has frequently been suggested that the vocabularies of all human languages can be analysed, either totally or partially, in terms of a finite set of semantic components which are themselves independent of the particular semantic structure of any given language. According to this view (which has been a commonplace of philosophical and linguistic speculation since the seventeenth century) the semantic components might be combined in various ways in different languages (and thus yield "senses" or "concepts" unique to particular languages), but they would themselves be identifiable as the "same" components in the analysis of the vocabularies of all languages. To quote Katz, who has put forward this view in a number of recent publications: "Semantic markers [*i.e.* semantic components] must . . . be thought of as theoretical constructs introduced into semantic theory to designate language invariant but language linked components of a conceptual system that is part of the cognitive structure of the human mind."

Little need be said about the alleged universality of semantic components, except that it is an assumption which is commonly made by philosophers and linguists on the basis of their anecdotal discussion of a few well-chosen examples from a handful of the world's languages.

Chomsky has suggested: "It is surely our ignorance of the relevant psychological and physiological facts that makes possible the widely held belief that there is little or no a priori structure to the system of 'attainable concepts.' " The first point that should be made about this remark is simply that the belief that there are few, if any, "universal, language-independent constraints upon semantic features [*i.e.* semantic components]" is probably most widely-held among those linguists who have had some experience of the problems of trying to compare the semantic structure of different languages in a systematic fashion: many have tried, and failed, to find a set of universal components. The second point is that, although Chomsky's own work contains a number of interesting, and probably correct, observations about certain classes of lexical items (*e.g.* "proper names, in any language, must designate objects meeting a condition of spatio-temporal contiguity," "the color words of any language must subdivide the color spectrum into continuous segments," "artifacts are defined in terms of certain human goals, needs and functions instead of solely in terms of physical qualities"), such observations do not go very far towards substantiating the view that there is "some sort of fixed, universal vocabulary [of semantic components] in terms of which [possible concepts] are characterized."

It may well be that future developments in semantics, psychology, physiology, sociology, anthropology, and various other disciplines, will justify the view that there are certain "language invariant but language linked components of a conceptual system that is part of the cognitive structure of the human mind," as Katz has suggested. Such empirical evidence as there is available at the present time would tend to refute, rather than confirm, this hypothesis.

COMPONENTIAL ANALYSIS AND CONCEPTUALISM

It is obvious that the value of componential analysis in the description of particular languages is unaffected by the status of the semantic components in universal terms. It should also be realized that componential theories of semantics are not necessarily "conceptualist," or "mentalistic." This point is worth stressing, since not only Katz and Chomsky, but also Hjelmslev, Jakobson, and many others who have advocated a componential approach to semantics, have done so within a philosophical and psychological framework which takes it for granted that the sense of a lexical item is the "concept" associated with this item in the "minds" of the speakers of the language in question. For example, Katz introduces the notion of semantic components (or "semantic markers") as follows: "Consider the idea each of us thinks of as part of the meaning of the words 'chair,' 'stone,' 'man,' 'building,' 'plant,' and so forth, but not part of the meaning of such words as 'truth,' 'togetherness,' 'feeling,' 'shadow,' 'integer,' 'departure,' and so forth—the idea that we take to express what is common to the meaning of the words in the former group and that we use to conceptually distinguish them from those in the latter. Roughly, we might characterize what is common to our individual ideas as the notion of a spatially and contiguous material thing. The semantic marker (Physical Object) is introduced to designate that notion."

We have already suggested that semantic theory should avoid commitment with respect to the philosophical and psychological status of "concepts," "ideas" and the "mind." Here it is sufficient to observe that what Katz has to say about the difference between the two groups of words can be stated without employing the term "concept" or "idea." The first group of words denote things which are, or can be, described in English as "physical objects" (the expression "physical object" is of course itself made up of English words); the second group of words do not. Whether the correct application of the first group of words to their referents presupposes that the speaker has some "idea" of "physical object" in his "mind" is a psychological question which we may leave on one side. The important question for the linguist is whether there are any facts pertaining to the acceptability or unacceptability of sentences, or to the relations of implication which hold between sentences, which can be described by assigning to all the words of the first group a distinctive semantic component, which we will agree to call "(physical object)." The answer to this question carries no implications whatsoever for the dispute between various schools of philosophy and psychology about the status of "mental concepts."

APPARENT ADVANTAGES OF THE COMPONENTIAL APPROACH

At first sight, the componential approach to semantics would seem to have one striking advantage over other approaches: in terms of the same set of components one can answer two different questions. The first question has to do with the semantic acceptability of syntagmatic combinations of words and phrases: whether a given combination is to be generated as significant or excluded as meaningless. The second question is this: what is the meaning (*i.e.* the sense) of a particular combination of lexical items? We will take each of these questions in turn.

We have said that the significance of grammatically well-formed sentences (and parts of sentences) is traditionally accounted for in terms of certain general principles of "compatibility" between the "meanings" of their constituent lexical items. One way of stating this notion of semantic "compatibility" is to say that the relevant semantic components of the lexical items in the syntagmatic combination generated by the syntax must not be *contradictory*. Let us assume, for example, that the word *pregnant* contains a component which restricts it to the modification of nouns which contain the component "(female.)" On the basis of this fact ("modification" being interpreted by the syntactic rules of the language) such phrases as *the pregnant woman* or *a pregnant mare* would be generated as significant and such phrases as *the pregnant man* or *a pregnant stallion* would be excluded as meaningless ("uninterpretable"). Whether such phrases as *the pregnant duck* are significant would presumably be decided with reference to further components of sense associated with the word *duck* and further restrictions imposed upon the combinability of *pregnant* with nouns.

There is no doubt that this is an elegant way of accounting for the combinatorial restrictions which hold between lexical items in particular grammatical constructions. It is to be noted, however, that any comprehensive treatment of the significance of sentences in such terms presupposes an adequate syntactic analysis of sentences and satisfactory rules for the semantic interpretation of the relevant grammatical relations. The example that has just been given, which involved the "modification" of a noun by an "adjective," is one which has never been regarded as particularly troublesome by semanticists. Its formalization within the framework of current syntactic theory is trivial by comparison with the problem of formalizing the vast majority of the relations of semantic "compatibility" which hold in the sentences of any language. In the last few years there has been a remarkable concentration of interest upon the problems attaching to the formalization of different relations of semantic "compatibility" (notably by Katz, Weinreich and

Bierwisch). So far the results are not impressive, despite the sophistication of the formal apparatus that has been developed; and it would seem that progress in this area is dependent upon the construction of a more appropriate theory of syntax than is yet available.

The second question that componential analysis sets out to answer is "What meaning does a given sentence or phrase have?" The general answer to this question is that the meaning of a sentence or phrase is the "product" of the senses of its constituent lexical items; and the sense of each lexical item is the "product" of its constituent semantic components. The meaning of a sentence or phrase is therefore determined by "amalgamating" all the semantic components of the lexical items according to a set of "projection rules" which are associated with deep-structure grammatical relations. It was suggested in the previous paragraph that current syntactic theory does not yet provide us with a satisfactory account of many of the relevant deep-structure grammatical relationships; and this was the main burden of our discussion of "grammatical functions" in Chapter 8.* It follows that we are at present unable to interpret the term "product" (or "compositional function"—to employ the more technical term) in the proposed definition of the meaning of a sentence or phrase as "the product of the senses of its constituent lexical items."

At the same time, it is clear that many of the semantic relations discussed in the previous chapter* might be reformulated within a componential theory of semantics. Synonymy, hyponymy, incompatibility and complementarity are obviously definable in terms of the semantic components of the lexical items in question. (For a componential approach to the definition of these relations the reader is referred to the works cited in the notes.)* What must be stressed, however, is the fact that the componential analysis of lexical items rests upon the prior notion of "implication" with respect to the assertion and denial of sentences. Componential analysis is a technique for the economical statement of certain semantic relations between lexical items and between sentences containing them: it cannot claim to circumvent any of the problems of indeterminacy that were discussed above in connexion with "understanding" and "analytic implication."

* References are to *Introduction to Theoretical Linguistics.*

THE "COGNITIVE REALITY" OF
SEMANTIC COMPONENTS

The most interesting work so far published in the field of componential semantics has come, not from philosophers and linguists,
but from anthropologists; and they have recently devoted considerable attention to what they have called the "cognitive validity," or
"reality," of semantic components. It was this question that we had
in mind, when we said earlier that we should have to examine what
was meant by "correct" in the context of componential analysis.

A good deal of the anthropological discussion makes reference
to the analysis of the vocabulary of kinship in various languages.
It has been shown, for example, that one can analyse the most common kinship terms of English in various ways. (In particular, *brother*
and *sister* can be regarded as having the same component, "direct
line of descent," as *father* and *mother* or *son* and *daughter,* as against
cousin, which shares the component "collateral" with *uncle* and
aunt, and with *nephew* and *niece;* alternatively, *brother* and *sister*
can be analysed as having the same component, "co-lineal," as
uncle and *aunt* or *nephew* and *niece,* as against *cousin,* which has
the component "ablineal.") The question is which, if any, of the
various possible analyses is "correct." Each of them is self-consistent;
each of them distinguishes every member of the lexical system from
every other member of the system; and each of them is "predictive,"
in the sense that it provides the anthropologist with a means of deciding, with respect to any member of the family, what his relationship is to other members of the family in terms of the lexical
system. But each of the alternative analyses rests upon a different
set of proportional equations:

either

father:mother::son:daughter::brother:sister

or

uncle:aunt::nephew:niece::brother:sister

It is therefore the "cognitive validity" of one set of proportions,
rather than the other, which should decide the question of "cor-

rectness" (if, indeed, this question is decidable). As far as the anthropological analysis of kinship is concerned, the "cognitive validity" of a particular proportion is determined, presumably, by the social status and roles assigned to the different classes of family relatives in the society; and this might well be reflected also in the linguistic "intuitions" of the members of the community.

But we can also consider the question of "correctness" from a more strictly linguistic point of view. Let us return, for this purpose, to the simple illustration of componential analysis with which we began this section. We assumed the validity of the following proportions

man:woman:child::bull:cow:calf
bull:cow:calf::rooster:hen:chicken
etc.

On the basis of these proportions, we "extracted" the semantic components (male) *v.* (female), (adult) *v.* (nonadult), (human) *v.* (bovine) *v.* (equine) *v.* . . . (sheep). We may now ask what is the linguistic status of these components.

At first sight, the opposition of the contradictory components (male) and (female) look satisfactory enough. If we know that someone is an adult, male, human being, then we know that the word *man,* rather than *woman* or *child,* is appropriately applied to him; if we know that a particular domestic fowl is an adult female of a given species, then we know that *hen,* rather than *rooster* or *chicken,* is the appropriate term of reference; and so on. But one might maintain that to differentiate *man* and *woman, rooster* and *hen,* and so forth, in terms of the sex of their referents is to give priority to but one of the many linguistically-relevant features which distinguish them. If one asks a young child (most of whose utterances are perfectly acceptable and manifest the same semantic relationships, as far as one can judge, as the utterances of his elders) what is the difference between men and women, he might answer by listing a whole set of typical characteristics—the kind of clothes they wear, how their hair is cut, whether they go out to work or stay at home and look after the children, and so forth. A totally unrelated set of criteria might be proposed for the differentiation of *rooster* and *hen,* of *bull* and *cow,* and so on. Why should one suppose that sex is the sole criterion even in adult speech? And how far is it true to say that *woman:child::cow:calf::hen:chicken*, and so forth?

Obviously, there is a certain class of sentences, the semantic acceptability or unacceptability of which can be accounted for in terms of this proportional equation: *That woman is the mother of this child, That hen is the mother of this chicken, and so forth,* v. *That man is the mother of this child, That woman is the father of this child, That woman is the mother of this calf,* and so forth. And the grammatical phenomenon of gender in English is partly determined by the sex of the referent. But this does not mean that (male) and (female) are the sole semantic features which differentiate the complementary terms *man* v. *woman, bull* v. *cow,* and so forth. The status of such components as (adult) *v.* (nonadult) is even more dubious: once again, there are sets of semantically-acceptable or semantically-unacceptable combinations that can be accounted for in terms of this opposition, but there are others that cannot.

The problem is undoubtedly related to the anthropologist's problem of "cognitive reality." Consider, for example, a society in which the role of men and women is so different that there are very few activities in which both will engage. Assume now that there are two lexical items in the vocabulary of that language, which can be translated into English as "man" and "woman" on the basis of their reference to male, adult human beings and female, adult human beings, respectively. Knowing this fact about the reference of the two lexical items, the linguist could apply these terms appropriately to men and women. He would be fairly sure that the translation of English sentences such as "The man gave birth to a child" (assuming that there is a term that can be satisfactorily translated as "give birth to") would be semantically-unacceptable. But there might be an enormous range of other sentences, including "The man cooked a meal," "The woman lit a fire," and so forth, which are equally unacceptable. Our own cultural prejudices and our own taxonomic classification of the physical world should not be taken as valid for the analysis of either the culture or the language of other societies, still less of any alleged "conceptual system that is part of the cognitive structure of the human mind."

A further point should be made. It is one of the concomitant dangers of componential analysis that it tends to neglect the difference in the frequency of lexical items (and therefore their greater or lesser "centrality" in the vocabulary) and the difference between lexical items and semantic components. For example, it is often suggested that *brother* and *sister* can be replaced with the "synonyms" *male sibling* and *female sibling*. But this is true only in the context of anthropological or quasi-anthropological discussion. The words *brother* and *sister* are extremely common words, known presumably to all speakers of English, whereas *sibling* is a technical term, coined for the convenience of anthropologists; and most English speakers probably do not know it. The fact that there is no common superordinate term for the two complementaries *brother* and *sister* is *prima facie* evidence that the opposition between the two terms is semantically more important than what they have in common. Similarly, the fact that there is a term *horse*, which has as its hyponyms the complementaries *stallion* and *mare*, is relevant to the analysis of the structure of the English vocabulary. Any theory of semantics which encouraged us to believe that the phrase *adult male elephant* stood in exactly the same semantic relationship to *elephant* as *stallion* does to *horse* would be unsatisfactory.

Componential theories of semantics do not necessarily fall victim to inadequacies of this kind. But there has been surprisingly little attention devoted to a discussion of the relationship between lexical items like *male* or *adult* and semantic components like (male) or (adult). One cannot avoid the suspicion that the semantic components are interpreted on the basis of the linguist's intuitive understanding of the lexical items which he uses to label them.

CONCLUDING REMARKS

Limitations of space prevent us from going further into the details of recent componential work in semantics. If our treatment of the subject has been somewhat negative, it should be realized that this has been by deliberate decision. I have tried to draw attention to some of the assumptions upon which componential theories of semantics are frequently based—in particular, the assumption that semantic components are universal. We have seen that the notion of componential analysis rests upon the establishment of proportional equations with respect to the sense of lexical items. The important question, which is not always considered, is the degree to which these proportions are "cognitively valid." It is too often assumed that these proportions can be set up simply on the basis of introspection.

Componential analysis has, however, made considerable contributions to the development of semantics. Apart from anything else, it has brought the formalization of syntax and the formalization of semantics (or some aspects of semantics) closer together than they have been in the past. That linguists are once again seriously concerned with the relations between syntax and semantics is due very largely to the impact made by the work of Katz and Fodor, taken up more systematically within the framework of "an integrated theory of linguistic descriptions" by Katz and Postal, and further developed by Katz in a number of subsequent publications. Although Katz and Postal tended to minimize the value of previous work in componential analysis, they were right to insist upon the importance of specifying the form of the "projection rules" and the manner of their operation "within the context of explicit generative linguistic descriptions." This had not been attempted before.

In a previous chapter, we raised the possibility of a *rapprochement* between "formal" and "notional" grammar; and much of our subsequent discussion of "grammatical categories" and "grammatical functions" would tend to suggest that further progress in the formalization of syntax depends upon this *rapprochement*. We may conclude the present work in the certain expectation that the next few years will see the publication of a number of books and articles directed towards this goal.

It is not unlikely also that a greater concentration of interest upon the theory of semantics will bring linguists back to the traditional view that the syntactic structure of languages is very highly determined by their semantic structure: more especially, by the "modes of signifying" of semantically-based grammatical categories. If this development does take place, one must be careful not to assume that linguistic theory has merely retreated to the position held by traditional grammarians. All future grammatical and semantic theory, however traditional its aims might be, must meet the rigorous demands of twentieth-century, "structural" linguistics. Revolutions may be followed by counterrevolutions; but there can be no simple restoration of the past.

Bibliographical Essay

CLASSICS

Readers interested in pursuing classics in empiricist semantics might begin with JOHN LOCKE's *An Essay Concerning Human Understanding,* Book III (London, 1695); GEORGE BERKELEY, *The Principles of Human Knowledge* (London, 1710); and DAVID HUME, *A Treatise of Human Nature,* Book I, Sec. 1 (London, 1739). *Classics in Semantics,* DONALD E. HAYDEN and E. P. ALWORTH, eds. (New York: Philosophical Library, 1965) contains a number of readings by philosophers, linguists, and literary scholars.

VERIFICATION THEORY OF MEANING

For further reading in this area see RUDOLF CARNAP, *Introduction to Semantics* (Cambridge, Mass.: Harvard University Press, 1959), Chapter 1; *Meaning and Necessity* (Chicago: University of Chicago Press, 1947); A. J. AYER, *Language, Truth and Logic* (New York: Dover Publications, Inc., 1952), and *Thinking and Meaning* (London: H. K. Lewis, 1947); BERTRAND RUSSELL, *An Inquiry into Meaning and Truth* (London: George Allen and Unwin Ltd., 1940) esp. Chaps. xv and xxii; ISRAEL SCHEFFLER, *The Anatomy of Inquiry* (New York: Alfred A. Knopf, Inc., 1963); RODERICK CHISHOLM, "Sentences about Believing," *Proceedings of the Aristotelian Society,* 56, 125–48 (1955–56) and reprinted together with a correspondence with WILFRED SELLARS in *Minnesota Studies in the Philosophy of Science,* Vol. II, HERBERT FEIGL, MICHAEL SCRIVEN, and GROVER MAXWELL, eds. (Minneapolis: University of Minnesota, 1958), pp. 507–39. *Readings in Philosophical Analysis,* HERBERT FEIGL and WILFRED SELLARS, eds. (New York: Appleton-Century-Crofts, 1949), pp. 29–115, contains five articles on this topic. See also CHARLES SAUNDERS PEIRCE, "How to Make Our Ideas Clear," *Popular Science Monthly,* Vol. 12 (1878); and WILLIAM JAMES, *Essays in Pragmatism* (New York: Hafner Publishing Co. Inc., 1948), pp. 141–76.

MEANING AND USE

Philosophical Investigations by LUDWIG WITTGENSTEIN, trans. by G. E. M. Anscombe (New York: The Macmillan Company, 1953) is a classic in this area. For further reading about Wittgenstein and his works, see *Ludwig Wittgenstein: The Man and His Philosophy,* K. T. FANN, ed. (New York: Dell, 1967) a collection of articles, and GEORGE PITCHER, *The Philosophy of Wittgenstein* (Englewood Cliffs: Prentice-Hall, Inc., 1964). The books by Pitcher and Fann both contain bibliographies of works by Wittgenstein and articles about his philosophy. Other works are JOHN AUSTIN, *How to Do Things with Words* (Cambridge, Mass.: Harvard University Press, 1962) and *Philosophical Papers* (Oxford: The Clarendon Press, 1961); G. E. MOORE, *Principia Ethica* (Cambridge: Cambridge University Press, 1929); C. L. STEVENSON, *Ethics and Language* (New Haven: Yale University Press, 1960); R. M. HARE, *The Language of Morals* (Oxford: The Clarendon Press, 1952).

THE WORD "GOOD"

Many philosophers have been interested in the meaning and use of the word "good." In addition to the works mentioned above by Moore, Stevenson, and Hare, readers might wish to look at PAUL ZIFF, *Semantic Analysis* (Ithaca: Cornell University Press, 1960); J. J. KATZ, "Semantic Theory and the Meaning of 'Good,'" *Journal of Philosophy* 61, 739–66 (1964); and ZENO VENDLER, "The Grammar of Goodness," *Philosophical Review* 72, 446–65 (1963).

RECENT PHILOSOPHICAL WORK
IN SEMANTICS

SOLL GOTTLOB FREGE, "On Sense and Reference," translated by M. Black, in *The Philosophical Writings of Gottlob Frege*, P. Geach and M. Black, eds. (Oxford: Blackwell, 1952), also in FEIGL and SELLARS; JERROLD J. KATZ, *The Philosophy of Language* (New York: Harper & Row, Publishers, 1966); PAUL ZIFF, "Understanding 'Understanding Utterances,'" in *The Structure of Language*, J. FODOR and J. KATZ, eds. (Englewood Cliffs, N.J.: Prentice-Hall, Inc., 1964); H. P. GRICE, "Meaning," *Philosophical Review* 66 (1956); JONATHAN L. COHEN, *The Diversity of Meaning* (London: Methuen & Co., Ltd., 1962); ROGER BROWN, *Words and Things* (Glencoe, Ill.: The Free Press, 1958); LEONARD LINSKY, ed., *Semantics and the Philosophy of Language* (Urbana: University of Illinois Press, 1952); W. V. O. QUINE, *Word and Object* (Cambridge, Mass.: M.I.T. Press, 1960); LOUIS B. SALOMON, *Semantics and Common Sense* (New York: Holt, Rinehart & Winston, Inc., 1966); and RICHARD RORTY, ed., *The Linguistic Turn* (Chicago: University of Chicago Press, 1967).

MEANING IN LINGUISTICS

JOHN LYONS, *Introduction to Theoretical Linguistics* (Cambridge: Cambridge University Press, 1968). Chapters 9 and 10 provide a good introduction to a number of aspects of meaning. W. V. O. QUINE, "The Problem of Meaning in Linguistics," in *From a Logical Point of View* (Cambridge, Mass.: Harvard University Press, 1953); reprinted in *The Structure of Language*, FODOR and KATZ, eds. This anthology also contains other articles of interest.

For additional reading on the collocational approach, see M. A. K. HALLIDAY, "Lexis as a Linguistic Level," in *In Memory of J. R. Firth*, BAZELL *et al* ed. (London: Longmans, Green & Co. Ltd., 1966); and MARTIN JOOS, "Semology: A Linguistic Theory of Meaning," *Studies in Linguistics* 13, 53–71 (1958).

On the field theory see SUZANNE ÖHMAN, "Theories of the Linguistic Field," *Word* 9 (1953); and JOHN LYONS, *Structural Semantics* (Oxford: Blackwell, 1963).

On componential analysis, see SIDNEY LAMB, "The Sememic Approach to Structural Linguistics," *American Anthropologist* 66 (1964); URIEL WEINREICH, "Explorations in Semantic Theory," in *Current Trends in Linguistics III* (The Hague: Mouton, 1966); and J. KATZ, "Recent Issues in Semantic Theory," *Foundations of Language* 3 (1967).

TRANSLATION

Translating from one language to another creates special theoretical problems. Readers interested in translation should look at EUGENE NIDA, *Toward a Science of Translating* (Leiden, Holland: Brill, 1964); R. A. BROWER, *On Translation* (Cambridge: Harvard University Press, 1959); J. C. CATFORD, *A Linguistic Theory of Translation* (London: Oxford University Press, 1965), and QUINE, *Word and Object.*